Yale Agrarian Studies Series
JAMES C. SCOTT, *Series Editor*

D1563282

"The Agrarian Studies Series at Yale University Press seeks to publish outstanding and original interdisciplinary work on agriculture and rural society—for any period, in any location. Works of daring that question existing paradigms and fill abstract categories with the lived-experience of rural people are especially encouraged."

James C. Scott, *Series Editor*

For a complete list of titles in the Yale Agrarian Studies Series, visit www.yalebooks.com.

# The Politics of
# Food Supply

U.S. Agricultural Policy
in the World Economy

**Bill Winders**
**Foreword by James C. Scott**
**With a New Preface by the Author**

Yale University Press   NEW HAVEN & LONDON

Set in Ehrhardt Roman type by Tseng Information Systems, Inc.
Printed in the United States of America.

ISBN 978-0-300-18186-9 (pbk.)
Library of Congress Control Number: 2011940587

A catalogue record for this book is available from the British Library.

10  9  8  7  6  5  4  3  2

# Contents

# Foreword

The task Bill Winders sets himself is sharply etched but, at the same time, dauntingly ambitious. How can one account for the demise of the trinity of production controls, price supports, and export subsidies that guided agricultural policy in the United States for more than a half century from the New Deal to the mid-1990s? The bookends of this enterprise are Franklin Roosevelt's Agricultural Adjustment Act (AAA, 1933), which instituted supply management, and the Federal Agriculture Improvement and Reform Act (FAIR Act, 1996), which abandoned it. Explaining this convincingly, as Winders does, requires a high order of interdisciplinary skills, including a firm grasp of partisan congressional politics, of agrarian movements throughout the country, of international trade, and of economic history. These skills alone might suffice for a competent account of this historic shift, but Winders's knowledge of crop histories and his use of Karl Polanyi's insights into the dialectic between market forces and protective regulation make this volume a distinguished contribution to Yale University Press's Agrarian Studies Series.

In place of explanations that have relied largely upon the vagaries of partisan politics and commodity prices to explain major policy shifts, Winders substitutes a particularly sophisticated version of class and sectoral politics. The three crops—corn, cotton, and wheat; those who grow them, market them, and buy them; and above all, those whose political futures depend on keeping each crop's constituents content, are the key actors in Winders's drama. Each crop is distinctive in its geographical location, its class and ownership structure, its markets, and its political clout. The constituents of each have different political interests, which, furthermore, shift over time. The coalitions they forge and dissolve, Winders argues, form the most reliable weather vane indicating the probable direction of agricultural policy.

The historical dialectic that Winders traces among the constituents for the various crops, the policy outcomes, and the resulting shifts in the structure and interests of the growers and sellers of each crop is what gives his analysis its dynamic quality. In a discerning version of the adage "be careful what you wish for," Winders shows how a policy "victory" by, say, the growers of cotton or corn serves, in unanticipated ways, to transform their very structure, interests, and sway. This logic is worked out to great effect in the southern cotton sector. There, in a setting where serfdom, in the form of share-tenancy, had replaced slavery, landlords seized for themselves alone the crop payments mandated by the AAA. When they were required by law to share these payments with tenants, landlords responded by dismissing the tenants, moving to more capital-intensive production, and diversifying into growing soybeans and feed grains and raising livestock. This, in turn, helped touch off the great migration north by poor rural blacks and whites, setting the stage for the cotton lobby's decline and facilitating the civil rights movement. Eventually, the demise of the one-party South broke the seniority-based death grip southerners had exercised on congressional democrats since the Civil War. Recursive, dialectical analysis of this kind seems, in my view, to offer the most promising way forward for otherwise wooden and static class analysis. It also helps explain why the one genuine attempt at land reform to break the back of (largely) racialized peonage in the cotton South failed. FDR's agrarian reformers—Rexford Tugwell, Jerome Frank, and "Pat" Jackson—were, to use a contemporary expression, "thrown under the bus" when the full congressional power of the southern planters was brought to bear on the New Deal. Just as post–Civil War Republican Reconstruction was undone by white planters, so was FDR's post-Depression plan for a reconstructed and more equitable agrarian South undone by much the same forces. If Winders's analysis is read in conjunction with first-person victim accounts such as found in Theodore Rosengarden's *All God's Dangers: The Life of Nate Shaw*, it provides a powerful understanding, from top to bottom, of this decisive moment in U.S. agrarian history.

Winders understands, as did Polanyi, that no one, save a handful of theorists, loves perfect competition. The ultimate goal of all producers and wholesalers is some form of oligopoly or monopoly that allows price fixing.

Producers understand that the more "perfect" the competition becomes, the closer the rate of profit approaches to zero. The coveted shelter from "cut-throat" competition is, short of natural monopolies, available to small-scale producers only through political influence. North American cotton and wheat growers have for some time, in international markets, been price-takers rather than price-givers and hence have sought protection. Corn, on the other hand, because the United States is *the* dominant world exporter and because corn is an "input" feed grain for foreign and domestic livestock rearing, has generated a more complex set of interests. At any event, the representatives of agrarian producers have generally sought precisely what Boeing, Chrysler, Harley-Davidson, and Bear Stearns have sought: to privatize profits and to socialize losses. When prices were buoyant, the pressure for price and export subsidies diminished, and when prices plummeted, the political clamor for subsidies grew. Whether the producers had the political clout to legislate their profit insurance is a large part of Winders's story, but what has never been in doubt, following Polanyi, is their desire to be politically sheltered from a tumultuous market.

Stepping back from Winders's original analysis, we might wonder why an examination by commodity sector should prove so exceptionally fruitful. Surely, it is curious that, from at least the New Deal forward, U.S. agricultural policy has primarily centered on price supports for the major commodities: corn, cotton, wheat, tobacco, soybeans, milk, etc. That is, the place occupied in other countries by a *rural* policy has been usurped in the United States by *commodity* policy. Why this should be so is both intriguing and complex. One might argue that the early ambitions of the Tennessee Valley Authority were the embryonic beginnings—alas stillborn—of a genuine rural policy. After this failure, the issue of price supports dominated agrarian politics in Washington. Where the French, the Danes, the Germans, and the Norwegians have asked themselves what kinds of rural communities they wish to promote, what the rural landscape should look like, what land uses should be encouraged, and what rural services should be publically provided, Americans have seldom posed such questions, let alone addressed them until very recently. Until they are addressed, we may have a wheat or corn policy but nothing that remotely resembles an *agricultural,* let alone a *rural,* policy.

James C. Scott

# Preface to the Paperback Edition

Food has frequently been at the forefront of national and world news during the past several years. While people in countries like the United States have found a renewed interest in where their food comes from, how it is made, and its economic and environmental implications, perhaps the more serious headlines have been inspired by rising food prices and world hunger. Of particular note is the food crisis that hit the world economy in 2007 and 2008, when the price of staple foods such as rice and wheat reached historic heights. Wheat and rice prices each rose to more than 200 percent above 2004–2005 levels, leading to food riots around the globe and destabilizing politics in many countries. Of course, the most fundamental effect of the rise in food prices was a dramatic increase in world hunger: the Food and Agriculture Organization (FAO) estimates that more than 1 billion people were undernourished in 2009, representing a dramatic increase from fifteen years before, when fewer than 800 million people were hungry.[1]

Food prices declined in 2009 but rose again in 2010 and early 2011. In fact, the FAO's food price index (a composite look at food prices) was higher in February, March, and April 2011 than at any other point in the previous twenty years. Part of this increase in food prices was again due to the rising cost of wheat and rice.[2] Protests rocked the Middle East in the first three months of 2011 and continued in some countries through the summer. This "Arab Spring" began in January with food riots in Algeria, which were soon followed by protests in Tunisia, where rising food prices also played a role. In addition, Egypt and Yemen—two countries that also experienced significant political upheaval and change—have been two of the top importers of U.S. wheat.

The world food crisis has led to riots, protests, more world hunger, political revolutions in the Middle East, and food prices on the rise once again. What does all of this have to do with the history of U.S. agricultural policy? A lot. Most explanations of the food crisis have focused on the immediate context, including the shift to biofuels and ethanol production, speculation in the commodities futures markets, recent weather patterns, and oil prices. While these kinds of factors no doubt played a part in the food crisis, we have to put this crisis in a broader historical context to gain a full understanding of it.

*The Politics of Food Supply* focuses on the long-term trajectory of U.S. agricultural policy, which for much of the twentieth century used supply management principles to try to reduce market volatility. Beginning in the 1970s, as this book shows, an important shift occurred that helped to set the stage for the recent food crisis: deregulation in agriculture in both national policies and at the level of the world economy. Over the past forty years, regulations that had helped to stabilize agricultural prices and production were eroded or eliminated altogether. Recognizing the role of long-term deregulation also reveals an important insight about the recent food crisis: the instability and volatility of prices are as important as the existence of high prices.

How did supply management help to stabilize agriculture, especially at the level of the world economy? The U.S. food regime, as discussed in Chapter 6, set forth rules, norms, and institutions that regulated agricultural production, prices, trade, and even consumption across the globe. The regulations in this regime took several forms, and each helped to smooth out the normal volatility in the market. First, national policies of supply management—resting primarily on price supports and production controls—were one important form of regulation in this food regime. Price supports provided a minimum price for agricultural goods, thereby protecting farmers from severe downturns in the market. Production controls restricted the amount of acreage that farmers could devote to particular commodities (e.g., corn, wheat, cotton) but also regulated production in a manner that helped to guarantee a steady production of these commodities. Nations throughout the world adopted supply management partly because the General Agreement on Tariffs and Trade (GATT) exempted agriculture from its general program of liberalization, and partly because the policy enabled them to compete with subsidized and regulated agriculture from the United States. The adoption of supply management policy in Europe, North and South America, Asia, and parts of Africa helped to guard against extreme market swings.

Second, at the level of the world economy, international commodity agreements helped to regulate agriculture. These agreements regulated prices, production, and trade for a handful of commodities: wheat, coffee, cocoa, sugar, wool, and cotton, among others. The first International Wheat Agreement (IWA) went into effect in 1949, and it specified the minimum and maximum wheat prices. IWA exporting countries included the United States, Canada, and Australia, which together accounted for more than 75 percent of world wheat exports, part of which was sold through the IWA.

During this period, supply management policy helped to stabilize agricultural prices. The average annual difference in wheat and corn prices from 1949 to 1970, for example, was about 7 percent, and rarely did prices jump or drop by more than 20 percent. Food crises on the scale of the 2007–2008 crisis were absent during this period. Agricultural prices were relatively stable under supply management, but the creation of this policy was neither natural nor inevitable. Instead, supply management emerged out of political conflicts following World War II. The analysis that follows in this book explains how competing political coalitions struggled over the shape of agricultural policy.

So, what happened to supply management? The U.S. food regime, with its extensive economic regulation that helped to stabilize prices and coordinate production, was gradually dismantled during the last quarter of the twentieth century. This deregulation occurred at three levels: the breakdown of international commodity agreements, the incorporation of agriculture into GATT, and the retrenchment of national agricultural policies emphasizing supply management. The IWA broke down in 1970, the United States fundamentally changed price supports and suspended production controls in 1973, food aid declined and was replaced with commercial exports in the early 1970s, structural adjustment programs by the World Bank and the International Monetary Fund pushed agricultural liberalization in poorer countries, GATT began to include agricultural liberalization in the late 1980s, the World Trade Organization (created in 1995) pushed for agricultural liberalization, and the United States ended its policy of supply management in 1996. Supply management was disassembled, and this book explains that policy shift.

One fundamental effect of this policy shift was greater volatility in agri-

cultural prices, beginning with a food crisis in 1973, which saw food prices
and world hunger rise quickly. For the next twenty-five years, agricultural
prices showed much more volatility as supply management crumbled: the
average annual difference in wheat and corn prices, for example, was about
19 percent—more than double the average from 1949 to 1970.

The food crisis of 2007–2008 occurred in a context that was the result
of secular shifts in agricultural policy, both national and world-economic.
The sharp rise in prices at the core of this crisis was an extreme example of
the volatility that has existed since the demise of supply management. Furthermore, this policy trajectory was the outcome of political battles between
competing coalitions with divergent economic interests. That is ultimately
the link to the analysis presented in the following pages. Those political
battles created the context in which the 2007–2008 food crisis was possible.

In the end, *The Politics of Food Supply* helps to make sense of the fluid
direction of agricultural policy, especially in the United States but also in
the broader world economy, by highlighting the shifting political coalitions
that fueled the policy changes, including the deregulation that began in the
1970s. While the focus here is not on the food crisis of 2007–2008 or on what
seems to be an increasingly unstable world economy, the analysis in this book
shows both the context that allowed for the creation and spread of supply
management policy, which helped to stabilize agriculture, and the context of
the deregulation of the past forty years, which has destabilized agriculture,
especially in terms of commodity prices. It may be worth noting that supply
management was forged after a period of significant instability in agriculture,
the 1920s and early 1930s. The stabilizing policy response in the form of supply management was neither automatic nor perfect. It came nonetheless, and
it came through political conflicts over competing economic interests. That
is the story told in the following pages.

### Notes

1. FAO, The State of Food Insecurity in the World: Addressing Food Insecurity
in Protracted Crises (2009).

2. While the food price index was higher in early 2011 than in 2008, the prices of
rice and wheat were not. Wheat and rice prices in 2011 were still notably higher than the
average for 2004–2005, but they did not reach the heights of 2008. This, of course, means
that other food prices were higher than in 2008. See www.fao.org/worldfoodsituation/
wfs-home/foodpricesindex/en/.

# Preface

To many people, U.S. agricultural policy seems quite odd, especially within the context of a market economy. At the simplest level, the federal government has paid farmers not to grow crops in an effort to boost farm prices and income. Many people have also recently criticized this policy as lavishing farmers with extravagant subsidies. In doing so, the government has severely restricted the operation of market mechanisms in an attempt to manage the supply of agricultural commodities. Supply management was the basis of agricultural policy from the 1930s until the Federal Agriculture Improvement and Reform (FAIR) Act of 1996, which fundamentally changed price supports (which provide farm subsidies) and altogether eliminated production controls (which restrict production). After sixty years of trying, opponents of supply management finally won fundamental changes in U.S. agricultural policy. The FAIR Act represented a significant instance of policy retrenchment and contraction, and it was therefore a dramatic and historic shift away from supply management.

When the FAIR Act passed, I was a graduate student considering dissertation topics. I was, and continue to be, interested in understanding how politics, economics, social movements, and class conflict influence social change. More specifically, how do various political-economic contexts facilitate changes in national policies? For me, the roots of current national policy are found in underlying class conflict and political coalitions. Traditionally, class conflict has been seen as occurring between labor and capital, but most conflict occurs within classes, not between them. Competition within the market economy, for example, often pits segments of capital against one another. Likewise, workers have frequently been divided among themselves. My focus, then, tends to be on intraclass conflict and the resulting coalitions, which often reach across class divisions. This perspective emerged, in part, from my understanding of how social movements affect social change. To firmly grasp the policy formation process, we have to explore the long-term political and economic processes driving class conflict and the formation of coalitions. In this way, I explain national policies by placing them in the context of historical trends and developments—a long-term view, if you will.

The passage of the FAIR Act provided an opportunity for applying this perspective to an instance of policy retrenchment. Many scholars try to explain this retrenchment by focusing on the immediate context of the act. My analysis, by contrast, places this recent shift in a much larger historical context that reaches back to the 1920s. Taking such a long view highlights the secular political and economic processes that facilitated the conflicts and coalitions that produced the FAIR Act. The end result, I think, is a fresh perspective on the trajectory of this policy. Not surprisingly, my analysis differs from many explanations of agricultural policy in important ways.

First, agricultural policy is driven by fundamental divisions within agriculture that emerge along regional lines: the South, the Corn Belt, and the Wheat Belt. To talk about "farmers" as a unified group, as frequently happens, hides fundamental differences in the economic interests, policy preferences, and political power of agricultural producers. Throughout the twentieth century, these regional divisions led to different political coalitions within agriculture. Some scholars acknowledge regional divisions, but most analyses tend to leave the divisions out of their theoretical explanations for why policy changes. Yet the underlying and enduring conflicts and coalitions within agriculture arise from these divisions. For much of the twentieth century, including the battle over the FAIR Act, a cotton-wheat coalition confronted corn producers over the shape of agricultural policy.

Second, changes in agricultural production and rural class structures can shape agricultural policy, and such shifts also influence the ebb and flow of conflicts and coalitions. Nowhere is this more evident than in the South: by about 1970, soybeans replaced cotton as the dominant commodity, and the plantation-tenant system that had been in place since the late nineteenth century gradually eroded and then disappeared. Through much of the twentieth century, southern planters (large landowners who rested atop the regional class structure) were a powerful force shaping a whole range of important national policies, including social security, labor rights, unemployment insurance, and numerous business regulations. The planters' influence on agricultural policy was no less evident or pervasive. A sizable literature has explored the influence of the South on the creation of supply management as well as the radical transformations that this policy brought to the region. Nonetheless, few studies of retrenchment in agricultural policy emphasize the effect of changes in southern agriculture. As southern agriculture changed, the political power of southern planters waned. Two primary factors drove this change: supply management policy and the civil rights movement. These two factors are closely related as supply management policy weakened the ties between planters and tenant farmers, helping to facilitate the rise of the civil rights movement. This social movement in turn posed a significant, and ultimately successful, challenge to the political dominance of southern planters, leaving supply management policy, which was the preferred policy of the planters, vulnerable to change. Explanations missing this history are necessarily incomplete.

Finally, agriculture in the United States (as well as in other nations) exists in the context of the world economy. The world economy influences, and in turn is shaped by, regional agricultural divisions and agricultural policy in the United States. Competition in the world economy, for example, shapes the interests and policy preferences of cotton, wheat, and corn producers. And whether the world economy is expanding or contracting likewise shapes the divisions and coalitions within agriculture. At the same time, U.S. agricultural policy profoundly affects the organization of agricultural production, trade, and consumption around the globe. Many other nations, for example, adopted supply management policy as well as the U.S. model of intensive agricultural production. However, this eventually led to changes in the world economy: greater competition within commodity markets, more barriers to the flow of agricultural trade, and shifts in nations' agricultural production. These world economic changes led to various pressures that facilitated changes in U.S. agricultural policy, in part by exacerbating some divisions within agriculture while easing others. Consequently, U.S. agricultural policy is intimately tied to the organization of agriculture in the world economy in ways that few scholars recognize.

In my analysis, I start with the divisions and coalitions within agriculture and then move on to explain these conflicts. Part of this explanation rests on dynamics in the world economy; part of it centers on the (often unintended) effects of agricultural policy; and part of it looks at the fundamental changes in the U.S. South and the hidden role of the civil rights movement in the trajectory of agricultural policy. This analysis, in other words, centers on the relations between class, state, and market. With this focus, my analysis follows the work of Karl Polanyi, who observed the ebb and flow of government regulation of the economy: at times, government regulation expands, and at other times it contracts. Polanyi referred to this process as the double movement of the market economy, in which some groups push for freer markets (toward a laissez-faire policy) as other groups push for greater regulation of the economy. U.S. agricultural policy demonstrates this double movement.

There are really two puzzles here: (1) how supply management policy lasted so long despite opposition, especially from groups within agriculture, and (2) why supply management policy ended when it did. One question is about policy longevity, and the other is about policy retrenchment. The solutions to each of these puzzles lay in the historical development of supply management—that is, in its policy trajectory. To focus on a particular moment of policy change, such as the passage of the FAIR Act, is tempting but shortsighted and ultimately incomplete. Instances of policy expansion or retrenchment are not discrete acts but rather are steps in larger policy trajectories. Analyzing these larger contexts is important for understanding given policy shifts.

As this book demonstrates, putting the FAIR Act into historical perspective reveals the fundamental influence that dynamics within agriculture have on national policy. Most important are the divisions and coalitions that have characterized agriculture for well over a century. Even instances of agricultural retrenchment, such as the FAIR Act, have resulted to a great extent from these divisions and coalitions within agriculture. Some groups within agriculture favor government regulation of the economy while others favor market mechanisms and liberalization. Which side has more political power, of course, goes a long way in determining the shape of agricultural policy. This is the basic double movement in agriculture.

This book sharpens our understanding of agricultural policy, but the analysis also lends insight into national policies, in general. Some aspects of agricultural policy are relatively unique, but this policy nonetheless reflects the experiences of many other policies. After all, the formation of supply management coincided with the creation of several landmark policies, including social security, unemployment insurance, and collective bargaining rights for workers. Similarly, the FAIR Act occurred alongside the retrenchment of other policies, most notably the end of Aid to Families with Dependent Children. Understanding the double movement behind agricultural policy reveals the dynamics that prompt national policies to expand and contract.

# Acknowledgments

A book bears the name of an author or authors, but behind most books lie hidden the help, suggestions, and patience of many people. This one is no exception. Over several years, many people helped this book to take shape. Its roots are found in my doctoral dissertation, but my research on agricultural policy extended well beyond the completion of my Ph.D. In fact, I have conducted so much additional research and gone in so many new directions that this book bears only a minimal resemblance to my dissertation. Consequently, as a graduate student and as a professor, I received various forms of assistance on this project. So, I owe many people thanks.

More than anyone else, Rick Rubinson deserves thanks and recognition. While I was a graduate student at Emory University, Rick introduced me to the insightful works of Karl Polanyi, Barrington Moore, Immanuel Wallerstein, and many others—works that clearly have shaped the theoretical perspective that informs the analysis of this book. Perhaps more importantly, Rick helped me to improve this analysis by lifting it to heights that it otherwise would not have achieved. Because he served as the chair of my dissertation committee and remained a mentor, close friend, and colleague after I graduated, Rick read countless versions of each chapter. This book would be far less without his generous comments, advice, and suggestions. In addition to Rick, I was fortunate enough to have a very thoughtful dissertation committee: Peggy Barlett, John Boli, and Regina Werum. Each of them brought an important viewpoint to this research. Although the analysis that I present here could still be improved, this book surely more closely reflects the ideals of that committee than did my dissertation.

I also owe a special debt to various government documents librarians and archivists. I made a number of trips to the National Archives in Washington, D.C., where Bill Davis, Tom Eisinger, and Ron Ross were most helpful. I am particularly indebted to Tom for his help in finding the 1958 House subcommittee hearing described in Chapter 1. After reading a reference to the heated exchange during this hearing, I tried to track down the original hearing of the House Committee on Agriculture. When the hearings that I initially looked at turned out to be dead ends, Tom found a box (RG 233, Box 661) containing minutes for all committee and subcommittee meetings and hearings of the Agriculture Committee in 1958. This led me to the correct hearing with this riveting exchange, and I am especially thankful for Tom's archival expertise. Closer to home, librarians at Emory University and Georgia Tech helped me track down various statistics, government documents, and congressional hearings. Martha Ebener at Emory's library was a terrific help in the beginning of my research journey. At Georgia Tech, I owe particular thanks to Bruce Henson, who not only helped me become familiar with Tech's library but also helped me find many government documents.

The day-to-day support that I received from Georgia Tech and its School of History, Technology, & Society (HTS) was important in moving this research beyond being a dissertation. The Ivan Allen College of Liberal Arts at Georgia Tech provided me with funding to conduct archival research, present my findings at academic conferences, and purchase numerous hard-to-find books. Chris Fehrenbach helped me to navigate all kinds of administrative mazes and has shared with me a good friendship. As chair of HTS, Willie Pearson gave me time and financial support to conduct this research and write this book. Ron Bayor, who became chair after Willie, was likewise supportive in the latter stages of this project. Two of my colleagues in HTS were particularly helpful while I wrote this book: Steve Usselman and Doug Flamming. Both Steve and Doug were amazingly generous with their time, reading and commenting on numerous papers, articles, proposals, and chapters. In general, they offered invaluable advice and guidance, and they have become ideal colleagues and good friends. I also received encouragement from Rachel Black and Ben Messer, two former HTS students who have moved on to better things. Other colleagues in HTS or in other schools at Georgia Tech encouraged me on this project, listened to my ideas, and attended presentations about this research: Laura Bier, Ron Broglio, Amanda

Damarin, Michelle Dion, Maren Klawiter, Hans Klein, Doug Noonan, and Sue Rosser. I was always impressed that Sue found time in her busy schedule as dean to come to my talks and give her perspective as someone who grew up in the Midwest when many of these political battles occurred. And, Michelle and Doug have become important friends and peers for me at Tech.

Many people beyond Georgia Tech helped me along the way, as well. A number of scholars commented on various articles, drafts of chapters, or aspects of the analysis that I present in this book: Pat Akard, Roy Barnes, Henry Bernstein, Len Bloomquist, Larry Burmeister, Harriet Friedmann, Jess Gilbert, Gary Green, Greg Hooks, Ira Katznelson, Kristin Marsh, Gerad Middendorf, David Nibert, Frances Fox Piven, Charlie Post, Harland Prechel, Peter Swenson, and Steven Vallas. Terry Boswell's belief that market prices were the answer pushed me to show that he was wrong (see Chapter 7). Early in my research, Marybeth Stalp and her family—especially Paul and Mary Claire Stalp—were generous in sharing their knowledge and experience as a farm family in eastern Nebraska. Portions of this book appeared in *Rural Sociology* in 2004, the *Journal of Agrarian Change* in 2006, and *Politics & Society* in 2005. Lastly, I owe a debt of gratitude to the folks at Yale University Press who helped to bring this book to press. Jean Thomson Black, an excellent editor, was always helpful. She and her assistant, Matthew Laird, patiently fielded my queries and guided me through the process. Jessie Dolch, my copy editor, did a wonderful job improving the prose and flow of the manuscript. I also appreciate the careful reading and useful comments and suggestions given by the three reviewers: Sara Gregg, Douglas Hurt, and Scott McNall. And, I am especially grateful to James Scott, who believed in this book enough to give it a chance to be in his series at Yale University Press.

Finally, I would have been unable to complete this book and the research behind it without the support of my family. In particular, my parents—Kathy and David Winders—have supported me in so many ways, and I appreciate the great patience and understanding that they showed me over the years. This book is partly a reflection of their encouragement. During my visits to the National Archives in Washington, D.C., my wife's parents—Sandra and David D'Unger—were always generous with their time. They not only gave me a place to stay while I was doing my research, but they also served as chauffeurs, cooks, counselors, dinner companions, purveyors of alcohol, and always gracious hosts. They gave me space to write during both winter and summer holidays. I am grateful for their understanding and generosity.

Above all, I am indebted to my wife, Amy D'Unger. She endured all my shortcomings, crises, joys, and sorrows as I completed this research and wrote this book—a process that took more time than either of us had anticipated. She learned far more about agricultural policy, the southern class structure, farm politics, and the world economy than she ever wanted to know. Nonetheless, she always patiently indulged my perpetual need for a sounding board for my ideas, discoveries, and arguments. She was also kind enough to read the entire manuscript and offer invaluable editorial advice. And, finally, she selflessly taught while pregnant one summer so I could finish this manuscript. I also appreciate various dogs who shared our home— Summer, Juneau, Denali, Eleanor, and Myrtle—and gave me time to think and work out writing-related problems on our many walks. And, last but certainly not least, I am grateful to our son, Samuel David D'Unger, who has brought unforeseen wonder and happiness into our family. Importantly, Sam gave me a definitive deadline for finishing this manuscript—his birth in August of 2006. He is my joy and inspiration.

Despite all of this support, advice, and counsel, however, this book bears only my name. And, in the end, the final responsibility for the arguments and the presentation of historical events and facts lies solely with me.

# Abbreviations

| | |
|---|---|
| AAA | Agricultural Adjustment Act |
| CCC | Commodity Credit Corporation |
| EEP | Export Enhancement Program |
| FAIR Act | Federal Agriculture Improvement and Reform Act |
| GATT | General Agreement on Tariffs and Trade |
| MMT | million metric tons |
| NAWG | National Association of Wheat Growers |
| NCC | National Cotton Council |
| NFU | National Farmers Union |
| PFC | Production Flexibility Contract |
| PL 480 | Public Law 480 (Agricultural Trade Development and Assistance Act, or international food aid) |
| USDA | United States Department of Agriculture |

# Abbreviations

# CHAPTER 1

# Introduction

## Agriculture between State and Market

> . . . we ought not to create any situation that pits one segment of agriculture against another.
> —BRYCE NEIDIG, PRESIDENT OF THE NEBRASKA FARM BUREAU FEDERATION, 1995

Throughout most of the twentieth century, agricultural policy in the United States veered sharply from free market principles by emphasizing *supply management*. Beginning with the Agricultural Adjustment Act (AAA) in 1933 as a response to the Great Depression, supply management policy rested on two programs: *price supports* and *production controls*. Price supports provided artificially high prices for certain field crops—most notably wheat, corn, and cotton. To receive these higher prices, however, farmers had to adhere to production controls, which restricted the production of these same commodities. To be eligible for cotton price supports, for example, a southern farmer might be limited to growing cotton on only 60 percent of the farm's acreage. The farmer might use the remaining 40 percent to grow corn or soybeans, to use as pasture, or to just leave idle. The point was to reduce the amount of land used in producing particular agricultural commodities. Through supply management policy, then, the federal government set minimum prices for and regulated the production of various agricultural commodities as a way to raise farm income.

Over the years, the contours of agricultural policy changed even as price supports and production controls remained the constant pillars. The federal government's influence on the market economy ebbed and flowed as supply management policy expanded and contracted. The most significant retrenchment came in 1996 with the Federal Agriculture Improvement and Reform (FAIR) Act—often called the "Freedom to Farm" Act. The FAIR

Act ended production controls by removing most restrictions on agricultural production: it allowed farmers to grow any commodity, in any amounts, and on any portion of their land.[1] This legislation also eliminated price supports, which are tied to market prices, and replaced them with fixed, declining payments. Therefore, the FAIR Act effectively terminated the policy of supply management. In 2002, the Farm Security and Rural Investment Act revived a version of price supports but not production controls. Without production controls, U.S. agricultural policy no longer manages supply.

So how can we explain the contours of twentieth-century agricultural policy? One place to start is at the political front lines: congressional hearings about farm policy. In such hearings, supporters and opponents of supply management policy — including politicians, individual farmers, agribusiness companies, and farm organizations — state their preferences and make their cases. These political battles lay bare the fundamental and recurring regional divisions within agriculture — particularly among the South, Wheat Belt, and Corn Belt.[2] Most often, the cotton-producing South allied with the Wheat Belt to support supply management policy, while the Corn Belt pursued more market-oriented policies. Such divisions had a profound effect on agricultural policy throughout the twentieth century. One hearing during the height of the Cold War particularly exposed the divisions between the South and the Corn Belt.

### Cotton versus Corn in the 1950s

In January 1958, a subcommittee of the House Agriculture Committee held public hearings to discuss the future direction of U.S. agricultural policy, focusing on programs for corn and other feed grains.[3] W. Robert Poage (D-TX), who chaired the subcommittee, favored supply management policy, as did most southern Democrats. The subcommittee heard testimony from representatives of the American Farm Bureau Federation — the largest and most influential U.S. farm organization — which, by 1958, had been expressing opposition to price supports and production controls for more than a decade. The Farm Bureau favored a more market-oriented agricultural policy that was at odds with preferences of members of the House Agriculture Committee. The differences, which were based on competing economic interests of corn farmers represented by the Farm Bureau and cotton farmers represented by southern Democrats, came to a head in these subcommittee hearings.

Chairman Poage opened the hearings by noting that "the committee will have to determine whether we want to follow a course that will give us high-priced feed or low-priced feed."[4] The former would likely rest on supply management, but the latter would not. Roger Fleming, the secretary-treasurer of the Farm Bureau, presented a proposal for changes in agricultural policy that included ending production controls for corn, reducing price supports for all commodities, and emphasizing exports.[5] Fleming also explained that production controls for other commodities, such as wheat and cotton, needed to be changed because "diverted acres from other crops [due to production controls] have gone into feed grains" and thereby distorted markets in the feed and livestock industries.[6]

Despite a cordial beginning, in which Poage told Fleming that the subcommittee was "delighted" to hear from the Farm Bureau, the exchange between members of the subcommittee and the Farm Bureau officials quickly became heated.

> M R .   P O A G E :  I just asked you whether you believe it would assist the livestock people and help them, to have the price of corn higher or lower than it is today.
>
> M R .   F L E M I N G :  Well, it is our recommendation to this committee that this proposal, which we have made and which is reported in dollar and cents at the top of page 11, would best serve the interests of the feed grain and livestock producers.
>
> M R .   P O A G E :  You still have not answered my question. If you don't want to answer it, all you need to do is say so—I asked you whether you feel that it would be advantageous to the livestock producers to have the price of corn higher or lower than it is at the present time.
>
> M R .   F L E M I N G :  . . . We have made specific recommendations in dollars and cents. I don't know how we can make it more specific than that.
>
> M R .   P O A G E :  Well, just assume that I am too ignorant to understand your printed recommendations. Just answer my question and tell me whether you people think it would be advantageous to the livestock producers to have the price of corn higher or lower than it is at the present time.
>
> M R .   F L E M I N G :  Well, first of all, you and I can get into an argument as to your ignorance—
>
> M R .   P O A G E :  No, assume I am ignorant.
>
> M R .   F L E M I N G :  I take the position that you are pretty smart.
>
> M R .   P O A G E :  Well, thank you, but go ahead, let us get your answer.
>
> M R .   F L E M I N G :  We are for the proposal contained at the top of page

MR. POAGE: I know, but are you in favor . . . of [a] higher or lower price of corn right now?

MR. FLEMING: If the price currently is below, the way our proposal would work out, then we are for it being higher. I suggest that you—

MR. POAGE: I think it is safe to say that you are the representative of the largest farm organization in the world. Don't you know the answer?

MR. FLEMING: Well, yes—

MR. POAGE: What I am asking you to do is to answer the question. . . .[7]

For much of the hearing, the committee and the Farm Bureau representatives wrangled in this manner over price supports, production controls, farm income, and previous policy positions of the Farm Bureau. This was largely because the Farm Bureau advocated significantly weakening supply management policy—eliminating many production controls, dramatically reducing price supports, and creating greater reliance on markets—while the committee, especially the southern Democrats, resisted such ideas. Tensions reached the boiling point, however, toward the end of the hearing, when the specter of communism emerged. The exchange over this issue began between Paul Jones (D-MO) and Frank Woolley, legislative counsel for the Farm Bureau.

MR. JONES: I have one question before we adjourn. Mr. Woolley . . . didn't you tell me then that the program we were suggesting of payments on cotton had been originally inspired by Communists, and that it was a Communist-inspired program—did you tell me that?

MR. WOOLLEY: No. What I said to you was that in 1955—and I am glad you asked that because—

MR. JONES: . . . did you tell me that?

MR. WOOLLEY: Now, Congressman, I want—

MR. JONES: I want you to tell me yes or no.[8]

Woolley said he could not remember whether he had brought up the issue of communism with Mr. Jones, but Woolley went on to discuss a pamphlet ____ion that was printed in 1955 by the Communist Party in the _____ Farm Crisis." According to Woolley, the pam- ____st Party "unequivocally supports produc- ____ge then joined the fray.

____ us get this straight.

____ng those comments charging communism in this ____you are doing, calling us Communists, because we are opposed to your proposal—let us lay it out on the table, and you just go ahead and name the people that you think are the Communists on the committee, and I want you to put that in the record; I don't want you to be going behind my back and, frankly, if you think I am a Communist, say so here and get it on the record.

MR. WOOLLEY: ... I told Mr. Jones ... that when I said that the Communists were supporting the production payment [program], ... this did not carry with it the idea that he or anybody else that was proposing production payments was a Communist. ...

The point I am trying to make ... [is] that if the Communists spend thousands of dollars propagandizing for a particular method ... doesn't it cause somebody to raise a question as to whether it might or might not be against our interest? That is the question, and it is not that you are a Communist—I know you are not—at least, I hope you are not.

MR. JONES: Are you inferring by your propaganda, are you trying to say that a bill that we introduced here was inspired by a Communist program? I resent that very much. ...

MR. FLEMING: Might I make a statement, Mr. Chairman?

MR. POAGE: [gaveling] This committee is going to adjourn right here and now, ... and I am sorry that anybody dragged communism into this, when it has nothing to do with the corn bill or the cotton bill or any other bill ... and I will not permit it to go any further.

MR. FLEMING: Just one sentence?

MR. POAGE: No; you can make it somewhere else, anywhere you want to. The committee is adjourned.[10]

Then, according to newspaper accounts, Poage shouted, "But if you want to discuss it further, I'll meet you in the alley."[11] In the end, some degree of civility prevailed as no confrontation occurred after the hearing: "The witness and Mr. Poage did not meet up after the session."[12]

The tone of this hearing and its degeneration into accusations of communism raise some important questions about national policies in general and twentieth-century agricultural policy in particular. How can we explain such extensive economic intervention by the U.S. government at a time when this country was the preeminent promoter of free market capitalism? Did supply management represent an "antimarket" policy won by opponents of capitalism? Was this policy the result of a unified "farm bloc" able to impose its will upon the federal government? Answering such questions is essential for understanding the contours of twentieth-century agricultural policy, and why this policy was frequently so politically divisive.

This heated exchange between members of the House Agriculture Committee and Farm Bureau officials provides an important introduction into the politics surrounding supply management policy. As committee members clashed with Farm Bureau representatives, the divisions between producers of different agricultural commodities, particularly corn versus cotton, emerged clearly. Thus, behind the tensions and flaring tempers at the committee hearing lie important political conflicts within agriculture.

Southern Democrats were the most important proponents of supply management, but they could hardly be labeled as liberals, much less as communists. Yet they unequivocally favored the extensive state regulation of the market economy found in supply management policy. This policy preference was not based on an "antimarket" position, but it instead resulted from economic interests created by the vagaries of the market economy. That is, southern Democrats were merely working to protect the economic interests of the cotton producers whom they represented. By the same token, Farm Bureau officials tended to adopt the policy preferences of large-scale commercial farmers in the Corn Belt, also working to protect the interests of the particular farmers they represented. This early attempt at agricultural retrenchment, at cutting price supports and production controls, was led not by urban consumers, taxpayers, or even free-marketeers; instead, this push to "get the government out of farming" was led by certain farm organizations, such as the Farm Bureau. Understanding the foundations of such divisions within agriculture, then, is important to explaining the development, expansion, and contraction of supply management policy. Finally, this early attempt at retrenchment failed. Why did the cotton South defeat the Corn Belt in this battle to shape agricultural policy? A large part of the answer lies in the political power of competing agricultural coalitions. Ultimately, this book argues that divisions and coalitions within agriculture were the driving forces behind the formation, expansion, and retrenchment of supply management policy.

## Supply Management Policy: An Overview

The broad contours of supply management policy are readily evident in the record of agricultural legislation, as shown in Table 1.1. This policy began as a response to the Great Depression of the 1930s, which hit agriculture particularly hard. During the depression, agriculture in the United States, and throughout the world economy, suffered from overpro-

**Table 1.1.** Landmarks in U.S. agricultural policy, 1933–2002

| | |
|---|---|
| 1933 | Agricultural Adjustment Act (AAA) |
| 1936 | U.S. Supreme Court declares AAA unconstitutional |
| 1938 | Second AAA passed (price supports between 52 percent and 75 percent of parity) |
| 1941 | Steagall Amendment (expanded commodities covered by AAA, increased parity to 85 percent) |
| 1942 | Stabilization Act (increased parity to 90 percent, extended this level two years past the end of World War II) |
| 1948 | Agricultural Act (maintained 90 percent parity) |
| 1949 | Agricultural Act (maintained 90 percent parity) |
| 1954 | Agricultural Trade Development and Assistance Act, or Public Law 480 (created export subsidies and international food aid) |
| 1954 | Agricultural Act (lowered price supports to 82.5 percent to 90 percent of parity) |
| 1958 | Agricultural Act (maintained minimum price support of 82.5 percent of parity) |
| 1964 | Cotton-Wheat Act (voluntary production controls for wheat and cotton) |
| 1970 | Nixon administration shifts from food aid to commercial exports |
| 1973 | Agriculture and Consumer Protection Act (removed concept of parity from price supports and suspended production controls) |
| 1985 | Food Security Act (reduced target prices, expanded export subsidies with Export Enhancement Program) |
| 1996 | Federal Agriculture Improvement and Reform Act (ended price supports and production controls but continued export subsidies) |
| 2002 | Farm Security and Rural Investment Act (continued income supports and export subsidies) |

duction, declining prices, and falling income. Between 1926 and 1933, for example, overall farm income plunged by more than 40 percent, cotton prices fell by about 50 percent, and wheat exports fell by more than 80 percent. Many farmers, economists, and public officials at the time believed that this economic turmoil in agriculture was caused by overproduction. With the passage of the AAA of 1933, the federal government sought to stabilize prices and support farm income by restricting the production of agricultural commodities. This policy of supply management was a clear departure from previous agricultural policy, which involved little intervention into the market economy, and it endured for more than sixty years with few changes.

Price supports and production controls initially applied to only a few "basic" commodities: wheat, corn, hogs, cotton, rice, and tobacco.[13] Peanuts were added in the late 1930s, and hogs were later removed. Under the AAA, price support levels were based on the concept of parity, which was an index of the purchasing power of one unit of an agricultural commodity. Parity was the price that gave agricultural commodities "the same purchasing power in terms of goods and services farmers buy that the commodities had" during the period 1909–1914, when agricultural prices reached historic heights relative to other prices.[14] Price supports, then, gave agricultural commodities parity with industrial prices, based on the ratio of prices between 1909 and 1914. The Supreme Court ruled the AAA unconstitutional in 1936, primarily because of a tax on processors of agricultural commodities (for example, food processors). In 1938, Congress passed a similar AAA without the controversial processing tax. In this second act, Congress set price support levels between 52 and 75 percent of parity with those of 1910–1914.[15]

From 1940 to 1954, supply management policy expanded beyond the boundaries of the New Deal. During World War II, price support levels increased to 110 percent of parity, providing greater income support to farmers. Supply management also expanded to cover a wider array of commodities during the war. Then, in 1954, export subsidies were created to help lower the price of agricultural exports, which had been artificially inflated because of price supports. *Export subsidies,* in the form of international food aid, became the third pillar of supply management policy, alongside price supports and production controls. By bolstering exports, these subsidies helped to reduce and therefore control agricultural surpluses. During this period, price support levels were raised substantially, existing programs (price supports and production controls) were expanded to cover many more commodities, and export subsidies were created to supplement price supports and production controls.

After this period of expansion, supply management policy experienced gradual retrenchment from 1954 to 1973. In 1954, price support levels were reduced and made flexible with the creation of a sliding scale. Then, production controls were eased in 1964. In 1973, the policy was weakened in three ways. First, the concept of parity was removed from price supports and replaced with target prices and deficiency payments. Second, production controls were temporarily suspended. And third, export subsidies in the form of food aid decreased and were replaced with commercial exports free of such subsidies.[16] Coupled with rising exports, the 1973 legislation resulted in significantly reduced support: direct payments to farmers fell from $3.7 billion in 1970 to $530 million in 1974. John Mark Hansen captures the retrenchment over this period by noting that "from the late fifties to the early seventies, the average support payments received by farmers diminished (in real dollars) by almost half."[17]

Supply management policy briefly expanded again between 1978 and 1986 in the midst of the worst financial crisis in agriculture since the Great Depression. In particular, payments to farmers reached record levels, production controls were strengthened, and export subsidies were expanded with the creation of the Export Enhancement Program (EEP). Turmoil in world agricultural markets was at the root of this economic crisis. As the world economic crisis eased, the gradual retrenchment resumed: by the early 1990s, payments to farmers decreased and production controls were again weakened.

Despite these notable expansions and contractions, the basic tenet of U.S. agricultural policy remained relatively constant: support farm income by raising prices for agricultural commodities through supply management to control surpluses. Price supports, production controls, and export subsidies were the constant pillars of agricultural policy—even through the periods of gradual retrenchment. During most of the twentieth century, then, the government extensively influenced market prices and production decisions in agriculture.

This all changed in 1996 with the passage of the FAIR Act, which ended price supports and production controls.[18] This legislation replaced price supports with fixed-income support payments tied to neither market prices nor production decisions. These payments, known as Production Flexibility Contract payments, decreased between 1996 and 2002 so as to ease farmers back closer to a free market in agriculture. The FAIR Act also ended production controls by eliminating acreage allotments and the Acreage Reduction Program, which administered set-asides.[19] Notably, the FAIR Act continued export subsidies under the EEP. Nonetheless, the FAIR Act ended the extensive government intervention in agriculture that had regulated both prices and production for more than sixty years. Opponents of supply management had tried to curtail the policy for five decades, but no previous efforts achieved the success of the FAIR Act. Consequently, the act returned U.S. farmers closer to the market from which they had been protected since the 1930s.

In 2002, however, the Farm Security and Rural Investment Act brought back some income supports linked to prices, but not production controls. Some restrictions on production remain, such as the Conservation Reserve Program, but they do not have the explicit goal of managing supply. Therefore, a central element of supply management has been eliminated. Even though the federal government continues to provide subsidies to raise farm income, restricting production is no longer part of the strategy. Agricultural policy today focuses on managing demand by promoting exports and creating new markets for U.S. commodities. This is a much more market-oriented strategy. Therefore, while some elements of supply management remain after the FAIR Act, U.S. agricultural policy has clearly retreated from the extensive state intervention into the economy that characterized supply management policy at its height in the mid-twentieth century.

The AAA and the FAIR Act represent two bookends of agricultural policy in the twentieth century. For more than six decades, then, the federal government directly shaped the market prices and production decisions of the agricultural sector of the economy. No comparable intervention into the market economy previously existed in agriculture, and the reach of the federal government shaped few other sectors of the economy so directly or fundamentally. How can we explain the contours of U.S. agricultural policy during the twentieth century? How, then, can we understand the "life" of this policy? What factors explain the shifts in agricultural policy? Why did supply management endure for sixty years, and why did it finally end in 1996?

## Understanding Supply Management Policy

The life of supply management as the core of U.S. agricultural policy presents an important case study. First, analyzing the long-term trajectory of supply management illuminates the politics and conflicts surrounding this policy. Were political battles over supply management policy, and the resulting expansions and contractions, primarily between agricultural and non-agricultural interests? Second, analyzing the contours of twentieth-century agricultural policy affords the opportunity for understanding the long-term trajectory of national policies, including both policy expansion and retrenchment. How can we understand the ebb and flow of state intervention into the market economy? And third, exploring the life of supply management policy allows for a close examination of the relationship between class and state. To understand shifts in national policy, we need to investigate not only how classes can influence policies but also how national policy can reshape class structures. By addressing each of these broad questions, this book sets forth an analysis of twentieth-century agricultural policy that is fundamentally different from existing studies.

## The Farm Bloc: Myth or Reality?

The expansion and retrenchment of twentieth-century agricultural policy is often understood as the consequence of battles between farmers and rural interests, on the one hand, and urban, consumer, and other interests on the other hand. That is, farmers fought to expand the support that they received from the government, while other groups, including taxpayers and consumers, fought to limit the generosity of federal farm programs. In this fight, farmers are often seen as a relatively cohesive group—the farm bloc. Certainly, there is some truth in this perspective, which derives in part from the experience of the New Deal when so many farmers coalesced around the AAA.

This focus on conflict between agriculture and other interests is especially prevalent among analyses of agricultural retrenchment, which tend to emphasize the "decline of agriculture." Scholars point out that the farm population declined dramatically between 1950 and 1980—the period when supply management suffered significant retrenchment.[20] In 1950, the farm population in the United States was more than 15 million, but it dropped to less than 3 million by 1980. This sharp decline in the farm population, some scholars argue, reduced the political power of farm interests because the number of representatives and senators from farm areas shrank as well.[21] Just as the political influence of farmers was declining, other groups representing urban and consumer interests began to challenge supply management policy.[22] While these issues are notable, the focus on political battles between agricultural and nonagricultural interests diverts attention from changes and processes within agriculture.

The battles between agricultural and nonagricultural interests were not the primary force behind shifts in U.S. agricultural policy. Instead, political divisions and coalitions within agriculture underlie both large and small shifts in agricultural policy. Even while many important segments of agriculture pushed for the creation of supply management, some segments opposed the policy from the beginning. Opposition to supply management existed within agriculture for virtually the entire life of the policy. At times this opposition was stronger, at other times it was weaker; but it persisted regardless of its political influence.

Within agriculture, one source of opposition to supply management was the general economic organization of agriculture. The South stood apart from the rest of the nation not only in terms of the commodities it produced, especially cotton and tobacco, but also regarding its regional class structure, the plantation-tenant system. For much of the twentieth century, agriculture in the South simply operated differently from agriculture in the rest of the nation. Yet even while the Wheat Belt and Corn Belt shared a similar class structure (based on independent family farms), the positions of wheat and corn in the world economy were different and promoted divergent policy preferences. Therefore, regional production was a central division within agriculture and sometimes created conflicting policy preferences among farmers.

Between 1950 and 1970, however, the structures and interests of these relatively distinct agricultural regions converged. In particular, the plantation system of the South faded away. Additionally, each region became integrated into the nation's "intensive livestock complex."[23] This altered the economic interests of segments of agriculture. Consequently, the gradual shift toward market-oriented policies was primarily a function of changes within agriculture. Despite appearances, then, the retrenchment of supply management policy did not represent an "antiagriculture" policy imposed by other groups; instead, the retrenchment was a policy shift favored by important segments of agriculture. Focusing on political battles between interests inside and outside of agriculture misses these important factors underlying the contours of twentieth-century agricultural policy in the United States.

Recognizing that divisions within agriculture undergird the contours of agricultural policy, how can we explain these divisions? What factors produce competing political coalitions within agriculture? And why do certain coalitions exert more political influence at particular times? The answers to such questions lie in the relationships between class, state, and market.

## State versus Market? National Policies and the World Economy

In his analysis of the social foundations of the market economy, Karl Polanyi put forth two important propositions. First, he argued that opposition to free markets and support for government intervention into the economy should be recognized as a normal market process.[24] Polanyi demonstrated that the market economy creates its own opposition: the market expands but is met by an opposing movement that is trying to create protections from the market. At times, the state becomes more involved in the market, while at other times it becomes less involved. Polanyi called this ebb and flow of state involvement a *double movement* of protectionism and liberalism, or state regulation versus laissez-faire.[25] In a market economy, various groups continually push for a free market unrestrained by government intervention; but as the market becomes less restrained, it begins to wreak havoc on people's lives. Eventually, then, a push in the opposite direction emerges: groups begin to call for the state to restrain the market forces and protect them from market vagaries. State intervention, however, can create its own problems: it begins to restrict profit, the accumulation of capital, and other "normal" effects of the market. Consequently, a new call comes forth to end state intervention and to allow the market to operate without interference. And so goes the expansion and contraction of state intervention in the market economy. Notably, this process occurs even among capitalists: while many capitalists push for free markets, others regularly seek national policies that offer protection from the market.[26] Whether promoting the free market or regulating the market, national policies will eventually prompt a reaction in the opposite direction.

Second, Polanyi argued that the market economy must be understood as a *world economy*. That is, the political economy of individual nations cannot be fully understood outside of the context of the world economy. The general context of the world economy, such as recession or expansion, influences the economic interests of groups trying to influence national policies. In addition, the position of groups in the world economy likewise shapes their economic interests. In the late nineteenth century, for example, U.S. cotton farmers, who dominated world markets, favored free trade; whereas U.S. sugar producers, who could be undersold by producers in poorer countries, such as Cuba, preferred tariffs. To understand the policies of any given nation, then, we must examine the policies within the framework of the world economy.

Polanyi's insights fit remarkably well with the development of agricultural policy in the United States during the past one hundred years. The twentieth century began with a relatively free market for agriculture: barriers to trade were low, and direct state intervention into pricing and production decisions was nonexistent. This laissez-faire approach to agricultural markets contributed to the economic turmoil of the Great Depression, in which farm prices and income fell dramatically, agricultural commodities were heavily overproduced, thousands of farm families were displaced as banks foreclosed on mortgages, and soil erosion from drought and unrestrained production created the Dust Bowl on the Great Plains. Importantly, the depression in agriculture, which began in the mid-1920s, affected the entire world economy, not just that of the United States. Many countries responded to this turmoil by creating policies to stabilize agricultural prices and production. New Deal agricultural policy was part of this response to the havoc wrought by the free market. Yet as Polanyi predicted, the policies of state intervention—price supports, production controls, and exported subsidies—created problems of their own. By artificially raising prices, restricting production, and obstructing trade, these state policies began to restrict profits and "limit economic freedom." A variety of groups then started calling for an end to such state intervention. Therefore, twentieth-century agricultural policy affords an opportunity for examining movement both toward and then away from state regulation of the market.

Polanyi's double movement helps to illuminate how the market, hampered and unhampered, contributes to political conflicts, but his analysis lacks an underlying explanation of this conflict. In other words, when does state intervention expand or recede? What determines the success or failure of each side of the double movement? More specifically for the case at hand, why did supply management policy end in 1996 and not earlier—or later?

## Class and State: National Policies and Class Structure Reshaping Each Other

Behind the ebb and flow of state regulation of the market economy lays the relationship between class structures and national policies. Class segments—factions of classes that share particular economic interests and policy preferences—are especially important in this relationship. To understand how class segments can influence national policies, we need to examine their economic interests. We must also look at how they use political power to translate their economic interests into national policy. At the same time, national policies can reshape class structures through the process of class transformation, which is also a fundamental element of the relationship between class structures and national policies.

The analysis of this book focuses on different segments of agriculture, as detailed later in this chapter. Production processes and class structures divide agriculture into segments (for example, large commercial farmers, farmworkers, family farmers, grain traders, fertilizer producers, etc.) that often have competing economic interests. That is, agricultural interests tend to be divided by competing commodities, position in the production process, and regional class structure. For example, southern planters—large landowners concentrated in the Cotton Belt of the South—tended to have economic interests different from medium-sized family farms in the midwestern Corn Belt and tenant farmers in the South. In addition, the world economy shapes the economic interests and policy preferences of class segments. Not only does the general context of the world economy influence economic interests, but the position of class segments in that economy also shapes their interests. For example, class segments that dominate their respective world markets are more likely to favor free trade than those that face competition. Likewise, shifts in the world economy can change the economic interests of class segments.

To transform these economic interests into national policies, segments of agriculture form political coalitions. Of particular importance are politically dominant farmers of cotton, wheat, and corn, who have been able to shape agricultural policy through farm organizations (for example, the Farm Bureau and the National Farmers Union [NFU]) as well as political parties. I refer to politically and economically dominant farmers within the South as the "cotton segment," in the Corn Belt as the "corn segment," and in the Wheat Belt as the "wheat segment." These three segments of agriculture represented the core of the political coalition behind the formation of supply management during the New Deal. The cotton, wheat, and corn segments also anchored the coalitions supporting and opposing price supports and production controls after World War II.

The structure of the state affects the ability of class segments to influence policy formation and implementation. Because the U.S. state is decentralized, competing class segments can try to influence policy formation at different points. The clearest example of this process is found in the disproportionate influence over national policy held by southern planters.

This segment had significant political power from the 1930s through the early 1960s because of its influence over the national Democratic Party and congressional committees. As a result, southern planters exerted extensive influence over the shape of national policies during this period.

Importantly, the relationship between class and state is not unidirectional. Rather, national policies favored by a particular class segment may later change the class structure of which that segment is a part. This process of class transformation may reshape the economic interests of class segments and alter the political power of competing class segments. Class transformation may also lead to shifts in political coalitions, especially when weaker classes organize, which may then result in pronounced changes in state policy.[27] Class transformation is most evident in the effect of supply management policy on the rural class structure of the South.

Understanding the ebb and flow of state intervention into the economy, then, requires an examination of changes in the economic interests and political power of class segments. As the interests of segments shift and their power waxes and wanes, state policy likewise changes. Behind this underlying class conflict is the world economy, which influences the interests of class segments. National policies can likewise reshape class structures, which may ultimately result in new policies.

The relations among class, state, and market constitute the core of this book's analytical perspective. So how do these ideas fit together? How can we explain why agriculture is segmented? How does this segmentation relate to the market economy, national policy, or class structures?

## Theoretical Underpinnings

Factions of social classes, such as large landowners or unionized workers, try to shape national policies to reflect their economic interests, which derive largely from a class segment's position within the production process, class structure, and the world economy. Of particular importance for understanding national policies is how class segments translate their economic interests into state policy through two processes: the formation of political coalitions and embedding interests within the state. At the same time, national policies can change the economic interests of class segments by reshaping the production process, class structures, and even the market economy. National policies therefore can contribute to the rise and fall of political coalitions. Thus, national policy trajectories, including that of agricultural policy, are heavily shaped by the dynamic relationships between class (class structures, class segments), state (national policies, state structures), and market (the world economy). This analysis differs from most explanations of U.S. agricultural policy, especially its retrenchment.

### Alternative Explanations of Agricultural Policy

Most analyses explain the expansion and retrenchment of agricultural policy by examining simple market shifts (for example, rising prices), partisan politics, and the political influence of farmers and farm organizations.[28] Some scholars argue that high market prices for agricultural commodities encourage farmers to accept cuts in supply management policy, while low market prices prompt them to protect supply management. The retrenchment of supply management in 1973 and 1996, for example, occurred during periods of high market prices for some commodities. Other scholars argue that retrenchment is most likely to happen when Republicans control the federal government, and supply management is likely to expand when Democrats are the dominant party. The idea here, of course, is that Democrats favor expanding federal regulatory and support programs while Republicans prefer little government intervention. However, the relationship between the trajectory of agricultural policy, market prices, and partisan politics is not always so clear-cut.

Finally, many scholars explain retrenchment in agricultural policy by pointing to two related trends that amount to a "decline of agriculture." First, they note that the farm population fell rapidly after World War II, as seen in Figure 1.1. Farmers represented about 25 percent of the total U.S. population in 1935, but they represented only about 12 percent in 1955 and less than 5 percent in 1970. Hansen argues that this decline in the farm population resulted in fewer members of Congress representing farm districts.[29] As a result, the political power of farmers declined, and they could no longer protect supply management policy as effectively as they had before.

The second aspect of the "decline of agriculture" is tied to interest group dynamics. Scholars often stress that, in the 1970s, interest groups outside of agriculture emerged that opposed supply management.[30] These scholars note, for example, that environmental and consumer organizations became critical of supply management policy for promoting intensive agricultural methods dependent on chemical fertilizers and for increasing food costs, respectively. The argument here is that the retrenchment of supply man-

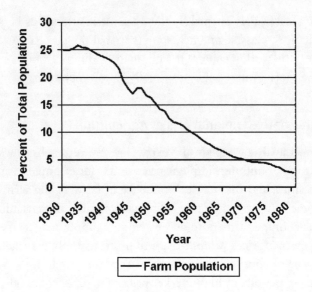

1.1. The decline in the farm population in the United States, 1930–1980. *Sources:*
U.S. Census Bureau, *Historical Statistics,* 157, Table K 1–16; Fite, *American
Farmers,* 101.

agement policy, especially during the mid-twentieth century, was partly the
result of interest groups opposed to the policy. Importantly, scholars point
out that this trend coincided with the shrinking of the farm population.
Therefore, the political influence of farmers declined precisely as the power
of other groups opposed to supply management policy increased. As a result
of this shift in political power, some argue, agricultural policy experienced
retrenchment. This general explanation, then, suggests that farmers lost political power because of demographic shifts and the appearance of nonagricultural interest groups opposed to supply management.

Interpretations that equate the expansion or retrenchment of agricultural
policy with periods of falling prices, which political party controls Congress,
or the size of the farm population overlook important divisions within agriculture and exaggerate the extent of political party coherence. In particular,
such standard explanations of agricultural policy ignore the secular changes
and recurring conflicts within agriculture, which are ultimately tied up with
regional commodity production and class structures, as well as with the dynamics of the world economy. Neglecting the effect of regional class structures is a particularly important omission. In short, such explanations are too
simplistic to account for the complex process of policy change.

This book, by contrast, takes a long-term view of the retrenchment of the FAIR Act. Such an historical perspective illuminates the importance of understanding secular relations among class, state, and market—three factors that undergird the contours of twentieth-century agricultural policy.

## Class, State, and Market

Class dynamics lay behind the rise and decline of supply management policy. When many people hear "class," they think of workers and capitalists, of the proletariat and bourgeoisie. In the case of agriculture, however, class often means farmers (that is, landowners) and farmworkers or sharecroppers, or a focus on agribusiness corporations.[31] Certainly, this is the core of the idea of class—that a group's relation to the production process is the group's defining social characteristic. And differing relations to the production process lead to competing economic and political interests, resulting in class conflict. Nonetheless, the idea of class is not limited to workers and capital, or to farmworkers versus landowners. Karl Marx himself made distinctions not only among workers, landowners, and capitalists, but also within classes, such as finance capital versus industrial capital.[32] The dynamics of the market economy shape such fissures within classes, as do state processes. Therefore, analyzing the relations among class, state, and market is imperative.

A class segment perspective strives to understand the transformation of class, of state, and of market. That is, this perspective aims to explain how class structures change, how national policies (as well as state institutions) change, and how the organization of the market changes—and how each one of these affects changes in the others. A class segment perspective centers on the power and interests of competing factions of larger classes, as well as on the structure of the state in mediating this influence. The focus is on class segments because classes per se rarely form, in part because the social organization of capitalism creates intraclass conflict as well as interclass conflict.[33] In fact, most conflict occurs within classes, while interclass conflict is relatively rare even though it is the underlying process in capitalism. Class segments have particular immediate interests that often conflict with those of other segments or with their class as a whole.[34] These interests tend to form along various cleavages, such as commodity differences (for example, cotton producers versus steel manufacturers), regional lines (southern versus midwestern agriculture), or position in class structures (large landowners versus small farmers). How competitive a commodity is in the world market shapes the economic interests and hence political preferences of producers.[35] Regional differences also influence the interests of producers and can create segments.[36] Such distinct social locations often encourage the formation of particular economic interests and political preferences.[37]

These three paths to fragmentation, and hence class segments, are evident in U.S. agriculture.[38] First, throughout most of the twentieth century, different regions specialized in particular commodities: cotton, tobacco, rice, and peanuts in the South; corn, soybeans, and hogs in the Corn Belt; and wheat in the Wheat Belt. Regional producers often developed competing economic interests, in part because of the different uses of the commodities. For example, wheat producers and corn producers often held competing interests because wheat is used for food, whereas corn is used for livestock feed. In addition, the competitiveness of each commodity in the world economy shaped the interests of producers.[39] The dominance of U.S. corn producers in world markets since the 1950s, for example, has led them to favor free trade and liberalization, but U.S. wheat producers faced much more international competition and consequently favored more controls in the world economy. Second, the particular class structure and political-economic context within each region shape the interests of producers, thereby creating segments. The regional class structures derive in part from different agricultural commodities, some of which have different labor requirements.[40] In the South before the 1970s, the plantation system centered on the relations between planters (landowners) and landless tenants and sharecroppers, with the former exerting extensive control over the latter's labor. The class position of the planters was one of economic and political dominance in the region.[41] In the Corn and Wheat Belts, however, owner-operated family farms were the center of the class structure. Many (petit bourgeois) producers engaged in simple commodity production, with control and ownership of the means of production but not of the labor power of others.[42] Yet some larger landowners were capitalists in that they could rent land, hire labor, and draw on far greater resources than most other farms. While political and economic power in the Corn and Wheat Belts was more dispersed than in the South, owners of large farms in these regions often dominated important farm organizations central to political influence. Third, the general production process in agriculture—inputs (fertilizer, machinery, etc.) production, primary production (planting, harvesting, etc.), and outputs (trading, processing, etc.)—shapes the interests of class segments, leading to fragmentation and even conflict.

Capital concentration in input and output processes has long squeezed primary producers within a relationship of unequal power.[43] Yet large agribusiness corporations tended to give little attention to agricultural policy until the 1960s.[44]

With such lines of division, then, a homogeneous "agricultural class" does not exist; instead, segments of agriculture emerge. Since competition within the market economy creates numerous divisions, deep schisms can emerge and weaken classes. How are conflicts between class segments resolved? The state often becomes the arbitrator among segments as they appeal to the state to protect their interests, but the power of competing segments is key.[45]

### Class Segments and Political Power

A class segment perspective examines how factions of social classes (for example, large landowners or unionized workers) attempt to shape policies to reflect their economic interests. Two processes are particularly important in transforming economic interests into state policy: *embedding interests within the state* and *coalition-building*. These two processes are the primary sources of political power for class segments. Furthermore, class segments form political coalitions with other segments.

First, class segments try to embed their interests within the state. This process can be understood as a continuum with a range of locations in the state that afford class segments varying degrees of influence over the policy formation and implementation processes. In the United States, class segments have access, albeit unequal access, to various state channels because the state is decentralized and permeable.[46] The porosity of the U.S. state allows almost all interests to express their views, thereby encouraging classes to act as segments rather than as unified classes.[47] Where these segments embed their interests within the state is important. Perhaps the most marginal location of embeddedness is participation in one of the more superficial of political dimensions: voting in elections, which is far removed from policy formation and implementation. A much stronger position of embeddedness can be found in access to key legislators, individual lobbying, or control over several legislators. In the South, for example, the planters' political dominance gave them great influence over the Democratic Party, regionally and nationally, until about 1970.[48] This influence over national politics was in part due to the electoral stability created by the region's one-party politics, which allowed southern senators and representatives to built up decades of seniority and thereby control important congressional committees.[49] By contrast, influence over political parties in the Corn and Wheat Belts was not as monopolized, but dominant producers in these regions tended to exert significant influence over farm organizations: the Farm Bureau in the Corn Belt and the NFU in the Wheat Belt.[50] In terms of political parties, the Republican Party tended to dominate in the Corn Belt, while the Wheat Belt was frequently split between Democrats and Republicans. These organizations gave corn and wheat producers access to the policy formation process. Another important point of access comes in the administrative bureaucracies and the implementation of policies. The corn segment, for instance, embedded its interests most effectively within the U.S. Department of Agriculture (USDA).[51] Examining where the interests of competing class segments were embedded in the state sheds much light on the shifts in twentieth-century agricultural policy.

Second, class segments form coalitions with one another since no single class segment can dominate the state.[52] Class segments that dominate industry, finance, and agriculture are particularly important for understanding state policies and the process of coalition formation. Barrington Moore points out that, as they try to shape state policies, some class segments will form center coalitions, or power blocs, that become the defining aspect of the political regime.[53] Such coalitions can create opportunities for weaker segments (such as farmworkers) to influence policy.[54] In the case of supply management policy, the civil rights movement played a surprisingly important role in this regard. From this perspective, then, discerning patterns in class coalitions is important for understanding policy formation and trajectories. Class coalitions in capitalism regularly shift because of the dynamism of the market.[55] An important factor in the durability of class coalitions is whether they are based on economic interests or political imperatives. Coalitions based on economic interests are often much more enduring because the shared interest is stable. Those based on political imperatives, however, tend to be much more tenuous, in part because the resulting compromises may eventually impinge on economic interests of segments within the coalition.[56]

As this book demonstrates, the political battles between competing coalitions within agriculture are central to understanding the expansion and contraction of twentieth-century agricultural policy. Behind the formation and shifting of such coalitions lie the changing economic interests of different segments within agriculture. To understand how such interests drive changes in coalitions and national policy, we need to look at the market—the world economy.

### Class Segments and the World Economy

The development of political coalitions and national policies occurs within the context of the market—that is, the capitalist world economy. Importantly, the world economy is *the* economy; it is not merely a backdrop to "national economies." Many scholars have argued effectively that a separation between domestic and international economics does not exist.[57] This is true not just of the current era of "globalization," but also of the history of the capitalist world economy, stretching back to its formation in the "long sixteenth century."[58] Economic events that appear to be domestic reflect occurrences in the world economy. At its root, the world economy involves an international division of labor in which nations fulfill particular functions. This international division of labor connects nations through a hierarchy—including the core, semi-periphery, and periphery—in which some nations (the core) engage in production and trade that is more profitable than that of other nations (the periphery).

National production and producers' interests, then, are formed in relation to the world economy. In particular, international trade and position in the world economy influence the economic interests of agricultural segments. We can see this in one of the basic characteristics of the world economy: the relative extent of free trade and protectionism. Agricultural segments play important roles in the process through which nations within the world economy periodically build up national trade barriers only to tear them down at a later date.[59] Thus, the world economy shapes the economic interests and policy preferences of class segments, leading to the formation of particular political coalitions.

Significantly, agriculture and the world economy have a reciprocal relationship: even as segments' interests in free trade or protectionism stem from this relationship, by achieving free trade or protections, they inherently alter the shape of the market. The world economy is not a haphazard conglomeration of individual nations, nor simply a reflection of national economic relations. Rather, international food regimes guide agricultural production and trade.[60] International regimes are the rules, regulations, and normative frameworks set forth in bilateral or multilateral agreements that guide trade and national policies in particular economic sectors. Scholars use the concept of international regimes to discuss and analyze different sectors of the world economy, such as industry, finance, and agriculture.[61] Food regimes do not necessarily follow the trade, production, or consumption patterns exhibited by regimes for industry, commerce, or finance. The shape and efficacy of a regime rest largely on the power of the hegemonic nation and competition between classes, or segments of classes, in different nations.[62] That is, the most powerful nation economically, the world economic hegemon, exerts significant influence over the shape of international regimes. And the structure of international regimes is shaped by class coalitions, especially those in the world economic hegemon. International regimes, however, are not permanent. Polanyi's discussion of shifts between economic regimes of free trade and regulation helps to shed light on the process through which regimes change.[63]

Surprisingly, many scholars fail to incorporate the role of the world economy into their analyses.[64] Even scholars whose analyses are comparative in nature often fail to examine this role in shaping national agricultural policy. For example, Adam Sheingate points out that the United States, France, and Japan shared a similar trajectory for agricultural policy: "During the nineteenth century, government policies were largely promotional; . . . In the 1930s governments intervened in agricultural markets . . . [and] in the 1990s . . . retrenchment became the focus of agricultural debates."[65] This policy trajectory, shared by diverse nations, suggests that something larger than the individual nation-state influenced the direction of policy. By heavily emphasizing political institutions in explaining this shared trajectory, Sheingate misses the central role of the world economy in shaping national policies, including agricultural policy. As Chapter 6 demonstrates, the world economy was the common thread in the trajectories of agricultural policy in various nations because the U.S. food regime set rules and regulations that facilitated the expansion of agricultural policy during the mid-twentieth century, as well as its eventual retrenchment in the 1990s.

### State Policy, the Market, and Class Transformation

National policies and the world economy not only influence the economic interests of class segments, but these factors can also reshape class structures. This process of class transformation is central to understanding the formation, development, and retrenchment of national policies. Perhaps most importantly, class transformation can fundamentally alter the political power of class segments. As a result, this process can lead to changes in political coalitions that undergird particular national policies. When this occurs, those policies become vulnerable to retrenchment.

Three processes often characterize the process of class transformation. First, as Polanyi showed, the market is a hazardous place even for strong classes. Market competition and fluctuations, and even the mere social organization of the market, compel classes, or segments of classes, to favor state intervention into the market.[66] That is, class segments try to influence the state to protect their economic interests. Second, state intervention in the market changes class relations. Ironically, national policies favored by a particular class segment may later change the class structure of which that segment is a part. Changes in the class structure can also create space in which weaker classes, such as tenant farmers, can organize. Third, class transformation alters the economic interests of classes and therefore alters class alliances. This process can result in a class segment opposing a national policy that it had earlier helped to create. Class transformation may lead to shifts in political coalitions, especially when weaker classes organize, which may then result in pronounced changes in state policy.[67] Furthermore, such changes in class relations can have the effect of freeing the forces of production, which may further reshape the market and class interests.

This book, particularly Chapter 5, demonstrates how class transformation is central to understanding the contours of agricultural policy in the twentieth century. In particular, class transformation in the South lies behind much of the retrenchment in supply management policy. Southern planters fell from power as supply management policy reshaped the southern class structure. The irony of this change is that the planters shaped the AAA to preserve their status atop the southern class structure. By reshaping the political economy of the South, the AAA created an opportunity for southern blacks to challenge racial segregation and, by implication, the dominance of the planters. Although the civil rights movement largely has been ignored in analyses of the retrenchment of supply management policy, it nevertheless played a fundamental role in the demise of the class structure of the plantation system and the transformation of southern planters into large commercial farmers. As a result, their ability to protect supply management policy also waned. Thus, New Deal agricultural policy became vulnerable to change in the 1970s because of the transformation of the class structure of the rural South.

Scholars who look at the transformation of the structure of agriculture tend to focus on three changes: the shrinking farm population, the declining number of farms, and the increase in average farm acreage. These trends were the important changes in the Midwest, and they occurred also in the South; however, the South experienced far more fundamental changes than these. Few scholars who try to explain twentieth-century agricultural policy pay close attention to the changing class structure of the rural South.

Class dynamics, market processes, and state policies are central to comprehending divisions within agriculture and how they influence supply management policy. Class transformation was a central part of agricultural retrenchment, particularly by changing the political power of some segments. The world economy played an important role as well, partly by creating divergent economic interests within agriculture. Analyses that pay insufficient attention to these factors fail to fully explain the trajectories of national policies.

Agricultural policy frequently pits one segment of agriculture against another. The roots of divisions within agriculture, however, lay in the very structure of agriculture and the dynamics of the world economy. The basic nature of a capitalist economy rests upon competition and the drive for profit as the source of its economic dynamism. These divisions surfaced in political conflicts over the shape of agricultural policy throughout the twentieth century.

Over the next several chapters, I demonstrate how a class segment perspective—with its emphasis on the relations among class, state, and market—explains the formation, development, and retrenchment of supply management policy. Along the way, each chapter addresses particular elements of alternative explanations, such as partisan politics and the "decline of agriculture." While unfolding in a manner that is roughly chronological, this book offers an analysis of agricultural policy that moves beyond a mere history. Part I, which includes Chapters 2 and 3, examines the process of national policy formation and expansion. Chapter 2 begins with the 1920s and explores the particular political-economic context that preceded the creation of supply management. This chapter focuses on why supply management policy did not emerge in the 1920s despite economic troubles in agriculture and political pressure for such a policy. Chapter 3 demonstrates how class, state, and market were important in influencing the timing of the formation of supply management policy, emphasizing how class power lay behind the efficacy of policy experts. This chapter also explores some of the opposition to the AAA and discusses the expansion of supply management during World War II.

Part II, which includes Chapters 4 through 7, is the core of the analysis and focuses on the gradual retrenchment of supply management policy. Chapters 4 through 6 explore the contours of agricultural policy during the middle of the twentieth century. Each chapter emphasizes a particular aspect of the overall analysis, with Chapter 4 focusing on shifting economic interests; Chapter 5 on changing political power, particularly of southern planters; and Chapter 6 on the dynamics of the world economy, especially the reciprocal relationship between the world economy and U.S. agricultural policy. In this way, each chapter provides a different lens through which to view and understand U.S. agricultural policy in the mid-1900s. Although the central theme of the relationship between class, state, and market runs throughout these three chapters, each chapter explains one facet of the story of how political coalitions underlie the contours of twentieth-century agricultural policy. Chapter 4 challenges the idea that partisan politics are a central factor in explaining the retrenchment of supply management policy between 1954 and 1975. Chapter 5 demonstrates how most understandings of political power in agriculture miss a fundamental aspect of agricultural retrenchment: the transformation of the rural class structure in the South. Chapter 6 shows that the relationship between national policy and the world economy is central to making sense of the retrenchment of supply management policy.

Chapter 7 critiques the argument that partisan politics and market prices explain agricultural retrenchment, particularly the FAIR Act. The three themes of economic interests, political power, and the world economy come together in this chapter to explain this act, the most significant and recent instance of retrenchment in agricultural policy. With the FAIR Act placed in the larger historical context of the life of supply management policy, the underlying importance of coalitions within agriculture is clear. Without a firm understanding of these coalitions, the substance and significance of the act are less clear.

Finally, this book ends with an epilogue that brings the analysis closer to today by discussing the Farm Security and Rural Investment Act of 2002. The general analysis of this book, especially the importance of agricultural coalitions, is reaffirmed by the content of this legislation.

For now, we begin with the early attempts to create supply management policy.

# PART I

# Creating State Intervention

# CHAPTER 2

# The Early Battles Lost

## Reaching for Regulation, 1920–1932

To allow the market mechanism to be sole director of the fate of human beings
and their natural environment indeed, even of the amount and use of purchasing
power, would result in the demolition of society.
—KARL POLANYI, *THE GREAT TRANSFORMATION*

From about 1900 through the 1920s, U.S. agricultural policy focused primarily on educating farmers, supporting agricultural research, creating periodic tariffs, and implementing government regulation of some agribusinesses, such as grain elevators. Agricultural policy exerted little direct influence on commodity prices or production decisions, which were both largely shaped by market mechanisms. Exploring this period can help to advance our understanding of the life of supply management policy. Despite the lack of extensive government intervention into agricultural prices or production, the political and economic context of the 1920s would seem to have been conducive to the creation of supply management policy: farmers faced market volatility in terms of prices and production; and farmers, farm organizations, and farm state politicians pushed for a policy that would help control overproduction. In fact, there were several attempts to create something close to supply management, but each ended in failure. Examining why this happened deepens our understanding of how supply management policy finally emerged.

### Agricultural Policy before Supply Management

At the beginning of the twentieth century, agriculture in the United States was guided primarily by the market economy. The federal government did not provide subsidies to farmers, set production guidelines, or support

market prices. Instead, national agricultural policy had three primary focuses: education and research, tariff protections, and agribusiness regulation.

First, education centered on informing farmers about new scientific
techniques and new technologies, such as tractors, combines, hybrid seeds,
and new rotation methods. This emphasis on education in agricultural policy
had roots reaching back to the Civil War, although the policy was also part of
the larger Progressive Era, ranging roughly from the 1890s to the 1920s, that
tried to bring more professionalization and expert knowledge to public life.
The government's focus on supporting research to make farming more scientific began in 1862 with the creation of the USDA and the system of land-
grant universities.[1] Then, in 1887, the Hatch Act established agricultural
experiment stations, which also searched for ways to make farming more
efficient or to improve agricultural technologies. Later, the Smith-Lever Act
of 1914 created a system of cooperative extension services to more effectively
spread the knowledge and technologies developed in the land-grant complex. Notably, this legislation was "almost as much a charter for the Farm
Bureau as it [was] for the Extension Service."[2] The Extension Service and
the Farm Bureau were created to communicate new technologies from the
USDA directly to farmers. Finally, the government also supported vocational education that trained farmers and farmworkers. Southern Democrats
were most supportive of vocational education legislation, such as the Smith-
Hughes Act of 1917.[3] The point of all of this legislation was to spread modern
scientific farming techniques, not to directly affect production decisions or
prices.

Second, in terms of trade and protection, the government left much of
agriculture largely to the market. Although the federal government raised
tariffs on many industrial goods during the second half of the nineteenth
century, relatively few agricultural goods were protected, in part because
U.S. producers of important commodities—particularly wheat, corn, and
cotton—fared well in or even dominated world markets. Nonetheless, relatively minor tariff rates were imposed on a few agricultural commodities:
barley, corn, eggs, potatoes, wheat, and wool.[4] Notably, southern agricultural
commodities were not protected by tariff, and the tariff issue divided agriculture. Farmers in the South so thoroughly dominated world cotton and
tobacco markets that they fully supported free trade. Farmers in the Midwest
and West, by contrast, believed that tariffs protected them from international
competition even though the United States dominated domestic and world

grain markets.[5] Particularly from 1890 through the early 1900s, protectionist segments of agriculture exerted influence over tariff policy through a
coalition with industrial capital. However, in 1913, the Underwood Tariff
"reduced rates on manufactured goods to pre–Civil War levels, with agricultural machinery placed on the free list."[6] Tariff levels remained low, leaving
the market as the primary influence on agricultural prices and production,
until the passage of the Smoot-Hawley Tariff of 1930, which raised tariff
rates dramatically.[7] For most of the early twentieth century, then, few tariffs
existed in agriculture.

The third element of agricultural policy before supply management
was the regulation of some agribusinesses. In 1905 and 1906, the regulatory
powers of the USDA expanded to include forest conservation, food and drug
regulation, and meat inspection.[8] As the First World War neared, the Cotton
Futures Act of 1914 and the Grain Standards Act of 1916 standardized the
grading of these commodities.[9] The Warehouse Act of 1916 created USDA-
regulated warehouses for the storage of commodities such as cotton. Then,
after the war, the Farm Bloc in Congress again increased government regulation in agriculture with the Packers and Stockyards Act of 1921 and the
Grain Futures Trading Act of 1922.[10] Although these and other pieces of
legislation helped to bring some economic stability by limiting many ex-
cesses, such regulatory activity affected the market economy primarily at
the margins. Relative to the supply management policy that would develop
during the New Deal, the federal government engaged in little economic
intervention in agriculture in the early twentieth century.

How did agricultural policy shift from such limited intervention to extensive market intervention? To fully understand the rise of supply management policy, we need to look at the economic troubles that agriculture
faced during the 1920s, as well as the policy solutions that were offered to
ameliorate those problems. Although a depression emerged in agriculture in
the 1920s, supply management policy did not begin until 1933. As agricultural policy before the New Deal demonstrates, supply management was not
simply the result of political pressure or economic turmoil.

### Agriculture in Crisis

During and immediately after World War I, agriculture prospered
as market prices for cotton, wheat, and corn increased significantly between
1914 and 1919: cotton rose from about 7 cents per pound to about 35 cents

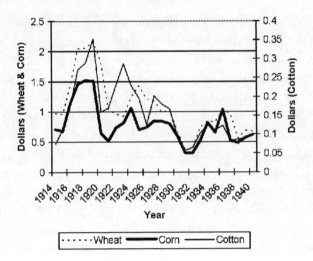

2.1. Market prices for wheat, corn, and cotton, 1914–1940. *Source:* USDA, National Agricultural Statistics Service, "Prices Rec'd by Farmers." *Note:* Cotton is on an axis with a different scale because putting cotton, wheat, and corn on the same scale minimizes the shifts in the price of cotton.

per pound, wheat went from 97 cents a bushel to $2.16 a bushel, and corn rose from 67 cents a bushel to $1.44 a bushel. Figure 2.1 shows this sharp increase in prices. Consequently, gross farm income more than doubled from $7.6 billion to $17.7 billion during this period.[11] This prosperity was interrupted by a short but intense depression from 1920 to 1921, when market prices fell by more than 50 percent: cotton fell to 17 cents a pound, wheat to $1.03 a bushel, and corn to 46 cents a bushel. Likewise, gross farm income fell to $10.5 billion in 1921—a drop of more than 40 percent in two years.

As Figure 2.1 shows, market prices rebounded for a few years after the collapse. By 1924, cotton prices reached 23 cents per pound, and corn prices climbed back to $1.06 per bushel. That same year, wheat prices rose to $1.24 per bushel and then climbed higher to $1.43 per bushel in 1925. Clearly, prices did not reach the levels of 1919, but they did recover somewhat from the short and intense collapse. This rebound ended, however, after 1925 when prices resumed their downward slide. Between 1926 and 1930, cotton prices averaged about 16.8 cents a pound, wheat prices about $1.10 a bushel, and corn prices about 80 cents a bushel. This represented a decline of at least 20 percent from the cotton and corn prices in 1924 and the wheat price in 1925. Furthermore, agricultural prices began a continuous decline in 1927 that would not end for about six years. A few years before the U.S. stock market crash in October 1929, then, agriculture began to slip into depression.[12]

After 1929, however, agriculture markets collapsed as the entire economy was enveloped by the depression. In 1932, agriculture hit bottom along with the rest of the economy. Wheat prices declined to about 98 cents per bushel in 1928, which constituted a drop of more than 30 percent since 1925. Even worse, wheat was a mere 37.5 cents per bushel by 1932—a decline of more than 70 percent from 1925. Cotton prices faired just as poorly. After rising to about 23 cents a pound in 1924, cotton prices fell to 5.7 cents a pound in 1931—a drop of about 75 percent in only seven years. Finally, corn prices experienced a similar decline: after reaching $1.06 in 1924, corn fell to 32 cents a bushel in 1932—a 70 percent decline.

The collapse in agricultural prices, of course, led to a sharp decline in overall farm income as this economic crisis affected everything from wheat to hogs to tobacco.[13] Gross per farm income fell from $2,051 in 1926 to $953 in 1932—a drop of about 54 percent in seven years.[14] Per farm income for cotton farmers fell even faster, by 68 percent between 1929 and 1932, from $1,245 to $397.[15] With farm prices and income in a free fall, farmers throughout the country increasingly faced bankruptcy and bank foreclosure on their farm mortgages. The rate of farm foreclosures and bankruptcies in the United States more than doubled from 18.7 per one thousand farms in 1931 to 38.8 per one thousand farms in 1933.[16] Thus, the depression of the late 1920s and early 1930s devastated U.S. agriculture.

What factors lay behind this depression? How did farmers come to be faced with prices that collapsed to a mere fraction of their previous levels? Part of the answer rests in U.S. agricultural production levels, and part of it is found at the level of the world economy.

### Behind the Depression

Cotton, wheat, and corn farmers began to face a serious economic crisis due to overproduction and declining exports during the mid-1920s. However, the relative importance of export and production levels differed for each commodity. For cotton, production and exports rose and fell together, but production increased faster than exports. By contrast, wheat production rose at the same time exports fell. The situation was slightly different for corn, though, because production declined slightly while exports fell dramatically. Regardless of whether production or exports was the crucial factor,

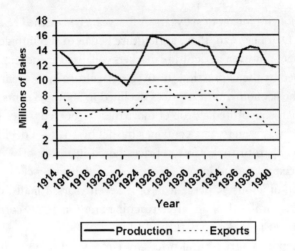

2.2. U.S. cotton production and exports (three-year averages), 1914–1940. *Sources:* USDA, *Agricultural Statistics, 1941;* USDA, *Agricultural Statistics, 1946.*

the end result was the same: a surplus drove down prices and, consequently, farm income.

Figure 2.2 shows changes in U.S. cotton production and exports in the early 1900s. Between 1920 and 1925, annual U.S. cotton production averaged about 12 million bales, and cotton prices averaged about 21 cents per pound. In 1926, however, cotton farmers produced a record 18 million bales of cotton. Over the next several years, cotton production declined slightly but still remained high, averaging more than 15 million bales between 1926 and 1931. At the same time, the average yearly surplus of cotton more than doubled from 2.5 million bales between 1921 and 1925 to 5.6 million bales between 1927 and 1932.[17]

Although cotton exports and production appear to mirror one another, the gap between production and exports was greater during the period 1926–1931 than 1921–1925. In the early 1920s, average annual cotton production was about 11.5 million bales, and average annual exports were about 6.7 million bales. Between 1926 and 1931, however, cotton production averaged 15.2 million bales, while cotton exports averaged 8.5 million bales. Therefore, even though cotton exports were higher between 1926 and 1931, the increase in cotton production still outpaced exports.[18] Thus, the collapse in cotton prices was fueled by expanding production but not declining exports.

Part of the cotton problem also stemmed from increased production in the world economy. Between 1921 and 1925, annual world cotton production

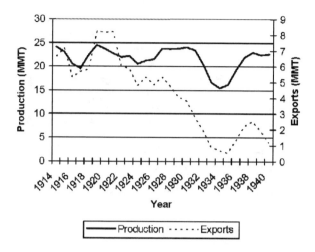

2.3. U.S. wheat production and exports (three-year averages), 1914–1940. *Source:* USDA, *Agricultural Statistics, 1962.*

averaged 20 million bales. However, world cotton production climbed to almost 27 million bales per year between 1926 and 1931. World cotton production increased 55 percent between 1922 and 1931. A significant portion of this increase in world cotton production came from the increase within the United States, which accounted for more than half of the world's cotton. Consequently, the rise in cotton production within the United States was a central cause for the surplus and depressed prices U.S. cotton farmers faced.

The situation for wheat production and exports differed slightly from that faced by cotton. Figure 2.3 shows that as wheat production increased between 1924 and 1928, wheat exports fell off dramatically. Production increased from 18.2 million metric tons (MMT) in 1925 to 25 MMT in 1928. Exports fell by 60 percent between 1920 and 1923 and then leveled off for a few years, only to decline further after 1927. By 1933, wheat exports amounted to only 1.1 MMT, a drop of about 90 percent from 1920. Thus, whereas cotton production outpaced rising exports, wheat production rose at the very moment when exports collapsed. The excess supply of wheat was due to the combination of rising production and declining exports.

Part of the decline in wheat exports was due to an increase in wheat production throughout the world economy, from 80 MMT in 1920 to 109 MMT in 1927. In particular, Canada, Argentina, Australia, and Russia each significantly increased their production of wheat. This crowded U.S. wheat

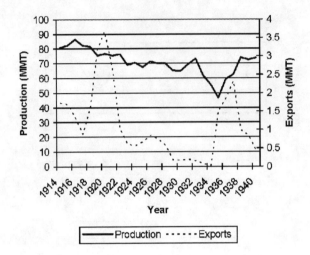

2.4. U.S. corn production and exports (three-year averages), 1914–1940. *Source:* USDA, *Agricultural Statistics, 1952.*

out of international markets, particularly Europe, thus contributing to lower wheat exports.

For corn, the situation was different still. Figure 2.4 shows that U.S. corn production remained relatively constant during the 1920s, but corn exports fell dramatically. Corn production declined slightly from 77 MMT in 1920 to 69 MMT in 1923 but leveled off thereafter until 1929. By contrast, corn exports fell from 5.3 MMT in 1921 to 0.3 MMT in 1924. Between 1925 and 1932, exports averaged only 0.5 MMT per year. Despite these trends, a surplus of corn still helped to drive down market prices.

In short, the trends in production and exports for these three agricultural commodities differed during the 1920s: cotton production and exports increased, but exports increased more slowly; wheat production increased as exports collapsed; and corn production remained relatively stable while exports fell. Several factors contributed to the increased cotton and wheat production, including "better seeds, improved control of diseases, more efficient specialization, and the adoption of mechanized equipment."[19] Perhaps most importantly, however, cotton and wheat acreage in the United States expanded. Cotton production expanded westward into Arkansas, Oklahoma, and Texas. In these states, cotton acreage increased from 15 million acres in 1921 to almost 27 million acres in 1926. In Texas alone, cotton acreage increased from 10.7 million acres to 18.3 million acres. Wheat acreage also increased by more than 20 percent between 1924 and 1929, from 52 million acres to 63 million acres. This expansion in cotton and wheat acreage led to increased production and contributed to surpluses that drove down the prices of these commodities.

Regarding exports, two factors created a context in which U.S. exports would be expected to decline. First, agriculture in Europe recovered from the devastation of World War I, meaning that fewer agricultural goods from the United States would make their way into Europe. Furthermore, many European nations began to rely on agricultural exports to help pay down debts accumulated during the war. As a result, European farmers began competing with U.S. farmers for export markets. Second, the United States came out of World War I as a creditor nation rather than a debtor nation, which it had previously been. This status increased the value of the dollar relative to other currencies, thereby increasing the cost of U.S. goods, including cotton and wheat. Thus, the nation's creditor status made U.S. exports less competitive.

Although cotton, wheat, and corn each faced problems of overproduction during the 1920s, the importance of shifts in production and exports differed for each commodity. First, the trends were different for these commodities. Production increased significantly for cotton and slightly for wheat, but corn production remained stable. Exports plummeted for corn and wheat, but actually increased for cotton. Second, exports were of varying importance for these commodities: more than half of all U.S. cotton was exported, as was about one-quarter of wheat, but less than 5 percent of corn was exported. Therefore, the rise in production for cotton and the collapse of exports for wheat had a much larger effect on producers of these commodities than did the shifts in corn production and exports. Despite the varying underlying effects of these trends, proposed political solutions focused on both production and exports.

### Political Solutions before the New Deal

The solution to a problem is generally determined by how the problem is defined. Competing definitions of the problem facing agriculture emerged during the 1920s and 1930s. One group of politicians and agricultural economists believed that the depression in agriculture resulted from overproduction, whereas a competing group "assessed the problem as general, resulting from the collapse of money and credit."[20] Yet another group of public officials believed the problem was one of economic and market organization. The attempted policy solutions, therefore, varied across time (corresponding in part to partisan shifts) as well as between the federal and state governments, depending on which explanation for the economic turmoil had more powerful supporters.

The initial political responses to the depression in agriculture came during the Republican administrations of the 1920s: Warren Harding (1920–1923), Calvin Coolidge (1923–1928), and Herbert Hoover (1928–1932). After Harding died in 1923, Coolidge became president and then won reelection in 1924. Hoover served as secretary of commerce in both Coolidge administrations and was influential in how the administrations approached agricultural policy.[21] In 1928, he was elected president. Each of these administrations opposed policy solutions that created significant intrusion into the economy, such as directly influencing prices or production. These administrations saw the problem in agriculture as deriving from a lack of economic coordination. Consequently, Coolidge and Hoover favored policies that centered on strengthening farm cooperatives to improve the marketing of agricultural commodities, and they opposed any proposal to have the government intervene in market prices or restrict production.[22]

By contrast, members of Congress from farm regions increasingly favored more extensive action by the federal government. In an effort to win such policies, senators and representatives from the South, Wheat Belt, and Corn Belt formed the Farm Bloc in 1921. The Farm Bloc reached across partisan boundaries, uniting some Democrats and Republicans. Yet southern support for extensive action by the federal government emerged much more slowly than it did in the Midwest. During the Harding administration, the Farm Bloc was initially quite successful at winning policies to increase government regulation in agriculture: the Packers and Stockyards Act, the Agricultural Commodities Act, and the Grain Futures Trading Act. Yet these policies did little to address the underlying problems of production, exports, and prices that agriculture faced after 1924. For this purpose, the Farm Bloc rallied behind a proposal to raise agricultural prices by controlling surpluses: the McNary-Haugen bill. This bill, then, was an early attempt to create supply management policy.

## The McNary-Haugen Bill

In 1921, George Peek, a farm equipment manufacturer from Illinois, wrote a policy proposal to address what he saw as the primary problems creating the economic turmoil farmers faced.[23] Peek was particularly focused on raising farm prices relative to industrial prices and controlling agricultural surpluses.[24] To these ends, Peek's proposal called for the government to raise agricultural prices by purchasing surpluses and selling them abroad at world market prices. Domestic prices would be protected by a tariff, further helping to raise agricultural prices relative to those in industry, which had long been protected by tariffs. The difference between the higher domestic price and the lower world price would be covered by an "equalization fee" charged to farmers based on their production.[25] As Douglas Hurt says, "Farmers would benefit to the degree that the domestic price, less the equalization fee, would be higher than the domestic price without dumping the surplus on the world market."[26] The equalization fee would not only help pay for the program, but proponents hoped it would reduce the risk of overproduction as well.[27]

In 1924, Senator Charles McNary (R-OR) and Representative Gilbert Haugen (R-IA) introduced Peek's proposal in the Senate and House, respectively. Initially, this proposal was supported by some farm experts and members of the Farm Bloc in Congress but not many farm organizations. Gilbert Fite states that the "major farm organizations lent only moderate support" to the bill and that they were "divided and confused" on proposals to control surpluses.[28] Most support for the bill came from the Corn and Wheat Belts, while southerners were reluctant to offer their support. One of the few farm organizations to offer early support for the bill was the Iowa Farm Bureau.[29] The lack of support from many farm organizations and the South in particular was in part due to the recovery, however weak, that followed the collapse of agricultural prices in 1920 (see Figure 2.1). Again, cotton prices increased from 17 cents per pound in 1921 to 29 cents a pound in 1923; though cotton prices fell again after 1923, they did not fall below 20 cents per pound until 1925. Consequently, southern Democrats did not necessarily feel compelled to support the McNary-Haugen bill in 1924. Similar trends existed for wheat and corn prices, leading many midwestern farm organizations to believe that such legislation was unnecessary.

In addition to the modest economic recovery, political opposition to the McNary-Haugen bill was immense in 1924. President Coolidge, Secretary of Commerce Hoover, grain traders, millers, bankers, the U.S. Chamber of Commerce, most economists, many newspaper editors, and even a number of farm leaders expressed opposition to the bill.[30] Against this political-economic backdrop, the McNary-Haugen bill was defeated soundly (155 yeas to 233 nays) in a House vote on June 3, 1924.[31] Southern Democrats, who voted overwhelmingly against the bill, were a primary factor in the bill's defeat.[32] More than 70 percent of southern congressional representatives voted against it, and the lack of support for the bill from southern senators also hindered its progress in the Senate.

After the defeat of the McNary-Haugen bill in the House, farm organizations increased their advocacy for the bill through the newly formed American Council of Agriculture (ACA). The ACA was an umbrella organization through which many farm organizations could concentrate their lobbying efforts and present a more unified farm voice. In this way, the McNary-Haugen bill became a "farm organization bill"; it became the preferred legislation of farm organizations. Nonetheless, the bill was defeated again in the House on May 21, 1926, and then defeated in the Senate on June 24, 1926. In contrast to the 1924 vote, however, passage of the bill in the Senate seemed quite possible.[33] The McNary-Haugen bill inched closer to passage partly because farm organizations had dramatically increased their political activities, largely through the ACA. Additionally, southern Democrats gradually gave more support to the bill as cotton prices declined to less than 13 cents per pound in 1926. More than half of southern Democrats in the House voted in favor of the bill. Southern support in the Senate was still lacking as two-thirds of southern Democrats voted against it.[34]

After the defeats in 1926, the McNary-Haugen bill was revised to cover six commodities: cotton, wheat, corn, hogs, rice, and tobacco.[35] The inclusion of the most important southern commodities—cotton, tobacco, and rice—and the worsening economic conditions for agriculture after 1925 combined to increase southern support for the bill. The Senate and House passed the bill in February 1927, but President Coolidge vetoed it.[36] This same scenario played out again in the spring of 1928: the House and Senate passed the bill, and Coolidge vetoed it again.[37] In both years, more than half of southern representatives voted for the bill in the House. In the Senate, however, southern support increased each year: in 1927, half of southern Democrats voted for the McNary-Haugen bill; and in 1928, more than 70 percent of southern Democrats voted for it. This was a dramatic turnaround from the defeat of the bill in the Senate in 1926, when most southern Democrats opposed it.[38] Southern congressional support was central to the passage of the bill in both years. Nevertheless, neither strong support from the South nor vigorous lobbying from farm organizations was enough to overcome the Coolidge administration's opposition. In 1928, the Senate tried to override Coolidge's second veto but failed to garner the required two-thirds majority.[39] This was the political end of the McNary-Haugen bill.

The politics of the McNary-Haugen bill reveal some important points about the formation of national policies. When one looks at policy formation, attention sometimes turns to who writes a particular policy—policy experts, interest groups, elites, or someone else? In the case of the McNary-Haugen bill, as already pointed out, farm experts—particularly George Peek—wrote and developed the proposed policy. And, at least initially, this was not a bill that gained the attention, much less the support, of many farm organizations. Thus, the bill was created without help from farm organizations; it was not a farm organization bill. Policy formation, however, is a process that includes more than the mere writing of a policy. More important, in fact, are the political and economic contexts that allow a proposal to become law. The progression of the McNary-Haugen bill toward becoming federal policy demonstrates the importance of the political-economic context in understanding policy formation, as well as the near irrelevance of authorship.

Table 2.1 summarizes the policy formation process for the McNary-Haugen bill. The fact that farm experts originally created and favored this bill, independently of farm organizations, could not win its passage in 1924. Nor could support from most farm organizations prevent the bill's defeat in 1926. Only when producers of the major commodities—cotton, wheat, corn, tobacco, and rice—coalesced behind the bill did it pass the House and Senate (and get a vote to try to override the presidential veto). Therefore, even though farm organizations had no hand in writing the McNary-Haugen bill, their support was important for its advancement. Furthermore, the addition of southern support was crucial, for it was only when the South swung in favor of the bill that it passed the Senate. Still, the political power of the farm organizations and southern Democrats was limited to Congress. The Republican Coolidge administration excluded these rural interests, opposed any policy that involved direct action by the government to raise prices, and instead favored proposals that focused on strengthening agricultural cooperatives.[40] In the end, the location of rural interests within the federal government was not strong enough to win their preferred policy. This would remain the case until southern Democrats gained influence within the executive branch and even more congressional influence during the New Deal. However, they would have to wait four more years for that political context.

**Table 2.1.** Highlights of the (failed) policy formation process for the McNary-Haugen bills, 1924–1928

| Date | Event | Political-economic context |
| --- | --- | --- |
| January 16, 1924 | Bill introduced in House and Senate. (Hearings from January to April.) | Only "moderate" support from farm organizations for the bill. |
| June 3, 1924 | House defeats bill, 155–233. | Most southern Democrats opposed to the bill. |
| July 1924 | Farm organizations form the American Council of Agriculture (ACA). | ACA formed to provide a unified lobby for agriculture in favor of the bill. |
| May 21, 1926 | House defeats bill, 167–212. | Support from the South increases as cotton prices fall. |
| June 24, 1926 | Senate defeats bill, 39–45. | |
| February 11, 1927 | Senate passes bill, 47–39. | Bill expands to include tobacco and rice. Southern support key to bill's passage. |
| February 17, 1927 | House passes bill, 214–178. | |
| February 25, 1927 | Coolidge vetoes bill. | |
| April 12, 1928 | Senate passes bill, 53–23. | Support continues to be strong from the South and from farm organizations. |
| May 14, 1928 | House passes bill, 204–117. | |
| May 23, 1928 | Coolidge vetoes bill. | |

In the meantime, this emerging agricultural coalition continued to lack the power to create a policy based on price supports and production controls during the Hoover administration.

## The Federal Farm Board

Advocates of state intervention on behalf of agriculture began to recognize the importance of their own lack of power in the presidential administration. In the 1928 presidential election, George Peek, the Iowa Farm

Bureau, and some Republican members of the Farm Bloc supported Illinois governor Frank Lowden for the Republican nomination.[41] Lowden supported federal farm aid and the McNary-Haugen bill.[42] Herbert Hoover, however, won the Republican nomination easily. In his acceptance speech, he declared the farm problem to be the most important problem facing the nation and promised to call a special session of Congress to develop legislation to address it.[43]

Nevertheless, many farm advocates and some Farm Bloc members were wary of Hoover because of his consistent and staunch opposition to the McNary-Haugen bills. Some farm advocates and organizations, including the Iowa Farm Bureau, even abandoned the Republican Party to support the Democratic candidate, Alfred Smith.[44] In particular, George Peek, a Republican his entire life up to 1928, campaigned aggressively for Smith in the Midwest. Smith, however, was tepid in his support of the principles of the McNary-Haugen bill, especially the equalization fee. Instead, he remained relatively vague about the nature of agriculture's problems and their solutions. As a result, there seemed to be little difference between the two candidates and party platforms.[45]

In the end, Hoover won the 1928 presidential election in a landslide, winning 84 percent of the electoral vote and 58 percent of the popular vote. Notably, Hoover carried every state in the Wheat and Corn Belts. Although Smith made inroads into parts of the rural Midwest and won more votes in the region than previous Democratic presidential candidates, he ultimately failed to win the support of enough farmers.[46] In fact, Republicans increased their hold over the Senate and the House with the 1928 election. In the 70th Congress (1927–1929), the Senate was closely divided, with forty-eight Republicans and forty-six Democrats, but after the 1928 election Republicans held fifty-six seats to the Democrats' thirty-nine. In the House, the Republicans went from a majority of 238 to 194 in the 70th Congress to a majority of 270 to 164 after 1928. The Republicans were firmly in control once again.

As president, Hoover remained opposed to legislation along the lines of the McNary-Haugen bill, following previous administrations in rejecting federal policies that would directly support market prices or restrict production. Instead, he favored efforts to help farmers through voluntary cooperative agreements and improved marketing. On April 15, 1929, Hoover called a special session of Congress to address the problems in agriculture, as well as the tariff. In a message to Congress on April 16, Hoover outlined his plans for agricultural policy. The centerpiece of his vision was federal assistance to agricultural cooperatives, but he also proposed the creation of "stabilization corporations" to protect farmers from "seasonal gluts and periodical surpluses."[47] Thus, Hoover acknowledged the need to address commodity surpluses, even if he was largely opposed to government intervention to control production. The president did not, however, propose a bill to Congress. Instead, he left it up to the House and Senate committees on agriculture to develop a bill that would meet his approval. In June 1929, Congress passed a bill that followed the plan outlined in Hoover's earlier message to Congress, and on June 15, Hoover signed into law the Agricultural Marketing Act (AMA).

The AMA centered on providing financial and managerial support for agricultural cooperatives. This, of course, was the policy each of the Republican administrations of the 1920s preferred.[48] Agricultural cooperatives would help to control the supply of agricultural goods by helping farmers to withhold surpluses from the market and thereby raise prices. This legislation allotted $500 million for loans to cooperatives "so they could make heavier advances to members than was generally the case and so they could market their holdings in an orderly fashion."[49] The idea was to help cooperatives become large enough to control large portions of the markets for grains, cotton, and other commodities. This, Hoover believed, would allow cooperatives to influence market prices through the orderly marketing of agricultural commodities.

Perhaps most importantly, the AMA created the Federal Farm Board, which oversaw loans to cooperatives and offered them professional assistance regarding marketing, management, and financial issues. The Farm Board also had the authority to create stabilization corporations to purchase seasonal surpluses of commodities, particularly wheat and cotton. Hoover, however, was more supportive of efforts to improve marketing and help cooperatives than he was of efforts to directly stabilize either prices or production.[50] In the end, the AMA differed from the McNary-Haugen bill (and the later AAA) in that the former sought to stabilize, rather than increase, agricultural prices and had no mechanism for controlling production. The AMA was merely a marketing policy that directly touched neither prices nor production. This was the AMA's downfall given the economic context of falling exports for wheat, rising production for wheat and cotton, and declining prices for most agricultural commodities.

The Farm Board ran into opposition where it most needed support, from cooperatives and grain traders, as it tried to develop national associations to coordinate regional and local cooperatives. Existing agricultural cooperatives were concerned that the board might intrude on their business and marketing decisions. Additionally, cooperatives had long competed with one another for members and market share. The Farm Board was not always capable of overcoming such relationships. In the end, the most accommodating cooperatives were those that needed financial assistance from the Farm Board. For their part, grain traders saw the board's national associations and stabilization corporations as threats to their economic well-being, and they labeled the board and the AMA "state socialism."[51] Thus, the Farm Board failed to coordinate effectively the cooperatives and traders in many commodities.

More importantly, the Great Depression shattered the United States, as well as the world economy, less than five months after the creation of the AMA. Between 1929 and 1932, prices for cotton, wheat, and corn plummeted by 60 percent (see Figure 2.1). Consequently, gross farm income fell by more than 50 percent. As discussed earlier, varying combinations of increased production and declining exports propelled prices downward (see Figures 2.2–2.4). The Farm Board was ill-equipped to deal with this economic collapse.

The Farm Board created stabilization corporations to purchase surpluses of wheat and cotton to stabilize prices for those commodities, but without mandatory reductions in production, farmers continued to produce more to make up for lower prices. Consequently, purchases of surplus cotton and wheat, and the consequent cost of storage, were draining the Farm Board's funds by 1931.[52] Yet production continued to rise, and prices continued to fall. Furthermore, the Farm Board lost more and more money on its loans to cooperatives, which were failing because of falling prices. The AMA's focus on improved marketing had led to its failure, and the Farm Board and President Hoover could offer only a weak alternative solution: they pleaded with farmers to reduce production.[53] Thus, Hoover and the Farm Board recognized that controlling production was necessary, but the president continued to believe that any such reduction had to be a voluntary move on the part of farmers.[54] Of course, farmers could not oblige the presidential pleas because the social organization of farming made voluntary reductions in production irrational.[55] The crisis continued unabated.

In 1931, the Farm Board attempted to reduce their stocks of cotton and wheat through exports after Hoover encouraged it to sell the surpluses to foreign governments on credit. Germany, for example, agreed to buy 600,000 bales of cotton and 7.5 million bushels of wheat.[56] The deal, however, could not make even a small dent in the mounting surpluses or the stocks held by the Farm Board, which had purchased 3.4 million bales of cotton and 275 million bushels of wheat by 1931.[57] The depression that now enveloped the entire world economy, and the resulting rise in tariffs, especially in Europe, made exports difficult even on credit. The Farm Board then tried a different approach, making a "commodity swap" in which it sent 25 million bushels of wheat to Brazil in exchange for 1 million bags of Brazilian coffee. This commodity swap, however, resulted in commercial U.S. wheat exports that normally went to Brazil being displaced.[58]

The situation was quickly worsening for cotton: production and carry-over reached record highs in 1931. The Farm Board tried to deal with the sharp increase in cotton production and carry-over stock by contacting governors of cotton-producing states to encourage them to cut cotton production. At Hoover's urging, the board suggested that the governors get cotton farmers to plow under every third row of cotton. However, the Farm Board would neither administer its cotton reduction proposal nor compensate farmers for reducing production. This elicited strong opposition from southern farmers and politicians, who believed that Hoover and the Farm Board were treating southerners unfairly.[59] Robert Snyder states, "Cotton farmers considered full compensation the only reasonable settlement."[60] But Hoover and the Farm Board were still opposed to any policy of mandatory production control with compensation.

By contrast, farm leaders and agricultural economists were formulating and gaining support for mandatory production control programs. These proposals went further than the McNary-Haugen bills, which used the equalization fee as an incentive against overproduction, and certainly went further than the administration's calls for voluntary reductions. At this time, however, the Farm Bureau opposed proposals for mandatory production controls, but some farm leaders, including George Peek and Henry A. Wallace (who would later serve as secretary of agriculture during the New Deal), were becoming convinced that such measures were necessary.[61] These efforts were, in part, preparation for the 1932 presidential election, although some attempts at controlling production were already emerging in the South.

## Calls for Production Controls in the South

While the Federal Farm Board was drowning amidst the turbulent market, public officials and farm leaders in the South grappled desperately with the cotton crisis. The dire economic situation in world cotton markets led many cotton producers and politicians in the South to advocate mandatory reductions in production to raise prices. In August 1931, Theodore Bilbo, governor of Mississippi, "proposed that the cotton-producing states attempt to alleviate their production and price dislocations by picking only two-thirds of the crop."[62] Two days later, the Farm Board made its proposal of plowing under every third row. With the backlash against the Farm Board, Bilbo's proposal did not go far. Nonetheless, even the board's unacceptable proposal could not dampen southern calls for controlling production.

Huey P. Long, governor of Louisiana, proposed a "cotton holiday" for 1932, during which the South would produce no cotton. Long proposed that southern states create laws mandating that farmers abstain from growing cotton in an attempt to reduce the surplus and raise prices. Long's proposal called for fines on those farmers who violated the holiday. A cotton holiday conference held in New Orleans in August 1931 was attended by state officials, planters, merchants, newspaper reporters and editors, and congressional representatives and senators from southern states. The conference endorsed Long's proposal, but the Farm Board warned against the likely deleterious effects of such a plan. Assuming that the cotton holiday had the effect of raising cotton prices, the primary beneficiaries of Long's proposal would be cotton farmers themselves. But such a plan would have negative effects on sharecroppers and tenants, local merchants, farm suppliers, and cotton ginners and their employees. In addition, a halt in U.S. cotton production would open international markets for cotton farmers in other countries, such as Egypt, which would thereby be encouraged to increase their own production. In this sense, then, the cotton problem needed to be addressed on the level of the world economy.[63]

Despite such drawbacks, the Louisiana state legislature passed Long's cotton holiday bill. The only state to join Louisiana in this endeavor, however, was South Carolina. Both states made their legislation contingent on other cotton states passing holiday legislation. The Texas state legislature followed a slightly different route, passing a plan to reduce, but not halt entirely, cotton production in 1932. Mississippi then passed legislation that would reduce the state's cotton acreage by 30 percent.[64] In the end, five southern states — Arkansas, Louisiana, Mississippi, South Carolina, and Texas — enacted mandatory cotton reduction legislation in 1931.[65] Alabama's governor, by contrast, refused to support such legislation. With several cotton states failing to pass reduction legislation, the cotton reduction movement in the South died.[66]

Although mandatory production controls were not put into place in the

South, the fact that five states passed and farmers throughout the South advocated for such legislation shows that a great many of the South's public officials and farmers supported a policy of supply management before 1932. Southern cotton growers, cooperatives, and politicians began to advocate for policies to directly support agricultural prices to levels of parity as well.[67] Snyder states that "virtually every issue central to the production control programs of the New Deal was discussed thoroughly in the mass meetings that were held across the South during the cotton crisis of 1931."[68] Thus, even before the creation of the AAA, the South already demonstrated that it favored the cornerstones of production controls and price supports. Still, the goal of supply management was elusive even with southerners firmly supporting the policy.

Supply management policy clearly broke with previous agricultural policy, which tended to focus on education, scientific farming, and technology. Nonetheless, that policy did not simply emerge in the 1930s out of nowhere. Instead, a series of attempts at forming supply management policy failed during the 1920s. Beneath the partisan battles were important dynamics of class conflicts and coalitions. The Republican Party was internally divided over the issue of agricultural policy at this time because the party rested on a coalition of segments of industry and agriculture. On the one hand, the national party was largely opposed to extensive government intervention into the economy, especially to raise prices or directly influence production. This position was reflected in the agricultural policies of Republican administrations during this decade. The Harding, Coolidge, and Hoover administrations all stood firmly against such proposals to increase government action directly into the market. On the other hand, congressional Republicans from the Corn and Wheat Belts advocated greater government intervention into the economy. The McNary-Haugen bills, which were early attempts at supply management policy, were Republican bills. The farm state Republicans in Congress, however, were unable to overcome the opposition, and veto, of their own party in the executive branch. Of course, without the eventual support of southern Democrats, this Republican bill would not have passed the House or Senate. Nonetheless, the formation of supply management policy had to wait for a more favorable Democratic administration in which southern planters would be able to exert much more influence over agricultural policy. That opportunity, of course, came in the form of the administration of Franklin D. Roosevelt and its New Deal after 1932.

CHAPTER 3

# Winning Supply Management
## A New Deal for Agriculture, 1933–1945

> . . . the liberal movement, intent on the spreading of the market system, was met
> by a protective countermovement tending towards its restriction . . .
> —KARL POLANYI, *THE GREAT TRANSFORMATION*

Although farmers, farm organizations, and politicians could not forge supply management policy in the 1920s, they finally won their battle during the Great Depression of the 1930s. The U.S. economy was devastated: between 1926 and 1933, the country's gross domestic product fell by about 25 percent, manufacturing wages fell by about 27 percent, farm income fell by about 47 percent, and the unemployment rate rose from about 2 percent to above 20 percent.[1] Poverty rose dramatically, in both urban and rural areas. Widespread hunger was seen in the dramatic expansion of soup lines; increasing homelessness was visible in the curbside belongings of families recently evicted from their homes; and the bank foreclosures on tens of thousands of family farms was evident in a great migration from the South and Midwest to California, as these families moved westward in hopes of finding employment and a fresh start.

In the depth of the depression, a time of dire need and despair, the federal government began to pursue a seemingly irrational policy: restricting the production and availability of many essential goods, including food. Furthermore, the point of restricting production was to raise prices during a period of falling incomes. So how did supply management policy emerge during this period? And why did this policy expand during the Second World War?

### The Pig Purchase Program

In August 1933, the federal government created the "pig purchase program" through which 4 million young pigs and 1 million pregnant sows

were to be slaughtered and pulled off of the market.[2] The government purchased the pigs based upon weight on a sliding scale of 5 to 9.5 cents per
pound, with the higher rate prevailing for the smaller pigs.[3] The program
aimed to reduce the supply of pork and thereby raise prices through two
means: (1) killing small pigs of between twenty-five and one hundred pounds
before they grew and became larger, and (2) killing pregnant sows before
they farrowed. Purchasing smaller pigs was intended to reduce the immediate supply of pork, and killing the pregnant sows was meant to reduce the
future supply of pork. This program was expected to remove about 2.6 billion pounds of pork from the market.[4]

The pig purchase program was to last from August to September 30,
1933. "The farrowing sow program failed to work out," however, because
farmers were reluctant to bring their pregnant sows to slaughter.[5] Consequently, the government decided to slaughter more young pigs. In the end,
6 million young pigs and two hundred thousand pregnant sows were slaughtered, with "practically all the leading packers in the country . . . working at
capacity killing and tanking pigs."[6] This program continued after September
1933, however, as the government periodically bought pigs off the market to
be slaughtered.[7] The government further expanded this program "by offering contracts to farmers to reduce . . . their hog production by 25 percent in
return for government benefit payments."[8]

The pigs slaughtered through this program were used for three purposes: fertilizer, hog feed, and meat for the poor.[9] According to Lawrence
Cheever, pigs weighing less than eighty-one pounds were to be "destroyed,"
while those heavier were to be "dressed, cured and later allocated to relief
agencies."[10] Approximately 100 million pounds of pork products were distributed for relief.[11] Fertilizer, however, turned out to be difficult to dispose
of: "Mountains of fertilizer—composed of ground up slaughtered pigs—are
piling up in the locality of the stock yards in various parts of the country . . .
and as a result masses are being taken to the 'dump yards' or thrown into old
quarries."[12] Thus, many of the slaughtered pigs went entirely unused. This
was not necessarily alarming to officials, however, because the central goal of
the program was to remove pigs from the market—not to provide relief for
people left poor and hungry by the economic collapse.

This same principle of restricting production and controlling surplus
amidst hunger and want was pursued throughout the agricultural sector of
the economy. In California, growers of oranges, peaches, lemons, and other
fruits organized cooperatives and created marketing agreements to reduce

production and dispose of surpluses by using them as by-products or sending them to the dump.[13] In the South, farmers plowed under more than 10 million acres of cotton and thereby destroyed 4 million potential bales of cotton, which served as the basic input for the U.S. textile industry.[14] And in the Midwest, the government asked wheat farmers to cut their harvest by 15 percent and corn farmers to take 20 million acres out of production.[15] Thus, the primary solution to agriculture's problems involved cutting back on production.

In a time of pervasive starvation and unemployment, the federal government destroyed many of the very things that were needed to alleviate poverty. This led to criticisms by "consumers who rightfully charged that people were starving while the federal government wasted food in order to prop up farm income."[16] John Simpson, president of the NFU, testified before the U.S. Senate that "the farmers are not producing too much. We need all this. What we have an overproduction of is empty stomachs and bare backs."[17] How did a policy so apparently mismatched with economic conditions emerge? Why did the federal government ask producers to restrict production and destroy much needed goods at a time when devastating poverty, hunger, and unemployment plagued the United States?

As with the pig purchase program, some of the commodities purchased under such programs went for relief to the needy: portions of surplus grain, butter, beef, and other agricultural commodities were distributed. However, "the quantities apparently needed [for relief] would not be sufficient to affect the market."[18] In other words, surpluses for many agricultural commodities were so great that they would remain even after relief efforts.[19] The primary purpose of the production control programs was to bring supply closer in line with demand.

The principle underlying these programs, seemingly so incongruous with the existing economic conditions, was the basis of the federal policy of supply management. This policy emerged during the New Deal of the 1930s and continued through the 1990s. Supply management, ironic as it may seem, preserved the market economy in agriculture and reinforced the structure of rural inequality.

### A New Deal for Agriculture

Democrat Franklin Delano Roosevelt defeated the Republican incumbent Hoover in the 1932 presidential election by a landslide; Roosevelt won 89 percent of the electoral vote and 57 percent of the popular vote. Unlike Alfred Smith in 1928, Roosevelt carried every state in the Wheat and Corn Belts. In addition, Democrats won substantial majorities in the U.S. House (313–117) and Senate (59–36). Roosevelt's New Deal brought national policies that significantly departed from those of the Republican administrations of the 1920s as he promised a more activist government, by which he meant a government more active in the economy. This was territory into which Harding, Coolidge, and Hoover were not willing to venture. And nowhere was Roosevelt's promise achieved as thoroughly as it was in agriculture.

## The Agricultural Adjustment Act

Shortly after his inauguration in 1933, Roosevelt called Congress into a special session to consider several bills to address various aspects of the depression, including the problems of agriculture. Roosevelt signed the AAA on May 12, 1933, and it was one of the first of his "alphabet programs" aimed at alleviating the depression.[20] The AAA set up two central programs, price supports and production controls, with the objective of raising farm prices by controlling the supply of agricultural commodities. This policy of supply management built on the experiences and programs developed during the previous ten years: the McNary-Haugen bills, the Agricultural Marketing Act, various production control proposals, and the cotton reduction legislation passed by southern states.

The Commodity Credit Corporation (CCC) was created in 1933 to administer price supports, which operated through "nonrecourse" loans. The CCC made these loans to farmers at about 60 to 70 percent of the parity price and stored the commodities. If the market price rose above the loan rate, then farmers could sell their crop and pay back the CCC loan, earning a profit on the difference between the higher market price and the loan rate. If prices remained below the loan rate, however, then the nonrecourse element of the loan operated: farmers had no recourse other than to forfeit their crop to the CCC, and the CCC could take no action against farmers who forfeited their crop. Consequently, farmers would receive an "adequate" price for their crop, and the CCC would effectively reduce the supply of commodities on the market with the expectation of stabilizing or even raising market prices. In essence, when market prices fell below price support levels, the CCC purchased basic commodities from farmers at the price support level as a means of pulling the commodities off the market, controlling supply, and raising farm income.

Price support levels were meant to raise agricultural prices, and hence farm income, relative to other consumer and industrial prices. Therefore, price supports were based on "parity," which aimed to give agricultural commodities "the same purchasing power in terms of goods and services farmers buy that the commodities had" in the period 1909–1914, when agricultural prices reached historic heights relative to other prices.[21] Price supports, then, gave agricultural prices parity with industrial prices, based on the ratio of prices between 1909 and 1914.

Production controls were administered by the Agricultural Adjustment Administration and were a means of limiting the supply of agricultural commodities. The AAA required farmers to adhere to acreage allotments, which were determined by growers' historical production of basic commodities. For example, farmers who had historically grown cotton on large numbers of acres were given large cotton allotments. Farmers who did not adhere to production controls would not receive price supports. Because historical production levels determined acreage allotments, the AAA was biased in favor of larger farms. The AAA also created set-aside programs that paid farmers to leave land idle.[22]

In addition to restrictions on acreage, the AAA created marketing agreements between farmers and processors. The secretary of agriculture could mediate the terms of the agreements to limit the supply of commodities that farmers could market and impose a fine on farmers who exceeded their marketing allotment. In this way, if farmers ignored controls on acreage, the USDA could still head off any potential surplus by limiting how much made it to the market.[23] Whether through restrictions on acreage or marketing, production controls under the AAA sought to eliminate surpluses and their degenerative effect on agricultural prices and farm income.

Under the AAA of 1933, government subsidies to farmers from price supports and production controls were funded by a tax on processors of agricultural commodities. Because the basic commodities—wheat, corn, cotton, tobacco, hogs, and rice—all needed to be processed in some fashion before they could be consumed, the processing tax was easy to administer. (The required processing also made it relatively easy to monitor production levels.) The secretary of agriculture set the level of the processing tax based on the difference between farm prices and parity prices. The "tax was placed on the 'first domestic processing' of agricultural commodities"—except for cotton ginning, which was exempt from the tax.[24] The aim of the processing tax was to prevent the cost of payments to farmers from straining the federal budget.

These two components, price supports (through CCC loans) and production controls (acreage allotments and marketing agreements), were the central elements of supply management policy under the AAA. But as will be seen shortly, the processing tax was the most controversial part of the policy. Before addressing the controversies created by the AAA, however, we should explore an important question: what factors influenced the shape of the AAA and Roosevelt's decision to pursue a policy of supply management?

### Shaping the AAA

Numerous scholars have analyzed the formation of the AAA, so my focus here is not to present an in-depth analysis or restate previous debates.[25] Instead, I merely focus on a few factors that stand out as particularly important in the shape of the AAA: previous agricultural policies and proposals, policy experts inside and outside the federal government, farm organizations, and southern Democrats and planters. One notable influence was the legacy of the battles over the McNary-Haugen bills of 1927 and 1928, which covered the same "basic" commodities as the AAA: wheat, corn, cotton, rice, tobacco, and hogs. Likewise, the processing tax of the AAA was similar to the funding mechanisms for earlier proposals, particularly the equalization fee of the McNary-Haugen bills.[26] Perhaps most notably, the concept of parity between agriculture, industry, and labor was the foundation of the McNary-Haugen bills of the 1920s. Thus, the legacy of the McNary-Haugen bills, and the political battles that surrounded them, clearly shaped the AAA.

The USDA played an important role in formulating the AAA as well. Roosevelt named as his secretary of agriculture Henry A. Wallace, who had been an advocate of the McNary-Haugen bills and their goal of achieving parity for agriculture. The similarities between the bills and the AAA are not necessarily surprising in light of this. Wallace was also a supporter of M. L. Wilson's proposal for production controls through acreage allotments, which went further than the McNary-Haugen bills had. With the sharp rise in agricultural surpluses, especially of wheat and cotton, between 1929 and 1932, Wallace and other supporters of the McNary-Haugen bills began to recognize that more dramatic measures were needed to control surpluses. The AAA reflected this position.

As secretary of agriculture, Wallace held a conference with farm leaders to get their input on the impending legislation. Many farm organizations came from the conference supporting the administration's proposal, and some farm organizations even felt as if they had influenced the shape of the bill. Of the farm organizations supporting the AAA, the Farm Bureau was among the most powerful and enthusiastic about supply management. Under the leadership of new president Edward O'Neal, the Farm Bureau endorsed the AAA and even had some input into its formation. Unlike his predecessor, who opposed mandatory production controls, O'Neal, a cotton farmer from Alabama, saw a need for government intervention in agriculture, including in controlling production. After the AAA passed, the leaders of the Farm Bureau felt that "it was their program which the Roosevelt administration had adopted."[27]

Although these organizations may have exerted some influence, the "real authors of the bill" were Wallace, Undersecretary of Agriculture Rexford Tugwell, and the agrarian economist Mordecai Ezekiel.[28] None of these three had direct or strong ties to any particular farm organization. Furthermore, George Peek and a few other farm experts were also consulted on the bill, which was completed a few days after the conference of farm leaders. Nonetheless, farm organizations were not entirely absent as influences over the actual writing of the AAA. Most notably, the legislation was drafted by Frederick Lee, legislative counsel for the Farm Bureau, and Jerome Frank of the USDA.[29] Thus, the AAA was influenced by previous policy developments, farm organizations, and farm policy experts.

New Deal legislation also had to be acceptable to, and was influenced by, the southern Democrats in the House and Senate. In Congress, southern Democrats held powerful positions, including Senate majority leader (Joseph Robinson of Arkansas), House majority leader (Joseph Byrns of Tennessee), the chair of the Senate Committee on Finance (Pat Harrison of Mississippi), and the chair of the House Ways and Means Committee (Robert Doughton of North Carolina).[30] The dominance of southern Democrats over such key legislative positions gave them much influence over the shape and substance of New Deal policies.[31] For example, the Social Security Act of 1935 and the National Labor Relations Act of 1937 both explicitly excluded agricultural workers. As a result, most southern blacks were effectively excluded from these federal policies. In each instance, southern Democrats were protecting the racial political economy of the South.[32] On national policies, then, southern Democrats no doubt looked out for the interests of the southern planters.

This was especially true on the issue of agriculture, as southern Democrats and planters welcomed the AAA. First, southern Democrats played key roles in its passage: Marvin Jones of Texas was the chair of the House Agriculture Committee, John Bankhead of Alabama headed the Senate Agriculture Committee, and Joseph Robinson of Arkansas guided the AAA through the Senate as majority leader.[33] Furthermore, more than 80 percent of southern senators voted for the AAA in 1933.[34]

Southern support for and influence over the AAA was likewise evident in the implementation of supply management policy. For example, Oscar Johnston, president of the largest cotton plantation in Mississippi, was the finance director of the Agricultural Adjustment Administration.[35] The creation of the CCC came about when Johnston "suggested government loans to cotton farmers at a rate above the market price."[36] In response to Johnston's suggestion, Roosevelt asked Jesse Jones, the chairman of the Reconstruction Finance Corporation, to create such loans. Jones then created the CCC to administer the loans.[37] Furthermore, southern planters dominated local agencies administering AAA programs.[38] Thus, the influence of planters pervaded the AAA from the federal government to the local administration.

The legislative and administrative influence of the South over the AAA was clear. With its focus on production control, the AAA displayed elements of the cotton holiday and reduction legislation enacted or considered by southern states in 1931. In 1933, the federal government paid cotton farmers to plow under approximately one-fourth of the cotton crop.[39] The policy imprint of southern planters was clear beyond the focus on price supports and production controls. For example, half of the basic commodities that were field crops were primarily southern commodities: cotton, tobacco, and rice.[40] In addition, the AAA payments were dispersed in such a manner that landowners were not required to share them with tenants.[41] Thus, understanding supply management policy is impossible without acknowledging the role of southern Democrats and southern planters in making the policy possible and influencing its shape. Supply management policy bore the imprint of the southern class structure.

The AAA in Action

The USDA and the Agricultural Adjustment Administration moved quickly to implement the price supports and production controls of the AAA. The cotton reduction program spent more than $200 million to pay southern farmers to plow under portions of their cotton crop, which had already been planted by the time the AAA was passed. The AAA was widely supported in the South, where the vast majority of cotton growers participated in the programs.[42] Southern cotton production fell from 13 million bales in 1933 to 9.6 million bales in 1934 and 10.6 million in 1935. And after averaging 39.5 million acres between 1929 and 1932, U.S. cotton production averaged 28 million acres between 1934 and 1936. The AAA cotton reduction program facilitated changes in the rural class structure of the South by pushing tens of thousands of tenant farmers and sharecroppers off the farm. (Chapter 5 analyzes these changes in detail.)

In the Midwest, the pig purchase program, which resulted in the slaughter of 6 million pigs, reduced the amount of pork available on the market. Yet Secretary Wallace recognized that the program would fail to raise pork prices if the production of corn and other livestock feed was not reduced. Therefore, corn and wheat farmers cut back their acreage and overall production. U.S. corn acreage fell from 110 million in 1932 to 93 million in 1936, and wheat acreage fell from 57 million to 49 million—a decline of about 15 percent for each commodity. Production levels fell even more dramatically: corn production fell from about 82 MMT in 1932 to 40 MMT in 1936, and wheat production fell from 25.6 MMT to 17.1 MMT during the same period. The decreased production was also in part due to a severe drought that hit parts of the Corn and Wheat Belts in 1934. Nonetheless, production controls seemed somewhat effective: between 1932 and 1935, cotton production fell by almost 20 percent, corn fell by 10 percent, and wheat fell by 25 percent.

This policy of supply management also achieved its goal of boosting farm income by making the state deeply involved in the market economy. Cotton prices almost doubled, and wheat and corn prices almost tripled between 1932 and 1936. Increased prices then led to higher farm income: after falling from $1,746 in 1930 to $953 in 1932, per farm income rose back up to $1,583 in 1936—an increase of more than 65 percent in four years.[43] Despite the apparent success of price supports and production controls, however, the AAA faced serious political challenges and created significant conflict within agriculture.

## Conflict in the First AAA

Many groups in agriculture welcomed the price supports and production controls of the first AAA, but other factions of agriculture opposed supply management. First, some farmers opposed the price-fixing and production dictates that the AAA created. Most such opposition came from the Corn Belt. While some southern planters opposed the AAA, most were staunch supporters of the policy. Second, conflict emerged over the extent to which the AAA would attempt to reform agriculture. Within the Agricultural Adjustment Administration, some officials believed that New Deal agricultural programs should aim to alleviate rural poverty and inequality, especially in the South, through social reforms. Third, and perhaps most important, many corporations that processed agricultural commodities—such as grain processors, cotton mills, and meat packers—opposed the manner of financing supply management. The processing tax created by the AAA rested squarely upon these corporations. Although each of these conflicts threatened the AAA to varying degrees, supply management policy emerged as the basic principle of long-term U.S. agricultural policy by 1940. Each of these conflicts reveal important dynamics—the staunch support of southern planters and some opposition from the Corn Belt and from agribusiness—that would influence agricultural policy for the rest of the twentieth century.

### Farmers against the New Deal

Some farm organizations opposed the AAA, and they tended to do so for one of two reasons: either because the policy failed to provide enough support to farmers, or because it went too far in imposing "regimentation" and government control upon farmers.[44] A few farm organizations argued that the AAA should provide farmers with support based on "cost of production" rather than parity.[45] The NFU, which was strongest in the Wheat Belt, was the largest farm organization to oppose the AAA for providing too little support to farmers; it instead favored support based on the cost of production. John Simpson, president of the NFU, criticized the focus on parity, which he argued would give farmers less than half of the cost of production.[46] The Missouri Farmers Association, led by William Hirth, and the Farmers Holiday Association, led by Milo Reno, also favored cost of production over parity. When the Senate was formulating the AAA, George Norris (R-NE) introduced an amendment that would pay farmers based on cost of production. The Roosevelt administration opposed any such measure, however, and Secretary Wallace got Congress to drop the measure from the final version of the bill, in part by asserting that the USDA was unable to calculate the cost of production for agricultural commodities.

After the passage of the AAA, these farm leaders and their organizations continued to criticize the administration's agricultural policy. Their primary criticism of the AAA remained focused on the use of parity in providing relief to farmers, but each organization likewise expressed opposition to production controls that left farm acres idle and destroyed livestock during a period of hunger and poverty. Both Simpson and Hirth argued that agricultural production should not be reduced until all Americans had adequate diets.[47] All of these farm leaders made their opposition to the AAA known in letters to Roosevelt, the Agricultural Adjustment Administration, and the USDA; through speeches and calls to farmers to protest the AAA; and in testimony during congressional hearings. In the end, such opposition failed to influence national agricultural policy. The Roosevelt administration, especially the Department of Agriculture, saw the solutions put forth by these farm leaders and organizations as too radical and responded with promises that were left unfulfilled.[48]

A variety of relatively small farm organizations opposed the AAA not because it failed to provide adequate support to farmers but because they saw it as imposing unnecessary and "un-American" controls on farmers. Most notable among these organizations was the Farmers Independence Council (FIC). Led by Dan Casement, who owned a large cattle farm in Kansas, the FIC expressed significant concerns that the federal government would take control of agriculture. Supported by meat processors, the FIC was particularly opposed to the government's corn-hog program and the processing tax that funded relief payments. Through such opposition, Casement and the FIC claimed to be protecting the liberty and independence of farmers from government control. Thus, organizations like the FIC opposed the AAA not because it failed to provide enough support but because supply management marked an unacceptable expansion of the federal government's reach.

Some farmers criticized the processing tax of the AAA, arguing that farmers ultimately paid this tax because processors simply paid lower prices to farmers to make up for the tax.[49] After the Supreme Court ruled the AAA and its processing tax unconstitutional in 1936, several small farm organizations emerged, including the National Farmers Process Tax Recovery Association (FPTRA), the Corn Belt Liberty League (CBLL), and the Farmers Guild. The FPTRA struggled unsuccessfully to get the federal government to return to farmers the money they had lost because of the processing tax on hogs. The CBLL organized farmers in opposition to production controls. Most, though not all, of the opposition of this sort came from farmers in the Corn Belt.[50]

Organizations like the FIC and the CBLL rarely had more than several hundred members, and the Roosevelt administration and the USDA responded to these groups with attempts to undermine them. As with the NFU and other more radical organizations, the administration tried to co-opt some of the conservative farm organizations that opposed the AAA. When such efforts failed, the administration turned to more direct tactics: threatening the organizations and using the Postal Service to investigate possible fraudulent activities; conducting congressional investigations into the organizations; directing county agents to oppose the organizations; attacking them in rural newspapers; and, of course, working to defeat legislation they supported.[51] In the end, the administration effectively quieted opposition by farmers, and supply management based on parity continued as national policy.

### Conflict over Rural Reform

The AAA also created conflict among segments of agriculture over another aspect of the policy: rural reform.[52] The most notable conflict emerged in the South between tenants and sharecroppers on the one hand and planters on the other. Disagreement existed over what portion of AAA payments, if any, tenants and sharecroppers should receive. Under the AAA, landowners signed contracts to restrict their acreage and limit production, and AAA payments were sent directly to landowners with the instructions that "a sharecropper was to receive one-half of the payments, a share-tenant two-thirds, and a cash-tenant all."[53] But many planters refused to share the AAA payments with their tenants or sharecroppers. Consequently, a political battle over payment distribution emerged both in the federal government's agricultural bureaucracy and in the cotton fields of the South.

Although some AAA administrators were concerned about the welfare of sharecroppers and tenants, who could be severely adversely affected by a reduction in production, there was a general acknowledgment that the cooperation of planters was fundamentally important for the policy's success. Southern planters' dominance over the political economy of the region meant that they could determine the success or failure of New Deal agricultural policy. Nonetheless, a division emerged within the Agricultural Adjustment Administration over the distribution of AAA payments. One group within the Agricultural Adjustment Administration opposed using agricultural policy as a means of rural reforms. This group included Chester Davis, who was chief of the Production Division; Oscar Johnston, who was head of the Finance Division; and Cully Cobb, who headed the Cotton Section. In particular, Johnston and Cobb were from Mississippi and had significant ties to southern planters. The primary focus of these conservative agrarians was raising farm prices through production controls; rural reform was largely absent from their agenda. As the head of the Agricultural Adjustment Administration, George Peek tended to agree with this group that supply management policy took precedence over rural reform.

Opposed to this group of conservative agrarians was a core group of "urban liberals," who were mostly lawyers from the Northeast who pushed for rural reforms.[54] Not only did the urban liberals argue that landowners ought to be required to share AAA payments with tenants and sharecroppers, but they also proposed redistributing some land to allow tenants and sharecroppers to become small, independent farmers. This group was led by Rexford Tugwell, who was the undersecretary of agriculture, and Jerome Frank, who was the general counsel of the Agricultural Adjustment Administration. Several members of this group, including Gardner "Pat" Jackson, were in the Consumer Division of the Agricultural Adjustment Administration.

Outside of the USDA, this conflict assumed the form of a sometimes violent battle between tenants/croppers and planters in the South. The Southern Tenant Farmers Union (STFU) was founded and led by H. L. Mitchell and Clay East, two socialist organizers, in Arkansas in July 1934. This group advocated for the rights of tenants and sharecroppers, particularly to share in the benefits distributed by the AAA. The STFU organized strikes and lobbied for assistance to tenants and croppers, but their efforts were met with violence and intimidation.

The STFU, for example, won little support for its struggle in Arkansas, which was the home state of Joseph Robinson, the Senate majority leader, who was central to the passage of Roosevelt's New Deal legislation. The president avoided offending southern Democrats, like Robinson, who were important to the success of his administration's policies. Likewise, the STFU found little support in the USDA or the Agricultural Adjustment Administration. Davis, Cobb, Johnston, and others opposed upsetting the organization of the rural South, and their contacts in the South told them that Mitchell and East were "Communists" trying to start "uprisings" among black tenants and croppers.[55] Furthermore, Secretary Wallace was particularly hesitant to pursue actions that would incur the wrath of conservative southern Democrats. Nor did the STFU garner much support from southern Democrats in Congress since neither tenant farmers nor sharecroppers had much access to voting. Finally, planters tended to dominate the local committees administering the AAA, while tenants were largely excluded from representation.[56] At every level of government, then, the interests of southern planters were generally protected.

The urban liberals, however, did advocate for the STFU and the interests of tenants, croppers, and poorer farmers. In February 1935, they made a valiant push to secure the interests of tenant farmers. With Davis, who had replaced Peek as the AAA administrator, away on a trip to the Midwest, Jerome Frank "issued a telegram to all state AAA offices in the South" to enforce cotton program contracts in a manner that favored tenants.[57] Davis quickly got word of this through "hundreds of complaints from planters, Extension agents, and Chambers of Commerce over the proposed legal interpretation."[58] Davis returned to Washington and demanded that Wallace "authorize him to request the resignations" of Frank, Jackson, and several other urban liberals.[59] Wallace agreed, largely because taking a stance behind Frank's interpretation of the cotton contracts would have cost Wallace his cabinet post and endangered other New Deal programs. Southern Democrats and planters were politically powerful enough to exact such a high price for undermining their interests. As a result, the STFU's strongest advocates were removed from government in what became known as the "liberal purge."

Tugwell responded to the purge by offering his resignation to President Roosevelt, who encouraged him to remain in the administration. Shortly thereafter, the president issued an executive order creating the Resettlement Administration (RA), which became the Farm Security Administration (FSA) and was independent of the Department of Agriculture. Like the urban liberal reformers, the RA/FSA "assisted small and tenant farmers, stood up for southern blacks, and generally represented the 'lower-third' in rural America."[60] And again like the urban liberals, such a progressive stance would eventually cost the RA/FSA its place in the federal agricultural bureaucracy during World War II.

Despite the liberal purge, legislation in 1938 required landowners to share AAA payments with tenants and sharecroppers. Following this legislation, however, planters frequently expelled tenants from their land and hired croppers and tenants as wage laborers, who had no legal claim to federal farm subsidies. In this way, the planters won the battle over the distribution of AAA payments. Here again, supply management policy, centered on price supports and production controls, solidified its position as the core of U.S. agricultural policy. Ironically, as Chapter 5 explains, this policy ultimately undermined the very system that planters and conservative agrarians fought to protect: the southern plantation system.

### The Revolt of Agricultural Processors

Arguably more threatening to the AAA than resistance from farmers or even the political conflict over rural reform was the staunch opposition from many agricultural processors. This group essentially paid for the subsidies through the processing tax. Importantly, the agricultural processors opposed the processing tax from the outset. Processors of wheat and livestock were prominent among opponents to the AAA. For example, Oscar Meyer, president of one of the largest meat processors, testified in opposition to the processing tax, "it is my firm conviction that a tax of this type, levied upon the processor is not collectible." In addition, he added, "any tax upon pork will almost immediately have to reflect itself in the form of lower hog prices, equivalent to the tax, so that, like all past legislation, legislative agricultural panaceas, this legislation will accomplish nothing; will, in fact, deepen the plight of the farmer."[61] Both Meyer and T. G. Lee, president of Armour & Co., testified that the processing tax would be harmful to meat prices and passed back along to the farmer, thereby undermining the policy.[62] Wheat processors also expressed objections to the processing tax.[63]

Despite such claims, Congress paid little attention to the opposition of agricultural processors and traders. The supporters of the nascent AAA — that is, the Farm Bureau, farm policy experts such as Peek and Wallace, and most importantly the southern Democrats and planters — were too well-embedded within the state and had too much power in the policy formation process to have their interests thwarted. This was the dominant coalition within agriculture.

Yet as with other portions of industry still opposed to regulation and government intervention, the interests of processors were embedded within the courts. The U.S. courts already had a long history of protecting the interests of business and private property. The very framework and language of property law ensured this. Additionally, seven of the nine Supreme Court justices (including the chief justice) had been appointed by Republican administrations, with the remaining two having been appointed by Democratic president Woodrow Wilson.[64] Franklin Roosevelt did not appoint a justice to the Supreme Court until 1937; consequently, the Court was the Roosevelt administration's "strongest visible opponent."[65] In May 1935, the Supreme Court ruled the National Industrial Recovery Act (NIRA) of 1933 to be unconstitutional. The NIRA set up industry boards to coordinate prices, wages, working conditions, and other aspects of industry. This was the administration's centerpiece of business legislation, and the Supreme Court's ruling hobbled the New Deal. The administration was anticipating similar court challenges to the AAA just months after the law was passed.[66] In fact, shortly after the Supreme Court voided the NIRA, Congress approved amendments to the AAA "to provide standards sufficient to meet the test of delegation of power, and to limit the control over agriculture to products which clearly entered interstate commerce."[67] The changes, however, left the processing tax unaltered. Therefore, while agricultural processors had little influence over the policy formation process, they could still try to protect their interests through the courts.[68]

Various processors sued the government, claiming that this tax was an undue burden and was therefore unconstitutional. Indeed, more than seventeen hundred lawsuits had been filed against the AAA by the end of 1935.[69] In December 1935, the Supreme Court heard the case of *United States v. Butler*, which challenged the constitutionality of the processing tax used to fund AAA benefits. The primary claimant was the Hoosac Mills Corporation, a bankrupt cotton milling corporation in Massachusetts.[70] William M. Butler was a cotton manufacturer and a receiver of Hoosac Mills. On January 6, 1936, the Supreme Court declared in a six to three decision that the AAA and its processing tax were unconstitutional.[71]

The administration defended the AAA on the basis of the government's right to tax and regulate interstate commerce. Because the Constitution gave the federal government these powers, the administration argued, the AAA was constitutional. The Court's majority, however, rejected this reasoning. Writing for the majority, Justice Owen Roberts focused on two central aspects of the AAA: the tax on processors used to fund subsidies to farmers, and the regulation of production by using acreage allotments tied to benefit payments. Roberts wrote that the processing tax was "the expropriation of money from one group for the benefit of another" and therefore was not covered under Congress's authority to tax as provided in the Constitution.[72] The processing tax, according to Roberts, was not used to provide for the general welfare of the nation but for the benefit of a particular group: "The whole revenue from the levy is appropriated in aid of crop control; none of it is made available for general governmental use."[73] Consequently, the Court majority ruled that the AAA could not be funded by the processing tax, which it deemed unconstitutional.

Just as important, the Court's majority ruled that the AAA's production controls were likewise unconstitutional because they infringed on the rights reserved for states in the Constitution.[74] As Justice Roberts argued, "The act . . . is a statutory plan to regulate and control agricultural production, a matter beyond the powers delegated to the federal government."[75] In addition, he argued that the production controls were not voluntary because the tax and benefit payments amounted to economic coercion.[76] Thus, Justice Roberts summed up the majority conclusion by stating that "Congress has no power to enforce its commands on the farmer to the ends sought by the Agricultural Adjustment Act."[77]

Justice Harlan Stone wrote a strong dissent that at times chastised Robert's "tortured" view of the Constitution.[78] He also criticized the majority for its zeal in invalidating the actions of the administration and Congress. In particular, Stone challenged the majority's assertion that the AAA payments amounted to "economic coercion."[79] Although justices Louis Brandeis and Benjamin Cardozo joined Stone in dissent, the New Deal had lost its agricultural program.

Some of the political connections behind this case are noteworthy. William Butler had been a campaign manager for Calvin Coolidge, Republican Party chairman in 1924, and a Massachusetts senator.[80] George Wharton Pepper was the lawyer for Hoosac Mills, and he was a "lifelong friend of Supreme Court Justice Owen Roberts," who wrote the court's decision. Some contemporaries felt that Justice Roberts ought to have recused himself. The dissenting justices included appointees by Hoover, Coolidge, and Wilson. Of further note, the dissenting Republican appointees, justices Stone and Cardozo, were both from New York, which was Roosevelt's home state. To whatever extent these factors were important or not, the most fundamental point is that supply management policy was lost, at least briefly, under pressure from agribusiness processors.

## Resurrecting Supply Management in the AAA of 1938

Congress responded to the Supreme Court's ruling on the AAA by quickly passing the Soil Conservation and Domestic Allotment (SCDA) Act in February 1936. This legislation—influenced by droughts in 1934, 1935, and 1936—paid farmers to reduce their production of "soil-depleting" crops, which tended to be defined so as to overlap with the commodities that were overproduced. Payments under the SCDA Act were funded by general treasury funds rather than processing taxes. In these two ways, the act avoided the two primary points of contention that the Supreme Court had with the AAA: federal intervention and regulation of agricultural production, which the Court majority saw as a state power; and processing taxes, upon which the Court looked unfavorably. The production controls were based on the claim that limiting the production of soil-depleting commodities was in the interest of the general welfare, thus strengthening the SCDA Act's constitutional standing.

Long-term agricultural policy, however, was framed by the passage of the second AAA in 1938, which set price support levels between 52 percent and 75 percent of parity for the basic commodities. Like the SCDA Act, the second AAA dispensed with the processing taxes and instead funded the benefit payments through general treasury funds. The AAA of 1938 used three methods of controlling production: soil conservation allotments, to limit the production of soil-depleting crops; marketing quotas; and acreage allotments. As in 1933, the new AAA was designed to meet the approval of farm organizations, especially the Farm Bureau, and southern Democrats. As before, a conference of farm leaders provided input on the policy proposals. And again, as with the first AAA, more than 80 percent of southern senators voted for the AAA in 1938.[81]

By 1938, the Supreme Court had issued rulings indicating that its position on federal intervention into the economy had shifted. In 1937, the Court upheld the National Labor Relations Act (that is, the Wagner Act), which enforced the right of workers to form unions and engage in collective bargaining with employers. In addition, the face and orientation of the Supreme Court changed before the passage of the second AAA in February 1938. Two conservative justices—Willis Van Devanter, a Taft appointee; and George Sutherland, a Harding appointee—retired, and President Roosevelt appointed two justices friendly to the New Deal: Hugo Black (in August 1937) and Stanley Reed (in January 1938), both southern Democrats. Additionally, in February 1937, Roosevelt proposed expanding the number of Supreme Court Justices from nine to fifteen, which would have allowed him to appoint six new justices presumably friendly to the New Deal. Although the Senate rejected Roosevelt's proposal, Gregory Hooks states that the "effort contributed to a reorientation of the Court."[82] With a more friendly Supreme Court, a Democratic administration, and a Democratically controlled House and Senate, supply management policy was no longer threatened in any serious way. The cotton-wheat-corn coalition was part of the dominant political coalition in the United States, and its economic interests were thereby well-embedded in the state.

## Wartime Expansion of Supply Management

During World War II, the position of supply management as the fundamental core of national agricultural policy was solidified in two ways. First, supply management policy expanded beyond the limits of the New Deal. In 1941, an amendment by Representative Henry Steagall (D-AL) increased the number of commodities eligible for price supports and production controls from six to twenty.[83] Before the war, supply management policy covered only the basic commodities: corn, wheat, cotton, rice, peanuts, and tobacco. The Steagall Amendment expanded the commodities covered by price supports and production controls to include hogs, eggs, chickens, turkeys, milk, butterfat, dry peas, dry beans, soybeans, flaxseed and peanuts for oil, American-Egyptian cotton, potatoes, and sweet potatoes.[84] This legislation also increased price support levels to 85 percent of parity for the six basic commodities. In 1942, the Stabilization Act again raised supports for the basic commodities, this time to 90 percent of parity. Section 8 of this legislation further "provided that the prices of basic commodities would be supported at 90 per cent parity for two years immediately" following the end of the war.[85] Section 9 provided the same guarantee for the nonbasic commodities specified in the Steagall Amendment. Additional legislation in 1944 raised price supports for cotton to 95 percent of parity. Finally, by 1945, supply management policy covered 166 agricultural commodities.[86] Thus, supply management policy expanded significantly during the war.

Second, alternative agricultural policies, specifically rural reform, that had contended for implementation during the New Deal were finally eliminated and forgotten during the war years. The FSA—which housed urban liberals who tended to side with tenants, sharecroppers, farmworkers, and poor farmers on policy questions—was weakened during the war (including having its budget appropriation withheld by the House Committee on Agriculture) and disbanded in 1946.[87] The Bureau of Agricultural Economics (BAE)—which housed the agrarian intellectuals who urged rural reforms, albeit at a slower pace than the urban liberals—was also weakened during the war and formally abolished in 1953. The elimination of these bureaucracies meant that agricultural policy would center on supply management through production controls and price supports, all tilted in favor of larger and more affluent farmers.

The fact that supply management expanded and solidified its place as national agricultural policy at this time is noteworthy because the war increased the consumption of agricultural commodities, thereby eliminating surpluses and raising farm prices. In other words, wartime demand solved the problems that farmers had faced during the previous two decades. In this economic context, supply management might seem to have been unnecessary. In fact, at the outset of the war, the USDA asked farmers to increase their production of particular agricultural commodities. Before farmers increased production, however, farm organizations sought assurances of price parity.[88] The memory of economic disorder in agriculture after the First World War was still vivid for many farmers, farm leaders, and politicians. The Steagall Amendment and the Stabilization Act met these requests for protection from market volatility by raising the price floor for agricultural commodities and extending these higher price supports for two years after the war ended.

With such protection secured, farmers expanded the production of agricultural commodities needed for the war effort. Wheat production increased from 22.1 MMT in 1940 to 30.1 MMT in 1945, an increase of 36 percent. Average annual wheat production during the war was 26.8 MMT compared with 20.3 MMT between 1930 and 1939. Likewise, corn production increased from 70 MMT in 1940 to 81.2 MMT in 1945. Average annual corn production during the war was 84.1 MMT compared with 65.9 MMT during the 1930s, an increase of 28 percent. Part of the increase in grain production occurred as southern farmers shifted away from cotton production. Cotton acreage declined by about 18 percent between 1939 and 1945.[89] Cotton production likewise fell. From 1920 to 1939, it averaged about 13.1 million bales per year, but it fell to 11.2 million bales between 1941 and 1945.[90] In fact, cotton production fell to 9 million bales in 1945, which was the first time since 1899 that it failed to reach 9.5 million bales. Much of the acreage shifted out of cotton went to producing soybeans and other oilseeds, grains, or vegetables. The federal government encouraged such shifts in agriculture by setting production goals and using bonuses, production payments, and high price supports—all to meet the food demands the war created.

In terms of farm income, however, "price supports and production controls were largely superfluous because the war effort greatly expanded [demand] for agricultural products."[91] In this light, the expansion of supply management during wartime prosperity indicates the political power of agricultural interests within the state. Even though the war increased agricultural prices, southern planters and the corn and wheat segments all pushed for (and won) higher price support levels. Price supports increased even though they "had some severe limitations during the war period when the need was great for an expansion of production and for a rapid shift from the lesser to more essential agricultural products."[92] Although cotton production declined, for example, Walter Wilcox asserts that "the outstanding example of misused human and other resources in agriculture during the war effort occurred in the Cotton Belt."[93] The average annual carry-over equaled 100 percent; a full-year's worth of cotton production was carried over each year, on average.[94] Therefore, cotton farmers could have shifted entirely to other crops for one year, and enough cotton still would have been available to meet the demand.[95] Even though cotton production far exceeded the increased demand during the war and many officials advocated a shift from cotton to other commodities that were needed for the war effort, southern Democrats won much higher price supports for cotton, which in turn contributed to continued overproduction.

Even wartime price control policies reflected the interests of agriculture: price ceiling levels on agricultural commodities were set at 110 percent of parity. To the extent that the government used price controls on agricultural commodities, farm organizations and congressional representatives made sure that they would be administered by "friends" of agriculture, namely the USDA. The Emergency Price Control Act of 1942 contained "an amendment to forbid the Office of Price Administration (OPA) director from setting price ceilings on any agricultural commodity without first gaining the approval of the secretary of agriculture."[96] This effectively weakened price controls on agricultural commodities.

Both increased price supports and favorable price control levels were in no small part due to the influence that the Farm Bureau and southern

Democrats had over key congressional committees. In addition, Chester Davis and Marvin Jones headed the War Food Administration, which administered supply management programs as well as the allocation of food during the war.[97] Davis had been the director of the Agricultural Adjustment Administration and had been a friend to the Farm Bureau. Jones had been a congressman from Texas who helped to lead the fight for the AAA. These two men worked to protect the interests of farmers (for example, high price supports), which often led to conflicts with the OPA in its effort to control prices.[98] Beyond these direct influences, the state depended on these segments for steady production of agricultural goods during the war, which granted these segments structural influence over agricultural policy.

These same forces helped to solidify supply management as the core of national agricultural policy. Southern Democrats, and their planter constituents, disliked and distrusted the FSA in particular because of this bureaucracy's tendency to support land reform and give aid to tenants and sharecroppers. Similarly, the Farm Bureau sought to undermine these bureaucracies. Hooks shows how "the changing balance of power at the core of the federal bureaucracy, and the marginalization of existing civilian agencies during the [war] mobilization left New Deal agencies vulnerable."[99] This context left the FSA and BAE vulnerable to attacks by southern Democrats, the Farm Bureau, and other opponents of agricultural reform: "Under the new conditions of World War II, despite the best efforts of USDA liberals, conservatives proved powerful enough to kill the agency."[100] With these two bureaucracies eliminated, supply management policy, centered on production controls and price supports tilted in favor of larger farmers, became the undisputed program of national agricultural policy.

Nonetheless, agriculture prospered during the war more than it had since before 1920. This was in part because supply management policy, in combination with heightened demand due to the war, proved successful at raising farm income. Between 1938 and 1952, gross annual per farm income in the United States increased by 330 percent, from $1,543 to $6,656.[101] Prices for cotton, wheat, and corn more than doubled during the war, contributing to the higher farm income. And the higher farm income helped to reduce the rate of farm foreclosures, which "fell swiftly throughout the war years and reached an all-time low by 1946."[102] Thanks to the Stabilization Act, the wartime expansion of supply management policy extended after the war, when agricultural divisions over supply management policy became particularly clear.

In response to the economic chaos of the Great Depression, the United States developed seemingly inappropriate national policies that increased prices and reduced production amidst reduced incomes and increased unemployment, want, and hunger. Within the context of a market economy, however, such policies do make some sense. In fact, as early as 1848, Karl Marx and Frederick Engels noted that one basic solution to capitalist crises of overproduction was "by enforced destruction of the mass of productive forces."[103] This would seem a paradoxical solution to a crisis created by capitalism, which Marx and Engels credited as the most dynamic organization of society because it engenders continual improvement in society's productive ability. Yet this is precisely how supply management policy overcame the agricultural crisis of overproduction: by restricting the productive ability of farmers.

On a fundamental level, Roosevelt's election overcame the last obstacle to the formation of supply management policy. Along with the new Democratic dominance in Congress, this administration increased the political influence of southern Democrats, who by 1933 were strong supporters of supply management, especially production controls. It is difficult to overstate the importance of southern Democrats in the formation of supply management policy. Largely representing the interests of southern planters, these Democrats dominated the House and Senate and heavily influenced the Roosevelt administration's policies. Thus, the political-economic context facilitated (in terms of economic interests) and allowed for (in terms of political power) the creation of supply management policy.

Importantly, the policy of supply management did achieve one of its goals: increasing farm income. From 1932 to 1947, gross farm income increased from $6.5 billion to $21 billion (in constant 1938 dollars). However, this policy raised farm income in a way that reinforced existing inequalities within U.S. agriculture. Supply management subsidies were based on historic production, current production, and acreage. Price supports gave greater income support to farmers who produced more bushels of corn or bales of cotton. That is, a farmer who produced six thousand bushels of corn received greater subsidies from price supports than did a farmer who produced four hundred bushels of corn. In this way, supply management was inherently biased in favor of economically larger farmers, such as southern planters.

This basis for the distribution of subsidies led supply management policy to be stupendously unsuccessful at its other goal: controlling overproduction. As Chapter 6 demonstrates, the combination of price supports and production controls had the ironic effect of creating and exacerbating overproduction. These programs generally failed to prevent surpluses, the other (if not ultimately *the*) principal goal of supply management.

Each of these aspects of supply management policy—its success regarding farm income, and its failure regarding surpluses—shaped the market economy in agriculture. This, in turn, affected the economic interests and policy preferences of segments of agriculture. The next chapter demonstrates how this combination of class, state, and market led to a particular trajectory for supply management policy after 1945.

# PART II

# The Politics of Retrenchment

Part

the Politics of Remembrance

# CHAPTER 4

# Shifting Agricultural Coalitions

## Sliding Back toward the Free Market, 1945–1975

Our price-support policy is a powerful force—one which can be designed to strengthen, to weaken, or even to destroy individual initiative and responsibility as the prime moving force in our economy.
—ALLAN KLINE, AMERICAN FARM BUREAU FEDERATION PRESIDENT, 1949

We as farmers look to God for seasons to grow our crops. We also look to our national Congress for laws to assure us a fair price for our crops.
—THEODORE STEED, ALABAMA FARMERS UNION, 1949

Supply management policy entered a period of gradual retrenchment after emerging in the New Deal and expanding during the Second World War. One final expansion of this policy occurred in 1954 with the creation of export subsidies. Nonetheless, a series of legislative changes in the 1950s through the 1970s lowered price supports, weakened production controls, and reduced export subsidies. Although supply management policy did not disappear during this period, the federal government became far less involved with agricultural prices, production, and trade. As a result, government support to farmers declined, as did market prices—although farm income did not fall.

How can we explain this trend in agricultural policy? Many scholars emphasize party politics in accounting for the contraction of supply management policy: Democrats tend to favor expanding government support, while Republicans try to limit federal intervention. Others argue that nonagricultural interests (for example, consumer and urban interests) led the offensive against supply management. However, just as the creation and expansion of supply management rested on dynamics within agriculture, so too did this gradual retrenchment. In particular, divisions and coalitions within agriculture shaped the partisan politics during this period.

## Behind the Partisan Politics

In 1952, the Republican Party gained control of both houses of Congress, and Dwight Eisenhower became the first Republican president in twenty years. Then, as now, the Republican Party stood largely as the party of the unfettered market, of laissez-faire capitalism, and this was evident in the party's position on agricultural policy. President Eisenhower appointed Ezra Benson to be secretary of agriculture. Benson argued that agriculture should be guided primarily by free and competitive markets, and he favored farm legislation that would reduce price support levels. The Farm Bureau supported Benson's positions wholeheartedly. With Republicans in control of the executive branch, the USDA, and the House and Senate agriculture committees, a dramatic policy shift might have seemed imminent.

Not surprisingly, many Democrats, especially from the South, opposed Eisenhower's proposal to roll back price supports; however, the administration's bill encountered another roadblock: congressional Republicans. Although some House and Senate Republicans supported the administration's proposal, others steadfastly opposed it; that is, members of the president's own party sought to prevent the realization of a more market-oriented agricultural policy. Importantly, some of the Republicans who opposed unleashing market mechanisms in agriculture served on the agriculture committees in Congress. Most notably, Representative Clifford Hope (R-KS), who chaired the House Committee on Agriculture, favored supply management. In 1954, this committee reported to the whole House its own bill maintaining high price supports rather than the administration's proposal to reduce price support levels. Eisenhower and Benson eventually pushed through modest checks on supply management policy, but nothing like they had anticipated.

In 1962, Democratic president John Kennedy proposed creating stricter production controls. Like Eisenhower's before him, Kennedy's party controlled both the House and the Senate. And, again like Eisenhower's, Kennedy's bill had the support of one of the most important farm organizations, the NFU. In contrast to Eisenhower's bill, however, Kennedy's aimed to strengthen supply management policy rather than weaken it. This legislation was meant to appeal particularly to southern Democrats, but some of them opposed the stricter control measures that he assumed they wanted. Thus, Kennedy encountered the same problem as did Eisenhower: members of the president's own party opposed the administration's policy.

What, then, is the relationship between partisan politics and the market economy? How can we make sense of this array of partisan support and opposition for supply management policy? Since the 1930s, the Democratic Party has been identified with government intervention into the economy, while Republicans have been associated with more market-oriented policies.[1] The traditional view of presidents captures this division: Democrats like Franklin Roosevelt, John Kennedy, and Lyndon Johnson favored social support programs, business regulations, and union protections; by contrast, Republicans such as Richard Nixon and Ronald Reagan sought to limit the role of the federal government in the economy.[2]

This partisan division has appeared in the realm of agricultural policy as well. Secretaries of agriculture in Democratic administrations—for example, Charles Brannan in the Truman administration and Orville Freeman in the Kennedy and Johnson administrations—have tended to favor expanding supply management policy. Republican administrations, however, have been more likely to have secretaries of agriculture—for example, Ezra Benson in the Eisenhower administration and Earl Butz in the Nixon administration—who sought to reduce the government's role in the agriculture market. Furthermore, in Congress, Democrats have been more likely than Republicans to support supply management policy.

Do such partisan differences help to explain the contours of U.S. agricultural policy in the mid-twentieth century? After 1945, agricultural policy started a gradual slide toward free market principles, leading government intervention in the market to diminish substantially by 1975. Price supports were lowered and weakened in 1954 and 1973, and production controls were relaxed in 1964 and 1973. Therefore, the period 1950 to 1975 represented a departure from the period 1932 to 1950, when supply management policy expanded significantly. At first glance, partisan differences might seem to account for this retrenchment of supply management policy: Democrats had more consistent influence over national policy during the earlier period. Upon closer examination, however, the relationship between politics and markets is actually more complex than this perfunctory partisan division over agricultural policy. For example, Republican administrations oversaw two of the three retrenchments (1954 and 1973), but a Democratic administration created the 1964 shift. Partisan differences over agricultural policy are even more muddled in Congress.

Previous chapters showed that Democrats and Republicans cooperated on agricultural policy in the 1920s through the Farm Bloc, joined to pass the

AAAs of 1933 and 1938, and together secured high price supports during World War II. In the next five decades, Republicans and Democrats protected supply management policy. In short, members of both political parties forged and protected a national policy based on extensive government intervention into the market economy: supply management. Even though Republicans were generally more likely to oppose supply management, party politics did not determine who favored it.

Still, this bipartisanship was not an indication of political consensus in toto. Quite the contrary, vigorous disputes existed within and between political parties over the shape of agricultural policy. The experiences of the Eisenhower and Kennedy administrations demonstrate this point. Some Democrats were ardent supporters of supply management, while others were steadfast opponents. Northeastern Democrats were frequently critical of supply management policy, whereas farm state Democrats (for example, from Iowa or Mississippi) tended to favor it. The same was true within the Republican Party: some farm state Republicans favored supply management policy, but Republican advocates of small federal budgets and free market ideology opposed such government expenditures to interfere with the market. Just as these internal party divisions made agricultural policy more bipartisan than many other policy arenas, they also created bipartisan opposition to supply management policy. Neither partisan boundaries nor party ideology was the key difference between advocates and opponents of supply management policy.[3]

Not surprisingly, a regional component lay beneath the internal partisan divisions: rural Democrats and Republicans were more likely to favor supply management policy than were Democrats and Republicans from urban areas. Thus, most of the bipartisan support for supply management came from the rural Midwest and South, while much of the bipartisan opposition came from the Northeast and other urbanized areas. This has tempted many scholars to focus on political battles pitting rural areas against urban areas. Agricultural retrenchment is often seen as the consequence of groups outside of agriculture gaining influence over agricultural policy. As the political power of farmers declined, other interests (for example, urban and consumer groups) began to challenge supply management policy. Even while this explanation looks past partisan politics, it nonetheless misses the underlying complexity of the retrenchment of agricultural policy.

Political and economic dynamics within agriculture are the real key to understanding the gradual slide toward the market. Although some segments of agriculture favored supply management policy, others opposed it. Chapter 3 showed this to be the case from the beginning of the AAA: food processors and some farmers fought price supports and production controls. Opposition to supply management within agriculture grew broader, especially in the Corn Belt, after the war. In fact, some of the same segments of agriculture that helped to forge the AAA later opposed the policy. A focus on the political battles between rural and urban interests misses this fundamental process within agriculture.

The political battles among segments of agriculture from 1945 to 1975 reveal important insights about the relations between class, state, and market in explaining policy shifts—especially how coalitions within agriculture reshaped national policy. The political power and economic interests of segments of agriculture are central to explaining the contours of agricultural policy during this period.

### U.S. Agricultural Policy, 1945–1975

From 1933 onward, agricultural policy rested on extensive state intervention into the economy through price supports and production controls. This policy of supply management changed gradually, subsiding significantly by 1975. During this period, then, agricultural policy gradually slid back toward free market principles. (See Table 1.1, which shows the initial expansion and then consequent retrenchment in agricultural policy.)

The AAA of 1938 set price support levels between 52 percent and 75 percent of parity for the basic commodities. During World War II, the number of commodities eligible for price supports and production controls increased from six to twenty under the Steagall Amendment of 1941. This legislation also increased price support levels to 85 percent of parity for the basic commodities. In 1942, the Stabilization Act again raised supports, this time to 90 percent of parity, and provided that price supports would remain at this level for two years after the war. Additional legislation in 1944 raised price supports for cotton to 95 percent of parity. Thus, supply management policy expanded between 1933 and 1945.

For the two years immediately following the war, price supports remained at 90 percent of parity as provided by the Stabilization Act. After these two years, price supports were to revert back to the scale of 52 percent to 75 percent specified in the AAA of 1938. The Agricultural Act of 1948 kept price supports at 90 percent of parity for another year, after which they were to be based on a sliding scale of 75 to 90 percent of parity. However, the Agricultural Act of 1949 kept price supports at 90 percent of parity until 1952, after which time supports would vary from 75 to 90 percent of parity based on supply. An amendment in 1952 once again kept price supports at 90 percent of parity for two more years.[4] Supply management policy, then, remained protected and stable until 1954.

During the 1950s, however, President Eisenhower's secretary of agriculture, Ezra Benson—"an enemy of the New Deal farm program"—led the fight for flexible price supports that would vary with market prices.[5] Secretary Benson argued that the "efficient farmer can more nearly get income parity if he is allowed to operate in a relatively free market."[6] Consequently, Benson championed the Agricultural Act of 1954, which created a sliding scale of 82.5 to 90 percent of parity for 1955 and 75 to 90 percent thereafter. This marked the first reduction in price support levels.

In 1954, the Agricultural Trade Development and Assistance Act, or Public Law 480 (PL 480), was also passed, adding a new dimension to supply management policy: export subsidies. PL 480 aimed to create new markets for U.S. agricultural commodities in the periphery of the world economy through the use of international food aid. Most export subsidies under PL 480 were directed at wheat, cotton, and dairy exports.[7] The act was meant to help reduce the growing surpluses, which supply management policy failed to control. (Chapter 6 discusses in detail how international food aid operated as well as its consequences.)

Production controls remained relatively strong until 1963, when wheat producers rejected the strict controls proposed by the Kennedy administration in a referendum on the wheat program for the next year.[8] This vote proved to be a death knell for such strict controls, which the Cotton-Wheat Act of 1964 replaced with more flexible controls.[9] This act marked a significant weakening in production controls.

In 1973, the Nixon administration proposed phasing out price supports but compromised well short of this goal with the Agriculture and Consumer Protection Act. This legislation introduced more market-oriented price supports based on a new target price system that worked similarly to traditional price supports, though without the connection to the idea of parity. Target prices were to be adjusted annually "to reflect changes in production costs."[10] This policy was intended to create prices that reflected market conditions.[11] Because of a shortfall in worldwide agricultural production at this time, the Agriculture and Consumer Protection Act also suspended acreage reduction requirements.[12] In doing so, this act moved toward the goals of the Eisenhower-Benson years.

Between 1945 and 1975, political battles raged over price supports and production controls, which were weakened during this period. These programs helped to raise farm income, but the trajectory of agricultural policy had clearly shifted by the 1970s. Price supports for the basic commodities fell (in real dollars) by roughly a third, and average payments to farmers fell (in real dollars) by almost one-half.[13] How can we explain this secular shift in agricultural policy? The agricultural coalition that originally supported New Deal agricultural policy changed in terms of its economic interests and its political power. The importance of the coalition is apparent in one of the failed attempts to change agricultural policy during this period—the Brannan Plan.

### The Failure of the Brannan Plan

In 1949, President Truman's secretary of agriculture, Charles Brannan, proposed a plan that would shift agricultural policy significantly in four ways. First, he proposed changing price supports from being based on parity, the basis of supports since 1933, to being based on "an 'income standard' as a method of computing price-supports."[14] In this proposal, government payments would have been based on a "moving ten-year base period (initially 1939 through 1948)" rather than on the traditional parity period of 1909–1914.[15] Notably, this formula worked out to about 100 percent of (traditional) parity, which was an increase over existing legislation that set supports at 90 percent of parity.[16] Second, Brannan proposed that subsidies for several perishable commodities go to farmers in the form of direct payments from the government instead of deriving from higher market prices. When prices fell below designated levels, the government would pay farmers the difference. In effect, this plan sought to change agricultural policy from raising market prices to emphasizing income supports. Third, the Brannan plan would have expanded the number of commodities supported to include animal products (for example, eggs, chickens, lamb, etc.) as well as any other commodity that the secretary deemed in need of support.[17] Finally, this proposal placed an "eighteen hundred-unit limitation on production eligible for support."[18] That is, Brannan proposed capping the subsidies for which farmers would be eligible. The Brannan Plan was an attempt to alter the direction of agricultural policy: dispatch with the notion of parity, allow prices to fluctuate, expand the policy to cover more crops, and cap subsidies with the aim of encouraging "family farms." Brannan's proposal ultimately failed as Congress opted to retain high, fixed price supports based on the parity formula. Just as with the failure of the McNary-Haugen bills of the 1920s, the failure of the Brannan Plan holds insights into the underlying importance of dynamics and coalitions within agriculture.

The NFU was the most notable supporter of the Brannan Plan.[19] As Virgil Dean states, "The similarity between the NFU's new farm policy position and the secretary's final statement to Congress is remarkable."[20] The Farm Bureau, by contrast, staunchly opposed the proposal, objecting to the idea of discarding parity as the basis of support as well as the suggestion that subsidies be capped. Other national farm organizations, including the Grange and the National Council of Farmer Cooperatives, likewise opposed various aspects of the plan.[21] Aside from the NFU, these farm organizations lobbied vigorously against Brannan's proposal.

Perhaps most importantly, however, southern Democrats also opposed the Brannan Plan. Like the Farm Bureau, southern Democrats and planters tended to oppose any effort to cap the federal subsidies that they might receive.[22] They also objected to the move away from parity. In the months after Secretary Brannan presented his proposal to Congress in April 1949, southern Democrats introduced no fewer than four bills that would maintain price supports at high, fixed levels.[23] These bills were meant as alternatives to the Brannan Plan, with only one bill being somewhat favorable by proposing a "trial run" on some elements of Brannan's proposal.[24] In the end, the Brannan Plan died in Congress, and a bill offered by Albert Gore (D-TN), which maintained price supports at 90 percent of parity, passed in its place.[25]

Only elements of the wheat segment favored this proposed shift in agricultural policy. (Some Wheat Belt politicians expressed doubts about and opposition to the Brannan Plan, despite the NFU's support.) Without an agricultural coalition, such as one involving southern planters, the Brannan Plan had little hope of passing. The divisions and coalitions within agriculture are also important for understanding why national policy changed at various times during the next three decades, when agricultural retrenchment occurred. In fact, the major changes in agricultural policy between 1945 and 1975 follow almost precisely the shifts in divisions and coalitions within agriculture.

### Conflict in Agriculture and the Slide
### toward the Market, 1945–1975

The period from 1945 to 1975 can be divided into three shorter periods, each marked by an important change in agricultural policy. First, price
supports were reduced and made flexible between 1945 and 1954. Second,
production controls were weakened between 1954 and 1964. Third, both
price supports and production controls were significantly changed in the
early 1970s.

## The Departure of Corn, 1945 to 1954

This period began with the farm bloc (corn, wheat, and cotton segments) favoring the price supports and production controls that formed during the New Deal and expanded during World War II. By the late 1940s,
however, the corn segment had dropped out of this coalition by opposing
high, rigid price supports and mandatory production controls. The Farm
Bureau, in particular, began advocating for more market-oriented policies.[26]
Between 1947 and 1954, the Farm Bureau continually called for flexible price
supports that would vary in the same direction as market prices: as market
prices rose, price support levels would also rise; as market prices fell, support
levels would likewise decline.[27] This would fundamentally alter the purpose
of price supports. Fixed price supports—for example, supports set at 90
percent of parity—offered a safety net that ensured farm income did not
fall with market prices. The Farm Bureau's flexible price supports were not
meant to support farm income directly. Instead, its proposal was aimed at
correcting discrepancies between supply and demand in agriculture. Thus,
the Farm Bureau, like Secretary of Agriculture Benson, sought to create a
more market-oriented agricultural policy.

The corn segment's preference for weakening price supports and production controls was particularly clear in the formation and passage of the
Agricultural Act of 1949. A 1948 Farm Bureau resolution stated, "We believe that the major provisions of this act, which provide . . . variable price
supports, are sound and in the best interest of American agriculture."[28] In
congressional testimony on the 1949 farm bill, the Farm Bureau's president,
Allan Kline, repeatedly stressed the organization's support of flexible price
supports.[29] For example, Kline stated, "We think the flexible price support

provisions . . . provide the foundation structure upon which we can build a really comprehensive long-range program."[30]

The Farm Bureau continued this position as Congress considered reducing price supports in 1954. For instance, Kline argued that provisions in the Agricultural Act of 1949 "requiring 90 percent of parity price support on the basic commodities without regard to supply should be allowed to expire at the end of the 1954 program."[31] In its official policy statement, the Farm Bureau stated, "we do not consider it the responsibility of the Government to guarantee profitable prices to any group."[32] Kline and the Farm Bureau also argued against production controls because "the shifting of acreage from protected crops under Government control programs creates serious problems for producers of these crops and has serious implications for the producers of unprotected crops."[33] That is, production controls on cotton, for example, might encourage southern farmers to grow more corn or soybeans, possibly leading to a larger supply and lower prices for the latter commodities. In this way, the corn segment viewed supply management as disrupting the market.

By contrast, the wheat and cotton segments opposed flexible price supports, favoring instead the retention of supports at 90 percent of parity. In 1949, James Patton, president of the NFU, testified: "Of the major alternatives before Congress, one would mean severe contraction of farm income. This is the alternative of letting the title II 'sliding scale' provisions [of the Agricultural Act of 1948] go into effect."[34] Beyond opposing flexible supports, Patton argued for continued and extensive government intervention into the market.[35] In 1952, the NFU continued to favor such an agricultural policy, adopting the following statement: "We look upon farm price and income assurance as one of the functions for the performance of which farmers and other citizens must call upon the government."[36] That same year, the NFU offered draft legislation to Congress that would repeal the sliding scale price supports of the Agricultural Act of 1949.[37] The NFU retained this stance in 1954, as indicated in one of its policy statements: "The substitution of 'flexible' 75–90 percent supports for what Secretary of Agriculture Benson calls 'high and rigid price supports' would not lead to sound adjustments in production, but only to further downward adjustments in farm income."[38] Additionally, Patton testified that his organization favored price supports at 100 percent of parity and stood in "complete opposition to the sliding scale."[39]

The cotton segment's opposition to flexible price supports is apparent in exchanges between southern Democrats and the Farm Bureau officials. The following exchange between Representative Pat Sutton (D-TN) and Kline is fairly typical:

> SUTTON: Can you show me one way how [flexible price supports] would help the American farmer . . . ?
>
> KLINE: You can read the whole statement [of the Farm Bureau]. It is all full of the philosophy of the method by which it would help.
>
> SUTTON: I followed your statement here. I cannot see how it would help the American farmer one bit. . . . I am indeed glad that the Farm Bureau of the State of Tennessee does not agree with [you]. . . . I believe they have the farmer at heart and not big business, as I feel your statement does.[40]

Later in Kline's testimony, Representative Harold Cooley (D-NC), chair of the House Agriculture Committee, and Representative W. R. Poage (D-TX) questioned Kline about how much support the Farm Bureau's program had from farmers in cotton states:

> COOLEY: Was [the Farm Bureau's policy proposal] sponsored by any of the cotton people in your organization?
>
> KLINE: Yes, sir.
>
> POAGE: How many of the cotton States in the Farm Bureau supported that at the convention?
>
> KLINE: I cannot give you the figures, Mr. Poage. I am not sure.
>
> POAGE: Mr. Kline, I am still faced with the situation these gentlemen are faced with. I just asked you how many of the cotton States—Texas, Louisiana, Mississippi, Alabama, Georgia, North and South Carolina—supported that in your convention in Atlantic City?
>
> KLINE: I do not know.
>
> POAGE: Do you recall any of them opposing it? . . .
>
> KLINE: Yes, but again I am not sure exactly how many states opposed it.
>
> POAGE: But you tell us that you did this simply to let the cotton people do what they wanted to do, to let the cotton people have the kind of program they wanted to have? . . .
>
> KLINE: That is an oversimplification. . . .
>
> POAGE: . . . I wanted to know who from the Cotton Belt wanted it handled this way.[41]

These exchanges also hint at the regional disagreements within the Farm Bureau, further demonstrating the split between the cotton and corn segments.

During this period, farm bureaus in southern states frequently disagreed with the national farm bureau, especially its advocacy for flexible price supports and market-oriented national policies. For example, H. L. Wingate, president of the Farm Bureau of Georgia, stated, "I . . . appear in opposition to the Aiken bill [and its flexible price supports] which the American Farm Bureau is supporting."[42] Instead, Wingate advocated maintaining high support levels. Thus, both the cotton and wheat segments continued to support supply management policy.

This cotton-wheat coalition, which favored supply management policy, won the battles in 1949 and 1952: in both years, new legislation delayed the use of flexible price supports while maintaining high and rigid supports. This changed in 1954. In this year, the House Committee on Agriculture reported a bill that maintained 90 percent parity, but the Eisenhower administration introduced a bill with the 75 to 90 percent sliding scale. An amendment raised the minimum to 82.5 percent for the first year, and it passed the House and Senate.[43] Therefore, price supports were finally made flexible on a sliding scale in 1954. Yet this sliding scale did not go down as far as either Secretary Benson or the Farm Bureau advocated.

This conflict within agriculture, between the cotton-wheat coalition and the corn segment, is also evident in the Senate votes on agricultural legislation. Table 4.1 shows the amount of regional support in the Senate for each major policy from 1933 to 1954. Legislation in 1933, 1938, and 1949 created or bolstered supply management policy, while the 1954 act was the first phase of retrenchment. The least amount of support for maintaining or expanding supply management from 1933 to 1949 came from the more urban Northeast, just as some scholars observe. And northeastern senators gave broad support to the Agricultural Act of 1954, which rolled back price supports. This suggests a battle between farm interests and urban interests. But we need to look beyond this observation to see the whole story. The underlying dynamics within agriculture are fundamentally important and reflect the divisions already discussed.

Southern support for supply management remained consistently high, with at least 85 percent of southern senators supporting each major policy in the 1930s and 1940s. Support from the Wheat Belt expanded significantly from 1933 to 1949, nearly matching the support from the South in 1949.[44] Importantly, no southern or Wheat Belt senators voted against or even expressed opposition to the Agricultural Act of 1949. Several senators from each region neither voted nor expressed support for or opposition to the

**Table 4.1.** Percentage of senators from each region supporting agricultural legislation

| Region | AAA of 1933 | AAA of 1938 | Agricultural Act of 1949 | Agricultural Act of 1954 |
|---|---|---|---|---|
| South | 86 | 91 | 86 | 36 |
| Corn Belt | 69 | 63 | 43 | 69 |
| Wheat Belt | 50 | 66 | 83 | 66 |
| Northeast | 33 | 28 | 38 | 89 |

*Sources:* Calculated using roll-call Senate votes in the *Congressional Record* (1933) 3121; (1938) 1881; (1949) 15008; and *Congressional Quarterly Almanac* (1954), 143.

bill.[45] In contrast, support for supply management from the Corn Belt fell by more than one-third, from 69 percent to 43 percent, between 1933 and 1949. This mirrors the decreasing support from the Farm Bureau for price supports and production controls. Corn Belt senators became increasingly opposed to supply management.

How did senators from these agricultural regions vote in the retrenchment of 1954? The most significant changes came in the support from the South and the Corn Belt. The majority of southern senators, 64 percent, opposed reducing price supports. Only 36 percent of southern senators supported the Agricultural Act of 1954—the lowest level of southern support for agricultural legislation since before 1933. Support from the Wheat Belt likewise fell, though not as sharply as that of the South. About 66 percent of Wheat Belt senators voted for the 1954 act, substantially lower than the support given to the 1949 act but as much support as the region gave to supply management in the 1930s. Most notably, support from the Corn Belt increased. Almost 70 percent of senators from the Corn Belt supported this retrenchment in agricultural policy. This was much more support than the region gave to legislation in either 1938 or 1949. Legislation to weaken supply management policy garnered much more support from the Corn Belt than did legislation to protect it. The policy preference of the corn segment stood in contradistinction particularly to that of the cotton segment.

In short, an important division existed between cotton-wheat and corn between 1945 and 1954. This raises two sets of questions. First, why did this split emerge? Why did the corn segment drop out of the coalition supporting high price supports? Second, why did the Agricultural Act of 1954 take the shape it did? If the Farm Bureau and the Republican Party opposed supply management, why was this retrenchment not more significant—especially considering that the Republicans controlled both houses of Congress and the presidency?

### Economic Interests and the Split in Agriculture

On the surface, the split between the cotton-wheat coalition and the corn segment resulted from a shift in Farm Bureau leadership. Through both the New Deal and World War II, the Farm Bureau had a southern president, Edward O'Neal, and a midwestern vice president, Earl Smith, representing a cotton-corn-wheat coalition within the organization. Allan Kline, a corn and hog farmer and head of the Iowa Farm Bureau, was elected president of the national Farm Bureau in 1947. Kline's election signaled the reassertion of the dominance of Corn Belt farm bureaus within the national federation. This shift, however, reflected more important underlying shifts rooted in economics. We have to look beyond the observable organizational disputes and examine the underlying class dynamics.

Importantly, the corn segment opposed high supports and production controls not only for corn but for cotton and wheat as well. That is, one solution to the conflict might have been to eliminate supply management for corn but retain the policy for other commodities. But this solution was unacceptable because the corn segment opposed supply management policy in general, not just for corn. Why? This position was based on the desire (1) to keep feed grain prices low and (2) to prevent production controls on other commodities from encouraging competing sources of soybeans and corn. We can see how these two interests led the corn segment to oppose supply management for corn, in particular, as well as for other commodities.

First, the corn segment's opposition to high supports for corn was tied to hog production. Between 1945 and 1975, the Corn Belt accounted for between 64 percent and 70 percent of all U.S. hog production. Just three Corn Belt states—Iowa, Illinois, and Indiana—accounted for at least 38 percent of national hog production between 1945 and 1975. This expansive livestock sector shaped the interests of corn producers, who received more revenue from hog production than from corn: "Corn producers . . . do not get their farm income directly from the sale of their crop. After all, between 85 and 90 percent of corn produced is sold in the form of livestock and livestock products."[46] This reliance on hog production created an interest in maintaining low prices for corn, which was the basis of livestock feed. Furthermore, meat consumption was increasing enough to prevent corn surpluses on the scale that cotton and wheat were experiencing. In fact, U.S. meat consumption increased swiftly and steadily over the next few decades (see Figure 7.1). Coupled with the emerging livestock complex, which rested on intensive and industrial production methods, this increasing consumption of animals made supply management policy less necessary for feed grains, especially corn. As Allen Matusow notes, "Since demand for meat is elastic (that is, sales rise more than proportionally as prices fall), many hog farmers saw no advantage in limiting supply to keep prices high."[47] Thus, the corn segment opposed high, rigid supports and production controls for corn.

Second, these same economic interests led the corn segment to oppose high supports and accompanying production controls for other basic commodities, not just for corn. Again, price supports were generally contingent on adherence to acreage allotments, which limited the number of acres a farm could produce of any particular crop. For instance, to qualify for price supports for cotton, a large landowner in the South might be limited to planting cotton on only 65 percent of the farm's total acreage. This removed sizable portions of farmland in the South from traditional southern crops and encouraged diversification. The corn segment feared that price supports and the accompanying production controls for cotton, in particular, might encourage increased grain production in the South.[48] This fear was well-founded because southern farmers often produced soybeans, wheat, and corn on land freed from traditional southern crops, such as cotton. For this reason, then, the corn segment opposed price support programs for other basic commodities as well as for corn.

Nonetheless, the wheat and cotton segments continued to favor price supports and production controls during the 1950s. For the wheat segment, this policy preference was rooted in two factors: demand in the world economy and how wheat was used. First, the end of both the Marshall Plan in Europe and then the Korean War led to reduced international demand for U.S. wheat, and a surplus of wheat ensued.[49] Consequently, the wheat segment favored both production controls and price supports, since the surplus drove down wheat prices. Second, unlike corn, most wheat was not used as feed but rather was sold for food, which was less elastic in price than was meat. Therefore, higher prices for wheat directly benefited wheat producers' incomes.

Perhaps more importantly, the cotton segment directly confronted the corn segment by favoring price supports and production controls not only for southern crops, but also for corn.[50] Southern planters favored subsidizing corn because the South could not match the Corn Belt's higher productivity in corn: "Iowa corn growers . . . generally were better situated for earning incomes than those in Georgia. . . . While the Georgia grower may only have covered costs of production with program benefits, the Iowa corn producer often found all subsidies to be profit."[51] Because the corn price supports benefited growers differently by region, the cotton segment likely had more invested in supports.

Southern planters also opposed the flexible price supports because the noncommercial corn area, that is, farms outside of the Corn Belt, received price supports at only 75 percent of the level of supports in the commercial corn area. Representative Stephen Pace (D-GA) described the situation for corn farmers in noncommercial areas, such as the South: "We get only 75 percent of the support that corn growers of Illinois and Iowa enjoy. As I see it, if marketing quotas were voted down by [farmers in] the commercial corn area, then the only support for corn in the noncommercial area would be 37½ percent of parity. Is that right? It would be 75 percent of 50 percent."[52] Thus, lower price supports for corn generally meant significantly lower supports for corn grown in the South. Consequently, the cotton segment was a proponent of high price supports for corn. The conflicting policy preferences held by the cotton-wheat coalition on the one hand and the corn segment on the other derived from these distinct market relations. Yet to understand why the resulting agricultural policy looked as it did in 1954, we have to examine the process through which these class segments attempted to translate their economic interests into state policy.

### Political Power and National Policy

Given these divergent interests, why did the Agricultural Act of 1954 take the form it did? The answer rests in the respective political power of each segment. Even when the corn segment cracked the coalition by turning against the New Deal policies, it could exact little change in these policies. This was largely because the cotton-wheat coalition persisted. Additionally, where each segment embedded its interest within the state was crucial.

The cotton segment's embeddedness within the Democratic Party and Congress virtually ensured the protection of its interests whenever this party held Congress or the White House. The Farm Bureau and the Republican Party each took up the mantle of flexible and reduced price supports, the preferred programs of the corn segment. The Republican administrations from 1953 to 1960 gave the Farm Bureau extensive access to the USDA.[53] Even when Republicans controlled the House and Senate, as they did during 1946–1948 and 1952–1954, the corn segment still had difficulty transforming its economic interests in political policy, in part because the wheat segment was likewise embedded within the Republican Party. This made the cotton-wheat coalition powerful regardless of partisan control of Congress. For example, Clifford Hope (R-KS) chaired the House Agriculture Committee from 1946 to 1948 and from 1952 to 1954, and he was supportive of high price supports and production controls.[54] This split between corn and wheat within the Republican Party prevented a unified party front to end supply management policy. As long as the cotton and wheat segments remained aligned in favor of price supports and production controls, the corn segment, and the Republican Party, could not eliminate the New Deal policies.[55]

In the end, the corn segment was successful in shifting price supports from being fixed at 90 percent of parity to a sliding scale of 82.5 to 90 percent of parity in 1954, in no small part because of the Republicans holding the White House, the Senate, and the House of Representatives. Despite the political power of the cotton and wheat segments, restoring price supports to their 90 percent level proved extremely difficult. President Eisenhower vetoed two attempts to restore price support levels to 90 percent in 1956 after Democrats regained control of the House and Senate. Nonetheless, with the cotton and wheat segments securely in control of the agriculture committees in both houses, price supports would not fall any farther until the 1970s.

This first phase of retrenchment highlights the importance of changes in political coalitions, where segments embed their interests within the state, and the role of southern planters. The corn segment's opposition to the cotton-wheat coalition created an opportunity for a policy shift. Without this division within agriculture, the retrenchment of supply management would have been far less likely. Therefore, looking beyond the opposition of urban interests is crucial. Despite the split in agriculture, the political power of the cotton-wheat coalition prevented the policy shift from being even greater. With southern planters so influential in Congress and the wheat segment splitting the Republican Party, the cotton-wheat coalition exerted substantial influence over agricultural policy.

## Changes in the Cotton-Wheat Coalition, 1954 to 1964

Although price supports were changed in 1954, production controls remained strong for about ten more years. The cotton-wheat coalition clung tightly to price supports and production controls in 1954, but by the mid-1960s their support of the latter began to wane. This is evident in the creation of the Cotton-Wheat Act of 1964, which instituted more flexible production controls for cotton and wheat.

For cotton, this legislation created a dual set of acreage allotments: farmers adhering to a smaller "domestic" allotment received high price supports, and those complying with a larger "total" allotment received lower price supports.[56] Farmers adhering to their domestic allotment received price supports up to 15 percent higher than those staying within their total allotment.[57] This flexibility was quite distinct from the previously strict production controls.

The cotton segment's weakened support for strict production controls became clear as the Kennedy administration proposed mandatory controls in 1961 and 1962. This legislation was meant to appeal to southern Democrats, some of whom supported the proposal. For example, Senator Allen Ellender (D-LA) and Representative Harold Cooley (D-NC) favored mandatory controls.[58] Yet other southern Democrats tried to weaken the control measures for both grain and cotton production. In particular, Representative Thomas Abernathy (D-MS) and Senator James O. Eastland (D-MS) sponsored amendments to exempt all feed grains fed on the farm where they were grown, about 75 percent of all feed grains, from controls.[59] Additionally, the state farm bureaus in the South voiced opposition to the policy of strict production controls.[60] In the final vote, 90 percent of southern senators supported the Cotton-Wheat Act. During the 1960s, then, the cotton segment increasingly favored flexible controls.

A more flexible program was also created for wheat producers. Though farmers complying with controls received price supports while those not complying received no benefits, the policy was more flexible in that noncompliance was no longer penalized.[61] The mandatory features of the controls were eliminated. The NFU supported this program in 1964, and wheat producers had voted down mandatory controls for wheat in a referendum in 1963.[62]

The Farm Bureau opposed a shift toward voluntary controls, favoring the elimination of controls altogether. The bureau's opposition to production controls was expressed by its president, Charles Schuman: "The basic fallacy of Government efforts to fix prices and control production cannot be overcome by shifting from compulsory to voluntary controls. . . . The only sure way to solve our feed grain and wheat problems is to let the market system guide production and consumption."[63] The Farm Bureau and the NFU continued to clash over price supports as well. While the NFU proposed setting wheat prices at 100 percent of parity, the Farm Bureau argued that the market should set prices.[64] The bureau favored price supports for regulating the supply of farm commodities, but the NFU favored price supports to raise farm income.

Although the cotton and wheat segments had favored high price supports tied to strict production controls since the 1930s, they began to look less favorably on production controls by the early 1960s. Since their interests changed almost simultaneously, though for very different reasons, the cotton-wheat coalition continued. Why did the interests of these segments change?

### Changing Economic Interests

An important change in the world economy reshaped the wheat segment's interests. After 1945, the United States exported little wheat as Europe raised trade barriers, thereby depriving the nation of one of its traditional markets for wheat exports. Recovering from this loss required new markets. To find, or more accurately to create, these markets, the United States relied on export subsidies through PL 480, or international food aid.[65] As Figure 4.1 shows, wheat exports more than doubled between 1950 and 1965, from about 10 MMT to almost 23 MMT. This growth in exports strongly influenced the wheat segment's view of production controls.

By the 1960s, food aid was one of the cornerstones of U.S. agricultural policy. While price supports and production controls failed to avert large grain surpluses, PL 480 reduced the surpluses by creating markets for U.S. wheat exports. Ken Kendrick, vice president of the National Association of Wheat Growers (NAWG), stated "without the use of Public Law 480, our wheat surpluses would have undoubtedly reached unmanageable proportions."[66] Food aid secured markets for U.S. wheat by changing diets and agricultural production in periphery nations.[67] With exports expanding, U.S. wheat growers could increase production rather than trying to control it. Consequently, the wheat segment increasingly favored exports and flexible

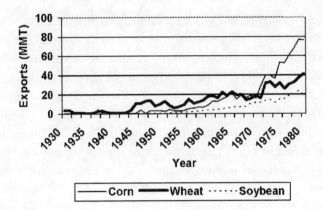

4.1. U.S. corn, wheat, and soybean exports, 1930–1980. *Source:* USDA (various years), *Agricultural Statistics*.

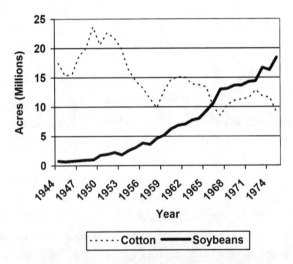

4.2. Acres of cotton and soybeans harvested in the South, 1945–1975. *Source:* USDA (various years), *Agricultural Statistics*.

production controls.[68] This policy preference might have created a second crack in the agricultural coalition had southern planters not experienced a shift in interests as well.

Southern agriculture began to change in the 1950s. Figure 4.2 shows that during the 1960s soybeans displaced cotton as the crop covering the most acres in the South. In 1950, the South produced 35 million bushels of soybeans, but production reached 432 million bushels in 1975. During this same period, the South's share of national soybean production rose from 12 percent to 28 percent. Also, by 1960 the value of soybean production in the South was behind only cotton and tobacco, and by 1975 soybeans led all other southern crops in value.[69]

Much of the expansion in southern soybean production occurred in states that had been the highest cotton producers. Georgia, Alabama, Mississippi, Arkansas, and Texas—the top cotton states from 1938 through 1950—accounted for about 60 percent of the South's soybean production from 1950 to 1975. Planters had been politically dominant in these states since the late nineteenth century. This shift from cotton to soybeans altered the planters' views of production controls and allotments. Even while favoring production controls for cotton, they worried that controls on soybeans and grains might affect their ability to expand production and move away from their reliance on traditional southern crops.[70]

Although price supports were weakened in 1954, production controls were strong until the economic interests of the wheat and cotton segments changed in the early 1960s. At this point, all three segments—cotton, wheat, and corn—favored less rigid production controls. U.S. agricultural policy facilitated this confluence of interests. First, PL 480 created international markets for U.S. wheat, which eased the need for production controls to ward off wheat surpluses. Second, production controls on traditional southern crops encouraged a shift to grain and soybean production, weakening the cotton segment's support for production controls. As with the 1954 policy shift, the roots of weakened production controls lay within agriculture.

## A New World Economic Context, the Early 1970s

Agricultural policy shifted again in the early 1970s. The Agriculture and Consumer Protection Act of 1973 removed parity from price supports and dropped acreage reduction requirements. Price supports were replaced with "target prices," providing income payments "based on cost-of-production consideration."[71] The act eliminated acreage reduction requirements but allowed for production controls if necessary.[72] Why did these changes occur at this particular time?

Does the rise of nonagricultural interests, namely, consumer and urban interests, explain policy shifts after 1970?[73] Even while the title of the 1973 act suggested the influence of consumer groups, they appear to have had little role in shaping the bill.[74] Weldon Barton examines the possible influence of

labor interests on this legislation.[75] The link between labor and farm interests is clear from the combining of food stamps and commodity programs
in 1965. Barton and others, then, argue that including the food stamp program in the farm bill increased urban support for farm bills—even if rural
Republicans often opposed the welfare and labor policies sought by urban
Democrats. In short, such arguments posit that groups outside of agriculture
played a central role in this retrenchment of supply management.

When we look more closely at this shift in agricultural policy, however,
we find that dynamics within agriculture were more fundamental to this retrenchment. Even though the inclusion of food stamps garnered some urban
support for farm bills, the move away from supply management principles
in 1973 rested to a much greater extent on changes within agriculture. This
is apparent even from the roll-call vote in Congress: a bipartisan coalition
of farm state representatives, not a coalition of rural-urban representatives,
secured the passage of the 1973 bill.[76] Table 4.2 presents regional support
in the U.S. House for the 1973 farm bill in two ways: (1) the percentage of
representatives within each region who voted in favor of the bill, and (2) the
percentage of the final "yea" vote that came from each region.[77] First, the
strongest support for the bill existed in the nation's agricultural regions—
the South, the Wheat Belt, and the Corn Belt, where 76 percent, 74 percent, and 63 percent, respectively, of representatives voted for the bill. By
contrast, only 23 percent of northeastern representatives voted for it. Unanimous "nay" votes came from the Connecticut, Maine, New Hampshire, and
Rhode Island delegations, and the vast majority of representatives from Massachusetts (75 percent), New Jersey (93 percent), and New York (76 percent)
also voted "nay."[78] Seventy-seven percent of all northeastern representatives
and 74 percent of northeastern Democrats voted against the 1973 farm bill.

Second, the support from the South, the Wheat Belt, and the Corn Belt
was crucial to the final passage of the 1973 farm bill: 73 percent of the "yea"
votes came from these regions. Of the 226 supporting votes for the bill, 166
came from the three major agricultural regions. Only 10 percent of the overall "yea" votes came from the Northeast. Most of the support for the 1973
farm bill, then, came from the South, Wheat Belt, and Corn Belt, while the
Northeast offered little support.

Consequently, there is little evidence of an urban-rural coalition around
the 1973 farm bill. The more urban Northeast played a very minor role in this
legislation. This is not to say that urban votes were not a factor in the passage
of the bill, but we must not ignore the continuing influence that agricultural

**Table 4.2.** Regional support in the U.S. House of Representatives for the Agriculture and Consumer Protection Act of 1973

| Region | Percentage of representatives supporting act | Percentage of total support for the act |
|---|---|---|
| South | 76 | 34 |
| Wheat Belt | 74 | 10 |
| Corn Belt | 63 | 29 |
| Mid-South | 61 | 6 |
| West | 42 | 9 |
| Northeast | 23 | 10 |

*Source:* Calculated using roll-call House votes found in *Congressional Quarterly Weekly Report* (1973), 2021–2022.

interests had over farm policy. To the extent that an urban-rural coalition existed, it existed within the major agricultural regions. This suggests that other fundamental factors have been overlooked in explaining this shift in agricultural policy.

Economic Interests in the 1970s

The Farm Bureau opposed the 1973 act because it was "a step away from the free market agriculture it advocates."[79] The Farm Bureau's policy statement announced its "objective to create a climate which will enable agriculture to return to the market price system."[80] The bureau supported an amendment, favored by the Nixon administration, to the 1973 bill to gradually phase out all subsidy payments.[81] Accordingly, of the three major agricultural regions, support was weakest from the Corn Belt.

An important reason for the corn segment favoring the end of price supports and production controls was the tremendous expansion in corn exports that occurred in the early 1970s. As Figure 4.1 shows, U.S. corn exports increased from 16 MMT in 1970 to 39 MMT in 1972 to 52 MMT in 1975. Beginning in the late 1960s, the volume of corn exports overtook and increased far beyond that of wheat exports. This increase was spurred on by shortfalls in world grain production, especially in Russia and China.[82] As a result, grain stocks in the United States fell dramatically. In this context, the

corn segment continued to oppose state intervention in agricultural production and prices, seeking instead to expand exports further by supporting the
Nixon administration's push for freer international trade.[83]

By contrast, the cotton and wheat segments favored the continuation
of price supports and voluntary production controls, thereby opposing the
administration and the Farm Bureau. For example, the legislative director
of the NFU asked "the committee to reject the recommendations of the
Nixon Administration for phasing out the present farm program."[84] Likewise, the president of Southern Cotton Growers, Inc., recommended that
"cotton farm programs with allotments and price supports be continued."[85]
Though these segments opposed the 1973 bill to the extent that it was not
strong enough, they ultimately supported the final bill.[86] The world economic context made this bill more acceptable than it otherwise might have
been.

The wheat segment benefited from a significant increase in exports, from
an average of 15.75 MMT per year from 1968 to 1971 to 30.5 MMT per year
from 1972 to 1975. Consequently, wheat prices rose from $1.33 a bushel in
1970 to $3.95 a bushel in 1973.[87] Wheat prices had not been so high since
1946, which made income and price supports appear less necessary to many
observers.[88] Although the wheat segment continued to view the favorable export situation as temporary, the dramatic increase in wheat exports reduced
the need for production controls and high price supports based on parity, at
least in the short run.[89]

The cotton segment favored retaining price supports and flexible controls for four reasons. First, this segment faced increasing competition from
products made more cheaply than U.S. cotton: synthetic fibers and cotton
from other nations. Susan Mann notes that synthetic fibers "were supplying
a sixth (by weight) of the world's textile needs in the early 1950s, a third by
the mid-1960s, and had taken over the lead of cotton in the 1970s."[90] Second, the cotton segment was more dependent on price supports than were
the wheat or corn segments. For the year 1972, wheat producers received
an average of $466 in federal subsidies, corn producers $94, and cotton producers $2,993.[91] Furthermore, "about one-third of cotton growers receive[d]
benefits of more than $20,000, compared to less than 5 percent of grain pro-
ducers."[92] Third, the importance of soybeans in southern agriculture grew
as soybean acreage increased. The value of southern soybean production
jumped from $860 million in 1970 to $2.1 billion in 1975, surpassing the

value of cotton and tobacco production.[93] The cotton segment opposed strict controls because of its continued expansion in soybeans. Finally, the cotton segment viewed production controls on cotton as less necessary because cotton exports had more than doubled between 1968 and 1973, from 2.4 million bales to 5.7 million bales. Thus, the world markets were good for U.S. cotton, just as they were for corn, wheat, and soybeans.

If the corn segment lined up against the cotton-wheat coalition, as it had in the 1940s and 1950s, then why did agricultural policy take the form it did in 1973? Why were target prices without production controls adopted rather than phasing out the programs altogether?

### Shifts in Political Power

Two issues emerge regarding power: power among segments of agriculture, and power between agricultural and nonagricultural segments. First, as seen throughout this period, the corn segment had difficultly asserting its interests when its preferences conflicted with those of the cotton-wheat coalition. The corn segment was allied with the Nixon administration and Secretary of Agriculture Butz, both of whom favored phasing out supply management policy. Yet achieving this was difficult because the cotton and wheat segments continued to favor this policy, particularly price supports.

Second, the political power of the cotton-wheat coalition had declined by the early 1970s. Many scholars rightly point out that farmers had lost some political power because of weakened farm organizations, congressional redistricting in the 1960s, a shrinking farm population, and fewer representatives and senators from farm districts.[94] Most scholars nevertheless miss the fundamental political and economic changes in the South that reduced the power of the cotton segment. The next chapter details the transformation of the class structure in the rural South and how it dramatically altered power within U.S. agriculture. Briefly put, this segment's power had been rooted in the planters, who dominated the South politically and economically through the plantation-tenant system that excluded most blacks and many whites from the political process. However, the New Deal programs weakened the plantation system by encouraging planters to replace tenants with hired workers, to mechanize, and to diversify their production. From the 1930s to the 1960s, this process transformed the planters into large commercial farmers, even if it did not fundamentally alter the concentration of land ownership. As a result, "cotton interests no longer [had] the strength in the House to pass any farm bill they [chose]."[95]

Two factors, then, were central to the formation of the Agriculture and Consumer Protection Act of 1973. First, the world economic context reduced the need for production controls or price supports, at least in the short term. Exports of cotton, wheat, corn, and soybeans flourished. Second, the cotton-wheat coalition suffered from a decrease in power. Southern planters had become large commercial farmers, losing their hold over regional politics and the Democratic Party. This made it much less likely that the cotton segment, even in an alliance with wheat, could get the farm program of their choice as they had in the past.

The retrenchment of agricultural policy between 1945 and 1975 was grounded in dynamics within agriculture. After World War II, the corn segment became increasingly opposed to price supports and production controls. This split within agriculture allowed for the retrenchment of supply management policy, but the coalition between the cotton and wheat segments curtailed this retrenchment. To understand the split as well as the coalition, we need to examine the economic interests and political power of these segments. To a great extent, the changing economic interests of segments of agriculture drove the retrenchment of supply management. Importantly, the changing world economy and supply management policy itself altered the economic interests of segments of agriculture, just as these class segments shaped the contours of agricultural policy in the mid-twentieth century. Therefore, we have to look beyond the partisan divisions and the battles between rural and urban interests.

Focusing on the relations between class segments and national policy also helps to make sense of the sometimes puzzling partisan politics of agricultural policy discussed at the outset of this chapter. Why did bipartisanship characterize much of the congressional activity concerning agriculture? And despite this bipartisanship, why were Democratic administrations more likely to favor supply management policy, while Republican administrations were more likely to oppose such intervention? Why was the Republican Party so divided regarding agricultural policy? Answering these questions requires an understanding of who wielded power within the political parties during the mid-twentieth century. Thus, the analysis offered here helps to answer questions that a focus on party politics leaves unsolved.

First, the bipartisanship found in agricultural policy was more complex than a rural-urban divide. The crux of this cooperation across party lines was the cotton-wheat coalition. The South was solidly Democratic, and the Wheat Belt was strongly Republican.[96] Despite their support for different political parties, the South and the Wheat Belt shared an economic interest in government protections from the market. This coalition, therefore, led to bipartisan congressional support for supply management.[97]

Second, the strength of the Republican Party in the Wheat Belt created that party's internal divisions on agricultural policy. On the one hand, Republicans from the Corn Belt tended to oppose supply management, and this policy preference fit with the free market ideology of the national party. Consequently, Republican administrations generally opposed price supports and production controls, much to the satisfaction of Corn Belt Republicans. On the other hand, however, congressional Republicans from the Wheat Belt frequently opposed their own party's presidents on agricultural policy by supporting supply management. Therefore, the Republican Party was split on this issue.

This conflict between the Corn Belt and Wheat Belt was also apparent in the differences between the Farm Bureau, strongest in the Corn Belt, and the NFU, strongest in the Wheat Belt. Between 1945 and 1975, the Farm Bureau was most influential in Republican administrations, and the NFU was most influential in Democratic administrations. Thus, in contrast to the corn and cotton segments, the wheat segment was split regarding politics: it voted Republican while supporting a Democratic-leaning farm organization. The Wheat Belt, then, was the source of bipartisanship on agricultural issues, but this is clear only when underlying economic interests are considered.

Finally, the reason for the Democratic Party's support of supply management is hardly a puzzle: the strength of southern Democrats in the national party pushed it solidly toward this policy. Unlike the Republican Party, there was really no agricultural interest among Democrats who opposed supply management. There was no major split among rural Democrats. This solidarity among southern Democrats, coupled with their disproportionate political power, was the key to the creation, expansion, and development of supply management policy.

The political power of the southern Democrats rested on the dominance of southern planters over the regional political economy. Southern planters molded agricultural policy to reflect their interests. This same policy, however, eventually reshaped the economic interests of southern planters by prompting a shift from cotton to soybean production. Yet supply management policy had an even more fundamental effect on southern planters: it undermined their political power. The next chapter examines this complex, and ultimately ironic, process.

# CHAPTER 5

# The Decline of the South

## Changing Power within U.S. Agriculture, 1945–1975

The plantation system involves the most stark serfdom and exploitation that is left in the Western world.
—NORMAN THOMAS, SOCIALIST AND TENANT FARMER ADVOCATE, 1936

C hanges in agricultural coalitions help to explain the gradual retrenchment of supply management, but changes in political power are likewise important. By focusing on the shrinking farm population, the weakening of farm organizations, or the reduction in the number of farm representatives in Congress, most scholars overlook the most important shift in power: the decline of southern planters. The political economy of the South changed as the plantation system gradually disappeared, altering the class position and political power of large southern landowners. The declining political power of the planters is embodied in the disintegration of the "solid (Democratic) South" and the rise of the southern wing of the Republican Party, both of which undermined the planters' influence over national, and even regional, politics.

Two primary factors drove this transformation in the rural class structure of the South: supply management policy and the civil rights movement. Although many scholars examine how supply management policy changed the South, very few recognize the hidden role of the civil rights movement in the retrenchment of agricultural policy. In brief, the AAA undermined the plantation system by promoting the replacement of tenants with wage laborers, as well as the mechanization and diversification of southern agriculture. This fundamental change in the southern agrarian class structure in turn facilitated the rise of the civil rights movement. Then, this movement for racial equality undermined the political power of the southern plant-ers—the most ardent proponents of supply management. Violent resistance permeated this transformation of the rural South, which was ironically ini-tiated by the southern planters themselves. This violence is epitomized by a campaign in Mississippi, the heart of the Cotton Belt.

## Freedom Summer and Violent Repression in the South

In the summer of 1964, the Student Nonviolent Coordinating Com-mittee and the Congress of Racial Equality organized Freedom Summer, an extensive civil rights campaign in Mississippi that focused on registering blacks to vote. More than one thousand students, most of them white, from northern colleges descended upon this rural southern state to participate. White Mississippians described it as an "invasion" and resented how these "hippie" students sought to disrupt the revered institutions governing local race relations.

Violence erupted immediately while many of the volunteers were still training in Ohio. On June 21, three civil rights workers—James Chaney, Michael Schwerner, and Andrew Goodman—investigated the burning of a black church in rural Neshoba County, and they were arrested by the county deputy after leaving the burned remains of the church. The three men were released from jail after ten o'clock that night and murdered by local whites shortly thereafter. Their bodies were discovered on August 4 in an earthen dam in rural Neshoba County.[1]

Although this was the most notorious instance of violent resistance, hundreds more incidents occurred in Mississippi that summer, including homes, cars, and churches bombed and set ablaze; false arrests and police harassment; threats, assaults, and even additional murders.[2] Yet in the face of this widespread violence and intimidation, Freedom Summer volunteers and organizers helped black Mississippians register to vote, ran Freedom Schools for local children, and set up community centers. Each of these activities challenged the Jim Crow system: to help blacks register to vote or to educate black children was to challenge the very bases of southern racial inequality.[3]

Voter registration was the heart of Freedom Summer, which aimed to crack open Mississippi's closed political system.[4] In 1964, only about one-third of all southern blacks were registered to vote, and far fewer in the rural

South were registered. Because the state Democratic Party was controlled by ardent segregationists, Freedom Summer organizers created the Mississippi Freedom Democratic Party (MFDP). About seventeen thousand blacks in Mississippi tried to register to vote that summer, though less than 10 percent of these attempts were ultimately successful.[5] Nonetheless, about eighty thousand black Mississippians voted in the MFDP primary election, which did not require registering with the state of Mississippi.[6]

In August, Freedom Summer ended at the Democratic National Convention in New Jersey. The MFDP asked to have the seats of the Mississippi "regular" delegates, who represented the racist political forces repressing the black vote through threats, intimidation, violence, and fraud. The MFDP argued that the Mississippi regulars did not represent the ideals of the national Democratic Party and therefore should not be part of the convention. The national Democratic Party, however, refused to give the seats to the MFDP delegates and instead proposed a compromise in which the MFDP would be given two at-large seats while the Mississippi regulars would retain all of their seats. In the end, all but three of the Mississippi regulars walked out of the convention because they refused to pledge allegiance to the national party. When the MFDP tried to claim the vacant seats of the Mississippi regulars, they were removed from the convention floor by national party officials.

Out of the turmoil and challenges of the summer of 1964 came the Voting Rights Act of 1965, allowing the federal government to send marshals to observe elections in states where intimidation and violence limited political participation. The voter registration project of Freedom Summer provided evidence that such legislation was necessary. This legislation helped to protect and bolster the political and social rights already affirmed by the Civil Rights Act of 1964.

What does this dramatic campaign in the civil rights movement have to do with U.S. agricultural policy? Everything. Freedom Summer illustrates how blacks challenged the traditional organization of southern society; how whites often violently resisted calls for racial equality; and how party politics, especially within the Democratic Party, gradually changed. The civil rights movement was one of the forces behind the fundamental changes in the South that altered political power within U.S. agriculture. Before exploring this change in the South, however, let us first look at the process of class transformation.

### National Policy, the Market Economy, and Class Transformation

Few scholars trying to explain twentieth-century agricultural policy pay attention to the changing class structure of the rural South. Southern planters tended to favor supply management policy, but their ability to protect this policy depended on their dominance over southern politics and national policies. The southern rural class structure, that is, the plantation system, allowed planters to dominate the South's political economy, which then gave them disproportionate influence over national policies. As this class structure changed during the 1950s and 1960s, however, the southern planters fell from their politically dominant position. After exerting great influence in Congress, the Democratic Party, and national politics from about 1932 to 1960, planters began to lose political power as the Republican Party gained influence in the South and blacks gained influence in the Democratic Party. This fall from power had important consequences for agricultural policy because the southern planters were among the most ardent supporters of supply management policy. Analyzing the demise of the southern planters highlights three processes that underlie class transformation.

First, the market prompts some class segments to advocate for the state to regulate the economy. The market economy is a hazardous place even for strong classes. Market competition and fluctuations, and even the mere social organization of the market, compel some classes, or segments of classes, to favor state intervention into the market. That is, class segments try to influence the state to protect their economic interests. As Chapter 3 demonstrated, the depression prompted southern planters, as well as farmers in other regions, to favor government intervention in the market. Southern planters influenced the formation of the AAA, which reflected their interests in production controls and price supports.

Second, state intervention in the market changes class relations. Ironically, state policies favored by a particular class segment may later change the class structure of which that segment is a part. Changes in the class structure can create space in which weaker classes can organize. In the case at hand, the AAA, which the planters supported, helped to reshape the plantation system upon which the planters' status rested, thereby jeopardizing planters' political dominance. In this case, southern blacks began to organize as they became increasingly removed from the terror and social control that were central to the southern plantation system.

Third, class transformation alters the economic interests of classes and therefore alters class alliances. This process can result in a class segment opposing a state policy that it had earlier helped to create, as seen in Chapter 4. Class transformation may lead to shifts in political coalitions, especially when weaker classes organize, that may then result in pronounced changes in state policy.[7] This chapter demonstrates how the transformation of the rural class structure of the South not only led to fundamental changes in regional policies, such as Jim Crow laws, but also how it allowed for changes in national agricultural policy. Furthermore, changes in class relations can have the effect of freeing the forces of production, which may further reshape the market and class interests.

This chapter details how class transformation in the South lies behind the retrenchment in supply management policy between 1945 and 1975. First, planters lost their *economic* class relation as the regional class structure changed, and then they lost their *political* class relation by becoming marginalized from the regionally dominant political coalition.[8] Thus they fell from power. To firmly grasp this process, we first need to examine how New Deal agricultural policy changed the class structure of the rural South. The irony is that the planters shaped the AAA to preserve their status atop this structure. By reshaping the southern political economy, however, the AAA created an opportunity for southern blacks to challenge racial segregation and, by extension, the dominance of the planters. Then, southern planters were transformed into large commercial farmers as the class structure of the plantation system disappeared. Large landowners in the South were no longer "planters" because their class position changed. The class structure of the plantation-tenant system that had given them political and economic dominance disappeared. With this fundamental change, their ability to protect supply management policy also waned. Thus, supply management policy became vulnerable to change during the 1970s because of the transformation of the class structure of the rural South. An important political process permeates class transformation: economic interests must be translated into national policy. This translation is crucial to the process of class transformation.

## The Southern Plantation System and the AAA

Southern planters were large landowners concentrated in the Cotton Belt, and they dominated the region's politics and economy from 1900 to 1940.[9] This political-economic dominance was based on the plantation system, which was built on tenancy and emerged out of class struggles and racial conflicts of the 1880s and 1890s.[10] This class structure rested on five elements: (1) the social relations between planters and tenants/sharecroppers, (2) labor-intensive agricultural production, (3) de jure racial segregation, (4) the exclusion of many social groups (especially blacks) from politics, and (5) the dominance of both the Democratic Party in the South and southern Democrats in the national party. The first two elements roughly account for the economic dimension of the plantation system, and the last three are central to the political dimension of the system.

First, planter-tenant relations defined the planters' economic class relation. Tenants and sharecroppers worked land belonging to planters, and each party received a share of the crop. The core of tenancy, then, was a tenant working land that belonged to someone else either through rental agreement or wage labor. Tenant farmers in the South rented portions of land and supplied the "cultivating power (usually mules) and implements and customarily [paid] two-thirds of the seed and fertilizer costs."[11] With sharecropping, in contrast, the landowner "[supplied] everything used in production (including housing) except labor and [furnished] half the cost of seed and fertilizer."[12] Some tenants were cash tenants, who did not share their crop with the landowner, but these were far less common than sharecroppers or share tenants.[13]

As some contemporaries pointed out, however, "The evil is not in renting land but in the traditions and practices which have grown up about it in the South."[14] The foundation of planter-tenant relations was the crop-lien system, which often put tenants in a cycle of debt that bound them to the plantation: "If a tenant could not pay his rent, the landlord had the right to collect the harvest in payment. If the crop did not cover the debt, the landlord had the right to the next year's harvest."[15] Nonetheless, the tenant system of the early 1900s was contractual, allowing tenants and sharecroppers to move between seasons.[16] Planters also had the ability to expel tenants, especially between seasons. The crop-lien system and the informality of contracts often put "absolute control of relationships in the hands of the landlord."[17]

Planters defended this system and their control over tenants and croppers by pointing to the paternalistic aspects of the system. As Donald Grubbs writes, "Religion, recreation, health and education were all the alleged products of planter paternalism."[18] Of course, planters spent much more on providing churches and holiday picnics than they did for health or education.[19]

Nonetheless, this paternalism, as marginal as it may have been, helped to strengthen the social ties between planters and tenants/croppers.[20]

This system of tenancy secured the supply of labor needed to cultivate cotton, which produced the greatest profit in southern agriculture.[21] Unlike the Midwest, which mechanized in the early 1900s, southern cotton production remained largely unmechanized until the 1960s. The percentage of cotton harvested mechanically in 1957 is telling: about 35 percent of cotton in Louisiana and Texas was harvested mechanically; only about 17 percent of the cotton in Arkansas and Mississippi was harvested mechanically; and less than 3 percent of cotton in Alabama, Georgia, the Carolinas, and Tennessee was harvested by machine.[22] As late as 1962, most southern states relied heavily on laborers to pick cotton by hand. Control over a sufficiently large supply of labor was therefore crucial, and this need to secure labor propelled the class structure. An added benefit of the plantation and crop-lien systems was that they diffused the risks involved in cotton production as well as controlled labor.

Second, regional politics supported the plantation system, thereby constituting planters' political class relation. Southern politics rested on racial segregation laws that constrained blacks' behavior and rights. Jim Crow laws became increasingly commonplace in the South by the early 1900s. Of particular note, numerous barriers, legal and otherwise, prevented most blacks and many whites, especially those who were not landowners, from voting.[23] For example, in the 1926 off-year election, only 8.5 percent of southerners voted.[24] As a result, planters dominated southern politics and held disproportionate influence in national politics.[25] The particular structure of southern politics, then, was a central element of the plantation system and, thus, of the class position of the planters.

Both the economic and political elements of the plantation system were central to the social organization of production and the control of labor. But the depression and the AAA initiated fundamental changes in this class structure.

### The AAA Transforms the South

Created in part to save southern agriculture, and planters in particular, from the depression and falling commodity prices, the AAA and its policy of supply management prompted changes in the rural class structure of the South. Figures 5.1 and 5.2 show one dimension of the shift away from

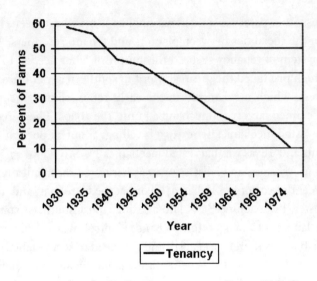

5.1. Change in tenancy rate in the South, 1930–1974. *Source:* U.S. Census Bureau (various years), *Census of Agriculture.*

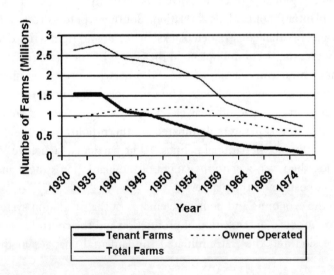

5.2. Number of southern farms, 1930–1974. *Source:* U.S. Census Bureau (various years), *Census of Agriculture.*

the plantation system between 1930 and 1974. Figure 5.1 demonstrates how the percentage of southern farms that were tenant farms decreased during this period, and Figure 5.2 shows the decline in the overall number of farms in the South.

The rate of tenancy in the South fell sharply from 1930 to 1974. In 1930, 59 percent of southern farms were tenant-operated, but the tenancy rate fell to less than 20 percent in 1964 and to 10 percent in 1974. The total number of southern farms also declined during this period, following national trends.[26] Yet the number of tenant farms fell more rapidly, dropping by almost 90 percent between 1930 and 1969, than did the number of other types of farms. There were 1.5 million tenant farms in the South in 1930, but only 72,000 such farms in 1974. Accompanying this decline in tenancy was an increase in the number of smaller, owner-operated farms. The percentage of owner-operated farms with fewer than 260 acres, that is, farms that were neither tenant farms nor plantations, increased from 36 percent of southern farms in 1930 to more than 70 percent in 1969. Nonetheless, after increasing between 1930 and 1950, the number of owner-operated farms declined steadily, though this decline did not approach the falling rate of tenancy.

Not only did the rate of southern tenancy decline, but the qualitative nature of tenancy also changed. Importantly, by the 1960s, tenancy was more likely to mean leasing farmland, that is, being a cash tenant, rather than being involved in the crop-lien system. Alternative forms of credit emerged to put the crop-lien system to rest. In particular, the expansion of credit through federal farm programs led to the gradual disappearance of this system.[27] Thus, the plantation system no longer characterized southern agriculture by the late 1960s. The class structure of the rural South came to reflect closely that of the Midwest: the majority of farms were smaller and owner-operated (that is, neither tenant nor plantation), and tenancy meant leasing land and comprised a small proportion of farms.

How did the AAA contribute to this fundamental change? Supply management policy weakened the plantation system by supplying federal subsidies that encouraged planters to replace tenants with hired workers and to mechanize. Furthermore, production controls prompted planters to diversify their production beyond southern staples such as cotton. Supply management, therefore, fueled the fundamental change in the southern agrarian class structure.

First, federal subsidies from price supports and production controls began to sever traditional social relations between landowners and tenants/croppers as planters tried to keep most, sometimes all, of the AAA payments. Cotton subsidies totaled $173 million in 1934, $115 million in 1935, and $163 million in 1936.[28] T. J. Woofter and his colleagues found that planters kept almost 90 percent of AAA payments in the early New Deal.[29] Some planters who scaled back production to receive federal payments let tenants and croppers go on federal relief given the reduction in work.[30] Other planters avoided sharing AAA payments with tenants simply by evicting them.[31] From 1930 to 1940, tenancy fell from 58 to 45 percent (see Figure 5.1), and by 1964 it was less than 20 percent, which was comparable to that of the Midwest.[32] In 1930, about 720,000 southern farms used sharecroppers, but this number had fallen by about 30 percent in 1940 and by about 90 percent in 1964.[33] AAA payments facilitated these trends by allowing planters to replace tenants and croppers with wage laborers.[34] In these ways, supply management undermined the plantation system by breaking the ties between tenants and planters.

Second, New Deal agricultural policy further helped to dissolve the traditional plantation system by fueling mechanization. AAA payments infused southern farmers, especially planters, with much-needed capital.[35] While plantations had long relied on tenancy and labor-intensive production methods, large southern farms slowly became more capital-intensive.[36] This happened in two phases: the adoption of the tractor for plowing, and the adoption of mechanical cotton pickers. The use of tractors for breaking land, planting, and cultivating expanded in the South between 1936 and 1946.[37] Moses Musoke states that "the number of tractors in the South rose from a mere 36,500 in 1920 to more than 271,000 in 1940, and during the next two decades, they increased . . . to more than 1.4 million."[38] Between 1948 and 1956, the use of mechanical cotton pickers became more widespread for harvesting. Although only 6 percent of U.S. cotton was harvested by machines in 1949, this figure rose to 23 percent in 1955, 51 percent in 1960, and 96 percent in 1968.[39] Such mechanization, funded in part by federal subsidies, gradually eliminated the need for tenants and sharecroppers as plantations shifted toward more capital-intensive production.

Third, supply management policy prompted diversification in southern agriculture, which also played a role in changing the class structure. Production controls required that farmers limit their production of basic commodities, including cotton and tobacco. Consequently, southern agriculture began to diversify as farmers grew other crops on land formerly used for cotton. Increased soybean production was at the heart of the diversification of southern agriculture after World War II.[40] This switch from cotton to soybeans played an important role in the transformation of the rural class structure.

As discussed in Chapter 4, southern soybean acreage expanded dramatically, and cotton acreage fell concomitantly between 1944 and 1975 (see Figure 4.2). Southern soybean production expanded from less than 700,000 acres in 1945 to 18.4 million in 1975. Conversely, the number of acres devoted to cotton production fell from a high of 23 million in 1949 to 8.9 million in 1975. Soybean acres surpassed cotton acres in 1966. Along with increased acreage, of course, came increased production: southern soybean production increased from 35 million bushels in 1950 to 432 million bushels in 1975. Much of this expansion occurred in states that had been the highest cotton producers: Alabama, Arkansas, Georgia, Mississippi, and Texas—the top cotton states from 1938 through 1950—accounted for about 60 percent of the South's soybean production from 1950 to 1975. Accordingly, the value of southern soybean production gradually increased from about $88 million in 1950 to $2.1 billion in 1975, when it surpassed the value of cotton production.[41] This shift toward soybean production, which was easily mechanized and not labor-intensive, also reduced southern agriculture's reliance on tenancy.

The consequences of New Deal agricultural policy—cash influx, mechanization, and crop diversification—contributed to a shift in the southern class structure by significantly undermining tenancy. The relationship between planters and tenants/sharecroppers changed. The rural South became less dependent on labor-intensive agricultural production and political control over tenants and croppers. By the 1960s, large commercial farms that were capital-intensive and hired full-time wage laborers were replacing the fading plantation system. Planters, tenants, and croppers were disappearing as class positions. This shift away from a plantation system demonstrates the first two processes underlying class transformation: the market became inhospitable and compelled planters to favor policies regulating the market, and these policies consequently changed the class structure of the South. This led to an opportunity for the rise of the civil rights movement, demonstrating how class transformation can create space for weaker classes to organize.

### The Fall of the Plantation and Rise
### of the Civil Rights Movement

Though supply management policy helped to initiate the demise of the plantation system, the New Deal left the system of racial oppression and political exclusion in the South largely untouched. That is, supply management policy changed the *economic* dimensions of the southern class structure—the planter-tenant relations, and the reliance on labor-intensive production; but it did not alter the *political* dimensions of this class structure—de jure segregation, a political system closed to most whites and blacks, and the dominance of both the Democratic Party in the South and southern Democrats in the national party. Still, the shift away from the plantation system created an opportunity for southern blacks to challenge the Jim Crow system that permitted violence against them and limited their political, social, and economic rights. This opportunity arose in part because the disintegration of the plantation system facilitated the migration of blacks out of the rural South.

The vast majority of blacks lived in the South in the early 1900s, but a "Great Migration" out of the region occurred from about 1915 through 1960.[42] In 1920, more than 75 percent of blacks lived in the South, but almost half lived outside of the South by 1960. Eight states were notable destinations for blacks leaving the South: California, Illinois, Michigan, Missouri, New Jersey, New York, Ohio, and Pennsylvania. These states accounted for about 12 percent of all blacks in the country in 1920, but by 1960 about 35 percent of all blacks lived in these eight states.[43]

Of blacks who remained in the South, a significant number moved from rural to urban areas. Whereas less than 23 percent of southern blacks lived in urban areas in 1920, almost 45 percent lived in urban areas in 1950 and more than 55 percent did so in 1960.[44] This is evident from the growth of the black population in southern cities between 1920 and 1960: Atlanta's black population increased from 62,000 to 186,000; Birmingham's grew from 70,000 to 135,000; in Memphis it increased from 61,000 to 184,000; and the black population of New Orleans expanded from 101,000 to 235,000.[45]

Part of blacks' migration out of the rural South was due to the demise of the plantation system. After 1930, the number of black tenant farmers in the South fell more than 20 percent by 1940, almost 50 percent by 1950, and 80 percent by 1960. The number of black sharecroppers followed this same trend, falling by more than 80 percent between 1930 and 1960. Between

1930 and 1960, then, most black tenant farmers and sharecroppers left the plantation system.[46]

This migration had three important consequences: it increased the importance of black voters, it removed blacks from the terror that enveloped much of the rural South, and it increased the concentration and independence of black communities. Thus, the migration of blacks out of the rural South increased their political power. As blacks moved to cities such as Chicago, Cleveland, Detroit, New York, and Philadelphia, they gained the franchise that they had lacked in the South. Between 1920 and 1960, black voters became more important in these cities as their share of the population increased from less than 7.5 percent to more than 24 percent in each city except New York, where the black population increased from 2 percent to 15 percent.[47] These cities were key to winning the electoral votes from New York, Illinois, Michigan, Ohio, and Philadelphia — which accounted for more than half of the electoral votes necessary for winning the presidency.

The importance of black voters, however, rested in more than their numbers in northern cities. Coming out of the New Deal, northern black voters favored the Democratic Party.[48] But as this party tried to balance the interests of southern whites, especially planters, with those of northern blacks, support from black voters decreased. Frances Piven and Richard Cloward point out that "the election of 1956 revealed that black allegiance to the Democratic Party was also weakening. . . . [Democratic presidential candidate Adlai] Stevenson had won about 80 percent of the black vote in 1952, but he won only about 60 percent in 1956."[49] This instability of the black vote in important urban centers in key electoral states increased blacks' political influence as both Democrats and Republicans courted the black vote by supporting civil rights — even if only in limited ways. In particular, President Eisenhower, a Republican, submitted a civil rights bill to Congress in 1956. Therefore, the weak attachment of black voters to the Democratic Party was as important as the emergence of a black voting bloc in northern cities.

When blacks left the rural South, they also escaped the violence and terror that had restricted their behaviors and rights for decades. The most extreme form of such violence was lynching. Between 1882 and 1968, 4,743 lynchings occurred in the United States, and 74 percent of these occurred in the South.[50] Furthermore, the top five cotton states — Alabama, Arkansas, Georgia, Mississippi, and Texas — accounted for almost half of all lynchings during this period. The number of lynchings decreased after the 1930s, but it was still a tactic of terror found primarily in the South.[51] And although northern cities were not havens of racial equality and democracy, they none-theless provided blacks with more social and political rights and presented a much smaller threat of violence than that which blacks faced in the rural South.[52] Even southern cities, where blacks continued to confront threats of violence and restrictions on their behavior, were a significant improvement over the rural South, especially the Cotton Belt. Escaping this social control increased the independence of southern blacks and allowed them to orga-nize.

Finally, black communities and organizations in urban areas were stronger than those in rural areas. In particular, the process of urbanization strength-ened black churches, black colleges, and southern chapters of the National Association for the Advancement of Colored People.[53] This was partially due to the increased economic opportunities and even the segregation that blacks experienced in urban areas. Aldon Morris notes that "black urbanization created densely populated black communities."[54] This expanded the mem-bership base and resources of black churches in urban areas. Doug McAdam argues that rural black churches were relatively weak because they generally had a small membership base, few resources, and weak leadership.[55] Most importantly, black urban churches and their leadership were financially and socially independent of the white community, allowing these churches to challenge segregation.[56]

In these ways, the demise of the plantation-tenant system in the South created an opportunity for blacks to organize. The emergence of the civil rights movement had fundamental consequences for the political power of the planters by undermining the pillars of the plantation system left largely untouched by the New Deal: the exclusion of blacks from politics, the domi-nance of both the Democratic Party in the South and southern Democrats in the national party, and de jure segregation. This further diminished the political power of the planters and therefore indirectly affected U.S. agricul-tural policy — which, ironically, had helped to set blacks free of the repressive rural South.

## The Civil Rights Movement and the Planters' Political Decline

Although supply management policy helped to transform the south-ern agrarian class structure, racial segregation and political exclusion did not automatically change as the plantation system crumbled. The demise of tenancy created an opportunity for southern politics to be reshaped, but it was the civil rights movement that propelled this portion of the transformation. The civil rights movement forced southern politics to expand and become more inclusive. The movement also pushed southern business to the center of regional politics. And finally, this movement weakened the position of planters within the national Democratic Party. In short, the civil rights movement challenged the political elements of the plantation system that the AAA did not.

### Expanding Southern Politics, Undermining Southern Planters

The plantation system had rested on minimal political participation and a bias toward rural interests. Between 1900 and 1944, the height of planters' dominance, voter turnout in the South for presidential elections averaged only 27 percent of the voting age population.[57] This reflected the exclusion of various groups, including most blacks and poor whites. Such low political participation allowed planters to dominate the political economy of the South, as well as U.S. agricultural policy.

The civil rights movement challenged this dominance by expanding political participation in the South. As seen in Figure 5.3, the proportion of southern blacks registered to vote increased dramatically during the 1950s and 1960s. In 1947, a mere 12 percent of blacks in the South were registered to vote, yet this figure climbed to 25 percent in 1956 and 65 percent in 1969. Supreme Court rulings, such as one outlawing white primaries, played a role in elevating registration levels, but the civil rights movement played a fundamental role in this process.[58] Kenneth Andrews finds that mobilization in Mississippi helped to increase voter registration after 1965.[59]

How (and why) did the civil rights movement increase voter registration and participation by blacks? The largest increase in southern black voter registration occurred during the Kennedy and Johnson administrations. Part of this increase came from attempts by these Democratic administrations to channel black protests into "normal politics," such as elections.

The movement engaged in disruptive actions, including bus boycotts, freedom rides, sit-ins, marches, economic boycotts, and demonstrations. Many of these collective actions raised the ire of white southerners, espe-

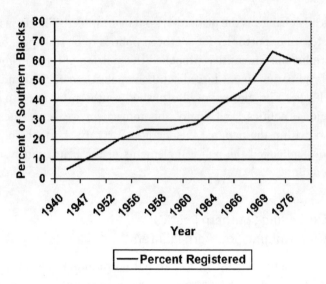

5.3. Percentage of southern blacks registered to vote, 1940–1976. *Sources:* Lawson, *In Pursuit of Power;* Matthews and Prothro, *Negroes and the New Southern Politics.*

cially the politically dominant planters.[60] Violence by whites frequently accompanied these actions, leading to intervention by the federal government. Such intervention caused dilemmas for the Kennedy administration, which relied on southern Democrats for support in Congress. To avoid direct conflicts with southern Democrats, the administration encouraged civil rights leaders to pursue "less disruptive" actions, such as voter registration drives. As Piven and Cloward put it, "the Kennedy Administration moved to reduce the level of conflict by attempting to divert civil rights activists away from confrontations over desegregation of schools, waiting rooms, restrooms, parks, and pools which so inflamed white southerners. They suggested instead that activists concentrate on voter registration."[61] This political maneuvering contributed to large-scale voter registration projects such as Freedom Summer in Mississippi in 1964.

The civil rights movement also boosted blacks' participation in southern politics by politicizing the community, particularly black churches in urban areas, which were the core of black communities.[62] In doing so, the movement brought politics into church members' everyday lives, which helped to increase individuals' political efficacy and thus their political participation.[63] All of this added up to increased political power for southern blacks, a group whose interests generally contradicted those of the planters.

## Pitting Business against the Planters

In addition to expanding political participation in the South, the civil rights movement was crucial to the political fall of the planters because it effectively pitted them against the emerging southern industrial class. The eventual fundamental division between the planters and southern industry further strengthened southern blacks, who forged a coalition with industry. Regional economic development was southern industrialists' primary goal; they wanted to build up the consumer market in the South.[64] Importantly, though, the system of racial segregation did not necessarily obstruct industrialization. In fact, the split labor markets and low-wage, antiunion aura of the South often helped the region's economic development. Only when the planters stood in the way of continued economic development did leaders in southern industry finally stand up and challenge the planters' power.

The civil rights movement created this conflict among the dominant class segments in the South. In the 1950s, whites' massive resistance to racial integration enveloped the South.[65] This resistance was led by the planters and disrupted economic activity and development, thereby conflicting with the interests of industry. The disruption of normal economics, not racial segregation in and of itself, brought some southern industrial and commercial leaders to oppose the planters.

The integration of southern schools demonstrates how the civil rights movement forced the industrialists to confront the planters. Many contemporaries felt that the South would adhere to the 1954 *Brown v. Board of Education* decision even if the region opposed it.[66] However, the Supreme Court put off creating a timeline for integration until 1956. Planters used this delay to mobilize resistance to *Brown*.[67] In Little Rock, Arkansas, massive resistance to the Court's school integration order led President Eisenhower to send in federal troops to enforce integration. The governors of Arkansas and Virginia shut down various high schools the next school year (1957–1958) to avoid integrating. An important result of the disorder caused by whites' resistance and school closings was that "Little Rock suffer[ed] a protracted lapse in plant openings, [and] statewide new-plant investment, which totaled $131 million in 1956, fell to $44.9 million in 1957, and then $25.4 million in 1958."[68] Other states faced similar economic disinvestment with such conflict over integration.[69] With negative economic growth, or even its prospect, leaders of industry and commerce in the South stepped forward, often winning elected positions. In Little Rock, "a businessman-sponsored slate of moderates" won election to the school board after the closings and reopened integrated schools.[70] Bruce Schulman states that "the ensuing strife [over the *Brown* decision], with its closed schools, boycotted businesses, and deployment of federal troops dramatized the benefits of moderation. . . . In that charged atmosphere, many pro-development racial moderates won election at the height of the desegregation conflict."[71] The conflict over black civil rights put southern industry at odds with the planters.

As southern industry began to assume a more significant, and moderating, role in southern politics to protect economic development and profits, they pushed southern planters aside.[72] The rise of industry and commerce in the South after 1940 facilitated the rebirth of the southern Republican Party, with the proportion of congressional Republicans from the South increasing significantly. In the House, Republicans accounted for 2 percent of the southern delegation in 1950, growing to 25 percent in 1974; in the Senate, there were no southern Republicans until 1962, but by 1974 about one-third of southern senators were Republican.[73] The growth of the Republican Party in the South reflected the path of industrialization: the "Outer South" (Virginia, North Carolina, Tennessee, and Arkansas) experienced economic development and the Republican rise earlier than did the "Deep South."[74]

The rebirth of the Republican Party's southern wing was not merely a consequence of economic development or portions of the business community shifting parties. The civil rights movement also played a role in southern whites, in general, bolting from the Democratic Party. As national Democrats reached out to southern blacks or advocated for civil rights and integration, southern whites became disenchanted with the party.[75] Importantly, the civil rights movement forced the national Democratic Party into a choice of supporting or opposing integration and racial equality. Although the national party did not always support racial equality and continued attempts to appease white southern Democrats, any concession on issues of race was too much for some southern whites to swallow. In this sense, then, the civil rights movement pushed the Democratic Party to act in ways that alienated southern whites and bolstered the Republican Party in the South.

The rise of southern Republicans had two important effects on planters' political power. First, the party shift meant that the South would fall lower in terms of congressional seniority. For years, southern Democrats and planters held disproportionate influence over national politics because of their positions within the state. Since the South was essentially uncontested Democratic territory with little political participation, southern Democrats built high levels of seniority and therefore had access to key positions in Congress. For example, a southern Democrat served as speaker of the House of Representatives for all but six years between 1931 and 1961. Southern Democrats also chaired important committees in the House and Senate, including the committees on agriculture and especially the House Committee on Ways and Means. The Senate majority leader was a southern Democrat for ten years between 1931 and 1961.[76] Given the planters' influence over southern politics, this meant that they held important power over national politics. The shift toward southern Republicanism undermined the seniority that was so crucial to planters' political power.

Second, the shift away from the Democratic Party during this period meant that planters maintained less control over party politics in the South. The southern Democratic Party from 1900 to 1945 was heavily influenced by rural interests (and planters in particular), but the nascent southern Republican Party rested on a more diverse social class base that included a growing business community. This meant that political actions could not interfere with the interests of southern industry, as discussed above. Thus, the planters' political sway within southern politics waned with the rise of competitive parties.

### Planters Marginalized Nationally

The civil rights movement also weakened the influence that southern planters had over national politics by challenging the latter's position within the Democratic Party. As the black vote became less solidly Democratic in the 1950s, national party leaders felt compelled to shore up this support, even at the expense of white southern voters.[77] Two factors prompted this action. As already discussed, millions of blacks migrated from the rural South to northern cities that constituted the heart of the northern Democratic Party. Losing the black vote in cities in key electoral states jeopardized the prospects of the national party.

Additionally, white southern Democrats had already demonstrated their propensity to leave the national party in the 1948 presidential election and in defections to the Republican Party in the Outer South. The South had voted over 70 percent Democratic in presidential elections through 1944, but in the 1950s Republicans captured 50 percent of the southern vote for president.[78] By 1968, Democrats won less than 40 percent of the presidential vote in the South. Thus, southern blacks appeared to offer a more stable voting base for the national Democratic Party.

The political power of the planters rested on the plantation system, including limited political participation by other groups. The fight by blacks, reluctantly supported by southern industrial and commercial leaders, expanded political participation to include a group whose interests directly opposed those of the planters. As Jack Bloom states, "In its bitter opposition to desegregation, the traditional ruling elite was fighting not only to retain the racial settlement of the past but also for the maintenance of the traditional social order, which was the condition for its rule."[79] The political changes brought by class transformation, including shifts in coalitions and the challenge of blacks, diminished the planters' influence over regional and national politics.

## Southern Planters Lose Supply Management Policy

How does this analysis of class transformation in the South help to explain retrenchment in supply management policy in the 1970s? Emphasizing southern class transformation reorients the analysis to focus squarely on competing segments of agriculture. Again, many analyses of agricultural policy during this period emphasize battles between agricultural and nonagricultural interests (for example, farmers versus urban interests). This misses the important political conflicts that existed within agriculture. This analysis also refines our understanding of the class bases of political power. Southern planters were the most powerful segment of agriculture and favored supply management policy. As the planters lost their economic and political class positions, their ability to protect supply management policy waned.

### Conflict over Supply Management

Even as agriculture and politics were changing in the South, planters continued to support supply management policy through the 1950s and 1960s. Chapter 4 discussed some of the reasons for this continued support: southern cotton farmers faced increasing competition from products made more cheaply that U.S. cotton (synthetic fibers and cotton from other nations), and they were more dependent on price supports than wheat or corn producers.

This policy preference put southern planters at odds with the Farm Bureau, which largely represented the interests of corn producers in the Corn Belt and which had tried to weaken the policy of supply management since the late 1940s. The Farm Bureau could effect only minor changes to U.S. agricultural policy during the 1950s because the political strength of the planters prevented significant retrenchment. This changed in the 1970s, when the Farm Bureau achieved its goal of fundamentally altering supply management policy. The Agriculture and Consumer Protection Act of 1973 eliminated acreage reduction requirements (that is, production controls) and significantly reduced price supports. The fact that supports were not eliminated entirely shows that the southern cotton producers had not lost all of their political power. Nonetheless, the reduction of price supports was not the preference of these producers.

Why did agricultural policy experience this shift that seemed to counter the preferences of the planters? This retrenchment was based on the change in the rural class structure of the South, which led the planters to lose power, both regionally and nationally.

### Class Transformation, Political Power, and Policy Retrenchment

The transformation of the rural class structure in the South affected both the economic interests and political power of the southern planters. The AAA prompted a shift from cotton to soybean production, which reshaped the economic interests of southern planters. From the 1920s through the 1950s, southern planters were ardent supporters of production controls. However, as soybean production became increasingly important to southern agriculture, planters feared that production controls might hinder their expansion in soybeans (see Chapter 4). In addition, the expansion of soybean production brought southern farmers into the growing livestock complex that characterized much of U.S. agriculture; that is, the economic interests of southern farmers became tied to feed grains by the mid-1970s (see Figure 7.1). Increased meat consumption, then, offered southern farmers a profitable alternative — livestock feed, particularly soybeans — to traditional crops such as cotton.[80] Consequently, their support for production controls weakened as supply management prompted a shift in agricultural production.

The process of class transformation also undermined the political power of the planters. This is evident in the changes in southern Democrats' grasp on leadership positions in Congress. Although southern Democrats dominated the leadership of the House and Senate agriculture committees, the House Committee on Ways and Means, and the House speaker and Senate majority leader positions from 1932 through 1960, this began to change in the 1960s. From 1961 to 1986, no southern Democrat served as the speaker of the House. The Senate majority leader from 1961 to 1977 was from the Wheat Belt state of Montana, and no southern Democrat held this position after 1961. Finally, southern Democrats lost the chairs of the House Committees on Agriculture and on Ways and Means in 1975. By the early 1970s, then, southern planters were no longer the dominating power in Congress that they had been between 1932 and 1960.

Additionally, the agricultural coalition that helped southern planters protect supply management policy during the mid-1900s severely weakened. Wheat Belt farmers, represented in part by the NFU, joined southern planters in fending off several challenges to supply management policy between 1947 and 1960. However, the cotton-wheat coalition was breaking down by 1970. Supply management policy reshaped the economic interests and policy preferences of wheat producers, reducing their support for production controls in particular.

At the very moment that southern cotton producers' political power was waning and the cotton-wheat coalition was weakening, Corn Belt producers experienced greater influence with the election of Republican Richard Nixon as president. The Nixon administration opposed supply management, thus favoring the view of the Farm Bureau.[81] Finally, the sharp increase in U.S. grain exports brought wheat farmers' economic interests in alignment with those of farmers in the Corn Belt. Consequently, the Farm Bureau, representing interests opposed to those of southern cotton producers, experienced an increase in its political power.

This shift in political power within agriculture is the underlying cause for the retrenchment of supply management policy in the 1970s. Class segments must translate their economic interests into state policy. Southern cotton producers were unable to do this because their political power had declined significantly by 1973. The power of cotton producers, who favored supply management, declined relative to the power of the Corn Belt and Farm Bureau, which opposed this policy. Importantly, this shift in power was grounded in the transformation of the southern rural class structure. Ignoring this process produces an inaccurate understanding of the shift in agricultural policy during this period.

We can see the importance of the transformation of the South by comparing the trajectory of agricultural policy during World War II with that of the early 1970s. With strong demand, high prices, and few surpluses during the war, we might have expected price support levels to decline since they were largely unnecessary. Yet price support levels steadily increased. Under similar market conditions in the early 1970s, price supports were significantly weakened — not expanded, as they were in World War II — and production controls were eliminated. Thus, the market conditions were similar to those of the early 1970s, but the policy outcomes were clearly different. What changed between these two periods? The fundamental change was in the political power of southern planters, which had been reduced considerably by 1970. The retrenchment of supply management policy in the early 1970s hinged heavily on the transformation of the southern agrarian class structure and the demise of southern planters.

The economic interests of key segments in agriculture — the cotton, wheat, and corn segments — changed between 1945 and 1975. By the end of this period, these segments no longer favored strict production controls or high price supports. This was particularly true for the corn segment, which opposed supply management beginning in the 1940s. But the cotton and wheat segments also became less supportive of this policy, especially production controls. The wheat segment was willing to accept the retrenchment of supply management because of favorable conditions in the world economy. This left the cotton segment alone in defending this policy. By the 1970s, then, the coalition supporting supply management had weakened in terms of its advocacy.

Perhaps more importantly, political power within agriculture had shifted by the 1970s. Whereas the cotton-wheat coalition held firm in protecting supply management, or at least the aspects that fit their economic interests, from 1945 through the 1960s, this coalition lost significant power. Not only did the coalition begin to break down because of changing economic interests, but the political power of the key member, southern planters, dwindled. By the early 1970s, the cotton segment was left to defend supply management policy at the very moment that its power was waning. This made supply management vulnerable to change by the corn segment, which had long opposed it. Political support for supply management had weakened, as had the power of the segments continuing to protect it. As a result, the corn segment was able to significantly weaken supply management policy.

Finally, the civil rights movement played a hidden though important role in the retrenchment of supply management. Supply management policy undermined the economic dimensions of the plantation system. One important effect was to allow blacks to leave the rural South, which helped to create an environment conducive to the rise of the civil rights movement. This movement for racial equality then challenged the lingering political dimensions of the plantation system as well as the political power of southern planters. Southern politics became more inclusive, and the Democratic Party began to support civil rights more fully. All of this reduced the power of southern planters over national policies, including agricultural policy. Thus, the transformation of the southern class structure was the underlying factor that allowed the retrenchment of supply management policy.

Before their demise, the southern planters not only shaped national policy through their political power but also exerted tremendous influence over the world economy. After World War II, the United States assumed a hegemonic position in the world economy that allowed it to shape the rules of global trade, production, and distribution to its own national interests. Because southern planters were so powerful within the federal government, they shaped the emerging international food regime—the rules for the international production, trade, and distribution of agricultural commodities—to reflect their economic interests. Yet as we have seen in several other instances so far, this intervention in the market economy ultimately turned on the planters and other segments of agriculture. The next chapter takes up this aspect of twentieth-century agricultural policy—how it fit within the world economy, and the reciprocal relationships that existed between class, national policy, and the world economy.

CHAPTER 6

# Agriculture and the Changing World Economy
## The U.S. Food Regime, 1945–1990

> Those . . . developing countries early on who made use of PL-480 are some of
> our very best customers around the world.
> —MERLIN PLAGGE, PRESIDENT OF THE IOWA FARM BUREAU FEDERATION, 1995

U p to now, we have focused primarily on political and economic
dynamics in the United States, but the market economy is
really a world economy that binds nations and classes closely together.
Furthermore, the world economy has a social organization, or structure, to
it. At a basic level, rules govern the production, consumption, and trade
of commodities, including agricultural commodities. These rules can have
profound effects for individuals, households, classes, and nations as a whole.
So what factors shape the structure of the world economy? Where do these
rules come from? And how great of an effect can the organization of the
world economy have? As in the United States, coalitions within agriculture
throughout the world have played a central role. One place to begin addressing these questions is the most significant world food crisis of the past fifty
years.

### The Food Crisis of the 1970s

In the early 1970s, the threat of hunger and food scarcity seemed pervasive. Several nations faced major famines: Afghanistan, Bangladesh, Chad,
Ethiopia, Kenya, Senegal, and Somalia, among others.[1] Experts warned that
the populations of at least thirty-two countries were threatened with starvation.[2] At the time, the Food and Agricultural Organization of the United

Nations estimated that four hundred million people throughout the world suffered from malnutrition.[3] Even in Western industrialized democracies, pockets of hunger and poverty were a constant problem.[4] These nations, including the United States, felt the effects of the food crisis as food prices rose to such levels that governments responded with price controls. Consumer organizations protested rising food prices, and the world appeared to have entered a new period of food scarcity.[5]

This world food crisis seemed to catch America and the world by surprise for two primary reasons. First, for decades the United States, and several other nations, faced an impending crisis that centered on having too much food, particularly too much grain. Chronic surpluses plagued farmers and constantly threatened to drive market prices, and hence farm income, down to dangerous levels. Though the United States had implemented a policy of supply management in the 1930s, it had largely failed to curtail surpluses of wheat, rice, and other commodities. In fact, in the 1950s and early 1960s, U.S. agricultural surpluses increased. Year-end supplies of wheat climbed fairly steadily from 5.3 MMT in 1948 to 35.9 MMT in 1962. Carry-over stocks fluctuated between 94 and 110 percent of annual wheat production from 1954 to 1958. In 1955 and 1956, government-held wheat reserves at the beginning of each year were larger than the harvest that farmers would produce by the end of each year.[6] Compounding the problem of this chronic surplus, annual wheat production in the country increased from 26 MMT in 1957 to 46 MMT in 1973, and it rose continually during the food crisis of the 1970s.[7] These trends were reflected in world grain production as well because other nations—particularly Argentina, Australia, and Canada—made similar gains in the production and productivity of grains.[8] Before the food crisis, then, agricultural production not only expanded, but it frequently exceeded consumption.

The second reason why this crisis seemed to be surprising was that the United States had offered various kinds of agricultural assistance to poorer countries for two decades. One kind of aid centered around improvements in agricultural technology. The United States had tried to foster a "green revolution" to improve agricultural production in several poorer nations. India, Mexico, the Philippines, and other nations received financial and technological assistance to "modernize" their agricultural production through the use of machinery, chemical fertilizers, hybrid seeds, and more efficient farming techniques. A primary goal of the green revolution was to enhance national agricultural self-sufficiency. And indeed, agricultural productivity and production did increase in these nations, at least for a time.[9] The United States also provided assistance in the form of food aid—which primarily included grain, rice, and dairy products—to many countries each year. Millions of metric tons of grain, mostly wheat, were shipped to nations around the world. Once again, other nations with abundant grains and other commodities pursued similar policies.

With such increasing production in and agricultural assistance from the United States and other industrialized nations, why did the world face a food crisis in the 1970s? Two obvious factors seemed to stand out at the time. First, there was a relative shortfall in world grain production in the early 1970s, partly due to natural occurrences such as droughts or floods, as well as a shortage in fertilizer in various regions.[10] Second, the world, especially poorer nations, experienced a "sudden population explosion" during the mid-twentieth century.[11] As a result, population growth seemed to exceed increases in agricultural production. Certainly, in many nations that faced food shortages at this time, poor harvests and population growth contributed to the crisis. Earl Butz, Nixon's secretary of agriculture, proposed a solution to the crisis that reflected this general analysis: remove government policies that restrict and constrain agricultural production in the United States.[12] If U.S. farmers could produce more, then such food crises could be eased if not averted entirely because food supplies would increase and prices would fall. To some extent, this was true. Ultimately, however, this understanding of the crisis remained at the surface and failed to get to the deeper roots of the problem.

Other observers at the time looked beyond population growth and agricultural production to discern the political and economic factors that contributed to the food crisis.[13] They often asked, how have U.S. policies contributed to such crises? One clear way was through the political use of international food aid. At times, the United States openly used its abundance of food as a "political weapon" to help achieve foreign policy goals. For example, in 1966 and 1967, just a few years before the world food crisis, India experienced a significant food crisis partly due to drought. President Johnson delayed food aid shipments to India because he "was known to be angry with [Indian Prime Minister] Gandhi and the Government of India for their disagreement with U.S. policy toward Vietnam, and he adopted a 'short-tether' policy of adjusting the release of aid . . . to India in relation to the responsiveness . . . of India to suggestions for changes in Indian agricultural policies and to U.S. foreign policy interests."[14] Food aid was used in similar ways to exert influence in a number of other countries, including Bangladesh, Cambodia, Chile, Egypt, Iran, South Korea, Vietnam, and even the Soviet Union.[15] Additionally, the United States scaled back its food aid programs during this food crisis.[16] Consequently, international food aid was often unreliable, even in dire times.

U.S. policies supporting the green revolution also contributed to the food crisis of the 1970s even though they helped to increase agricultural production in several nations. Intensive agriculture based on the U.S. model relied heavily on petroleum. By encouraging such intensive agriculture, which included the use of machinery and chemical fertilizers, the green revolution made nations more vulnerable to economic shifts such as the sharp increase in oil prices in the early 1970s. As a result, the rise in oil prices threatened agricultural production in countries like India that had been part of the green revolution. The cost of agricultural production and of food itself rose with the price of oil. Many observers and politicians at the time recognized this link between the oil crisis and the food crisis.[17]

Still, the roots of the food crisis of the 1970s go far deeper than poor weather conditions, population growth, the unreliability of U.S. food aid, or even the rise in oil prices. To truly understand this crisis, we must look to the very structure and organization of agricultural production, trade, and consumption in the world economy—or, the international food regime. The contours of the food regime following World War II were intimately shaped by U.S. agricultural policy and rested principally on the General Agreement on Tariffs and Trade (GATT) and international food aid (PL 480). Supply management policy depended on the particular shape of the food regime, and the food regime reflected the divisions in agriculture evident in battles over supply management policy. Ultimately, the food crisis of the 1970s signaled the crumbling of the food regime upon which supply management policy rested. The relationship between the world economy and U.S. agricultural policy deserves close examination because it helps to explain the retrenchment of supply management policy that occurred in the 1990s.

## International Food Regimes

A *food regime,* or international food order, is "a stable set of complementary state policies whose implicit coordination creates specific prices relative to other prices, a specific pattern of specialization, and resulting patterns of consumption and trade."[18] The food regime sets the market, which then structures the production and distribution of agricultural commodities throughout the world economy, thereby shaping the international division of labor in agriculture. Two of the fundamental aspects of a food regime include the extent of state intervention into the market (such as tariffs and subsidies) and the direction of trade flows (for example, from colonies to the hegemon). At different moments in history, the contours of the food regime vary: sometimes free trade predominates, but at other times trade barriers protect nations' agriculture; at times basic foodstuffs flow from poorer areas of the world to richer areas, but during other periods the trade flows in the opposite direction. To understand such different periods and the shift in food regimes, we need to examine the politics within and between nations. In particular, we must look at the dominant nation in the world economy, the world economic hegemon, because this nation largely sets the food regime.

These two aspects of food regimes, the extent of state regulation and direction of agricultural trade flows, also constitute the basic contradictions held within food regimes that can eventually burst them asunder and lead to changes in the regime. Polanyi's discussion of shifts between international regimes of free trade and state regulation helps to shed light on the process through which regimes take shape and change.[19] First, the extent of state intervention—whether assuming the form of national regulation or laissez-faire market self-regulation—calls forth forces that push in the opposite direction. Polanyi notes that on the one hand, attempts to achieve the utopian "orthodox" free market eventually wreak havoc on social life as well as on nature. As a result, movements opposing free market forces protect people and land to contain the destruction created by the market. On the other hand, "self-protection against the market limits the maneuver and, therefore, short-term profitability of capital."[20] This likewise creates opposition that seeks a change in the extent of state intervention. Therefore, opposition emerges within food regimes regardless of whether the regimes are oriented toward markets or regulation.

Second, the direction of trade shapes the production, consumption, and distribution of food throughout the world economy. In this regard, each food regime rests on a particular international division of labor. Of central importance is the flow of basic foodstuffs, such as grains, which can create dependence and fundamentally alter the basis of national economies. In other words, this aspect of the food regime influences the extent to which various nations maintain food security. For example, Sidney Mintz outlines how the nineteenth-century international sugar trade fueled Britain's industrialization by changing the diets of British workers, but this trade also reconfigured Caribbean economies to make them dependent on British imports.[21] By reorienting the international division of labor for agriculture, a food regime creates new patterns of economic competition that ultimately alter the balance of international trade.

In this way, a food regime also affects national economic and political development by shaping national economies. The world economic hegemon, however, influences the "preferred" path of national development: "The most powerful states have historically gained the capacity to set the rules, not only of international commerce, but also of discourse, including the discourse of industrial development, as the fetish of modern national civilizations."[22] Importantly, food regimes also help to solidify the position of the world economic hegemon by reinforcing its preferred patterns of production, trade, and development. Yet after a time, the dynamics of the regime begin to undermine the dominant position of the hegemon.

Yet Polanyi's analysis understates the importance of political power.[23] While this ebb and flow between state and market exists over time and helps to distinguish between food regimes, how can we explain the timing of shifts in state regulation or trade flows? Certainly, the market facilitates changes in the production patterns within nations, but we need to consider the competition between nations. One aspect of how nations compete within the world economy is the formation of national policy. As previous chapters have shown, we must turn to the underlying shifts in class coalitions to fully understand national policies. Thus, the shifting economic interests and political power of competing class segments flow beneath the shifts in international food regimes.

All of these dynamics are seen clearly in the rise and fall of the food regime that emerged after World War II. Behind the shift between protectionism and free trade hide the influences of political coalitions of agriculture in the United States and elsewhere. We have already seen how the agricultural coalitions in the United States shifted between the 1920s and 1970s. These shifts are important to understanding the changes in the food regime. Likewise, the food regime developed in such a way that it facilitated changes in U.S. agricultural policy. Before exploring the rise and fall of the U.S. food regime, however, we need to understand clearly its particular contours. What were the fundamental rules for the production and trade of agricultural commodities after 1945? Did agriculture follow the same rules as other sectors of the world economy? How was this food regime different from those that came before?

### The U.S. Food Regime

How the U.S. food regime differed from what existed before is informative. During the nineteenth century, Britain reigned supreme over the world economy. The food regime that Britain created during its hegemony rested on free trade: between 1840 and 1870, tariffs and trade barriers fell dramatically, and Britain maintained a free-trade stance on agriculture until the 1930s.[24] In addition, basic agricultural commodities flowed from the periphery to the core during the British food regime. Less powerful nations (such as the United States, Russia, and Mexico), settler colonies (including Australia and Canada), and colonial areas (such as Ghana and Algeria) sent grains and other basic foodstuffs to the European core of the world economy. The shape of this particular food regime reaffirmed Britain's industrial development and economic dominance.[25]

Emerging just after World War II, the food regime under U.S. hegemony diverged sharply from the British food regime in terms of state regulation and the direction of trade flows.[26] The U.S. food regime relied upon the regulation and protection of national agriculture, reflecting the domestic policy of supply management. The national regulation of agriculture centered around trade barriers and subsidy programs. The United States in particular intervened extensively into the market where agriculture was concerned by regulating prices, purchasing surplus commodities, subsidizing exports, and using production controls. These policies were adopted by numerous other nations: Argentina, Australia, Great Britain, Canada, India, Japan, Mexico, most of Europe, South Korea, and many others. Though some nations—including Australia, Canada, and Japan—developed similar policies during the Great Depression, the continuation and spread of these policies was facilitated by the particular trade rules set forth in GATT following the end of World War II. Notably, Europe's Common Agricultural Policy (CAP), which expanded agricultural subsidies and tariffs, was created in 1958.[27] This widespread state regulation of agriculture contrasts sharply with the British food regime that limited state intervention in agriculture. Although free trade helped to anchor the British food regime, nations throughout the world economy adopted subsidies and price supports based on the U.S. model after 1945.

In addition, agricultural trade, especially grains, flowed from the core to the periphery during the U.S. food regime.[28] Europe had been a primary destination for grains during most of the British food regime, but this changed dramatically after 1945 as grains increasingly went to developing nations. In such nations, wheat imports "rose from a base of practically zero in the mid-1950s to almost half of world food imports in 1971."[29] This flow of agricultural commodities reshaped diets and agricultural production throughout the world. Harriet Friedmann describes one fundamental change in diets: "while total per capita grain consumption in the underdeveloped world increased only 12 per cent per capita, consumption of wheat increased 60 per cent (for the world as a whole, the increase was 21 per cent for all grains and 32 per cent for wheat)."[30] Agricultural production in the periphery likewise changed as grain production declined dramatically in countries such as Colombia.[31] Driving this trade flow were export subsidies, especially food aid based on PL 480, which helped to create new markets for U.S. agriculture, in particular wheat, during the 1950s and 1960s. Once again, other grain-exporting countries followed suit. In terms of state regulation and agricultural trade, the U.S. food regime operated in a manner that was largely the opposite of Britain's food regime.

The essence of the U.S. food regime was a system of trade protections and farm subsidies that resulted in agricultural surpluses that were largely dumped in the periphery as food aid. The national policies and characteristics of agricultural production found in the United States shaped the production, distribution, and consumption of agriculture in the world economy. First, other countries began to develop their agricultural sectors according to the U.S. model. This meant, in part, adopting supply management policy. For example, Europe's CAP used a variety of farm and export subsidies to support the development of its own intensive, industrial agriculture sector. Second, peripheral nations began to import basic foodstuffs, initially in the form of U.S. food aid. These nations consequently experienced a collapse of their agrarian sectors, massive rural-to-urban migration, and political power concentrated in the hands of urban interests pursuing cheap food policies.[32] As a result, these countries became increasingly dependent on food imports despite often having a history of agricultural self-sufficiency.

The food regime based on national protection was to some extent unique in the world economy under U.S. hegemony. In contrast to the extensive regulations, tariffs, and subsidies found in agriculture, the United States generally fought for increased free trade and reduced state interventions into the economy.[33] Why did the U.S. food regime depart so much from that of British hegemony? And why was the food regime relatively unique in the broader U.S. attempt to liberalize the world economy? In short, how can we explain the contours of this food regime?

### The Formation of the U.S. Food Regime

Supply management policy was the foundation of the U.S. food regime based on national protection and agricultural trade flowing to the periphery. The international food regime reflected the policy of supply management, and this policy was likewise dependent on this particular food regime. Nevertheless, a food regime based on national protection and agricultural trade flows toward the periphery was neither automatic nor inevitable. Instead, the dominant agricultural coalition in U.S. politics, the cotton-wheat coalition, strongly influenced the shape of the food regime to correspond with its preferred national policy. Therefore, two factors are important for understanding the U.S. food regime: how the food regime complemented supply management policy, and how the cotton-wheat coalition shaped the food regime.

### Supply Management Policy and the U.S. Food Regime

The policy of supply management in the United States was successful in one important way: it helped to raise farm income substantially. Despite this success, however, the policy had one glaring failure: it actually encouraged overproduction, at the same time that it generally failed to control supply. The irony of this shortcoming is that by encouraging overproduction, supply management policy contributed to the very market instability against which farmers sought protection. This was, of course, a fundamental problem with the policy.

The root of this problem was the particular combination of production controls and price supports administered under the policy. Production controls were primarily based on acreage rather than on the actual volume of production; that is, farmers faced restrictions on the acreage that they could use in production but few limitations on the actual volume of commodities that they could produce on each acre.[34] As long as farmers adhered to restrictions on acreage, they could generally produce as much as possible. Importantly, price supports, which guaranteed minimum prices, encouraged farmers to do just that: produce as much as possible on each acre in production. In contrast to production controls that restricted acres, price supports were based on volume produced: if the price support for cotton was set at $0.35 per pound, farmers would receive that support price on all cotton that they grew within their acreage allotment. This inconsistent basis of supply management—production controls on acres, price supports on volume—produced a logic for individual farmers that undermined the primary function of the policy: managing the supply of commodities. This policy encouraged farmers to intensify their production on a smaller number of acres in order to receive the optimal benefit from price supports.[35]

After the Second World War, a technological revolution in chemical fertilizers, pesticides, and herbicides, as well as the spread of mechanization, allowed farmers to significantly increase their productivity (that is, production per acre). Between 1945 and 1970, productivity for most commodities increased significantly: corn productivity doubled from 33 bushels per acre to 72 bushels per acre, wheat productivity from 17 to 31 bushels per acre, and cotton productivity from 254 pounds per acre to 438 pounds per acre. With these increases in productivity came fairly constant increases in overall production: between 1945 and 1970, corn production increased from 81 MMT to 141 MMT; wheat production increased less dramatically, from 30 MMT to 37 MMT.[36] Cotton production remained relatively high through the 1950s but began to fall with the shift to soybeans in the 1960s. Consequently, despite this historic attempt to manage supply through production controls, overall production of agricultural commodities increased because of unprecedented improvements in productivity.

This increased production would be a problem only to the extent that demand for these commodities did not keep up with the growing supply. This is evident from the fact that overproduction became a problem for some agricultural commodities but not for others. In particular, cotton and wheat experienced the most significant problems. Surpluses were largely averted immediately after World War II because the war had decimated agriculture in Europe and much of Asia. Agricultural production in these regions began to recover by the early 1950s, and the demand for U.S. agricultural goods in the world economy weakened. Cotton producers faced large carry-over stocks in the early 1950s. Year-end stocks between 1946 and 1950 averaged

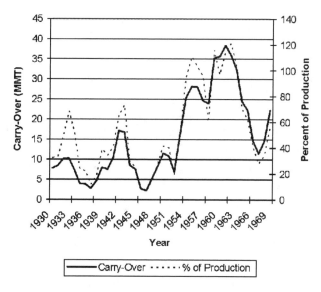

6.1. Overproduction of wheat in the United States, 1930–1969. *Source:* USDA (various years), *Agricultural Statistics.*

about 5 million bales, which equaled about 46 percent of average annual production. Carry-over stocks, however, rose significantly in the 1950s: between 1955 and 1959, year-end stocks averaged almost 11 million bales. During this later period, carry-over stocks represented approximately 84 percent of annual production. In fact, the carry-over of cotton surpassed actual production in 1956 and 1957. This overproduction of cotton contributed to market volatility and increased government spending on price supports and storage costs.

The situation was even worse for wheat producers, who faced a growing surplus between 1952 and 1961. Figure 6.1 shows this chronic overproduction of wheat. Carry-over stocks of wheat climbed fairly steadily, from 5.3 MMT in 1948 to 35.9 MMT in 1962. From 1946 to 1950, the annual year-end supply of wheat averaged about 6 MMT, but the annual surplus of wheat rose to an average of about 28 MMT between 1954 and 1959. From 1954 to 1958, carry-over stocks ranged between 94 and 110 percent of annual wheat production. Carry-over stocks exceeded production in 1955, 1956, 1959, and 1961–1963. Thus, production controls failed to prevent chronic wheat surpluses. Just as with cotton, this surplus of wheat created significant market instability and raised the cost of government farm programs.

Corn producers, by contrast, were relatively spared the problem of chronic surpluses. Because the production and productivity of corn increased, carry-over stocks did indeed increase during the 1950s, just as was the case with cotton and wheat. Yet carry-over stocks never accounted for more than 56 percent of annual corn production during this period. Corn producers did not face an overly burdensome surplus largely because of the expansion of the livestock industry, which consumed most of the corn produced as feed. The expanding livestock industry rested on intensive production methods by developing concentrated animal feeding operations, which consumed increasing amounts of corn, soybeans, and other feed grains.[37] Increasing per capita meat consumption (see Figure 7.1) influenced the economic interests of producers in the Corn Belt by preventing large surpluses of feed grains, particularly corn. Therefore, although surpluses of corn certainly existed at this time, they never reached the threatening level of cotton or wheat surpluses and were thus more manageable.

With such chronic oversupply of some agricultural commodities, the federal government looked beyond production controls to achieve its goal of managing supply and stabilizing the market. Since controlling production had failed so miserably, the government tried to increase the consumption of U.S. agricultural commodities by expanding international markets. Export subsidies were the primary tool it used to create new markets and expand old ones. At the center of this new strategy was PL 480, which subsidized exports to Africa, Asia, and Latin America. This shift toward subsidized exports helped to alleviate the chronic overproduction of wheat, cotton, and other commodities, particularly in the 1960s, when year-end stocks of wheat declined even while production increased by about 50 percent. Alleviating chronic overproduction through increased exports lowered the cost of government farm programs in various ways. For example, price support payments declined as market prices rose in response to reduced supplies. Also, exporting surplus commodities led storage costs to fall as government-held stocks shrank. Therefore, supply management policy depended on the flow of agricultural trade in the world economy, and export subsidies quickly became one of the main pillars upon which supply management policy rested. Thus, the policy rested on the contours of the food regime.

To understand fully how this food regime emerged, however, we need to look beyond the policy of supply management—to the political battles surrounding GATT and PL 480, which were at the center of the formation of this food regime. The trade rules outlined in GATT not only allowed the United States to retain supply management policy but prompted other nations to adopt the policy as well. PL 480 firmly established the flow of agricultural goods from the core to the periphery. These two political policies, then, provided the foundation for the U.S. food regime. Importantly, political struggles involving segments of U.S. agriculture lie behind the development of GATT and food aid.

### The General Agreement on Tariffs and Trade

Before the end of World War II, the United States began formulating policies to reestablish free trade as the basis of the world economy. It wanted to remove trade barriers that had emerged throughout the world economy during the 1920s and 1930s. Even Britain, the bastion of free trade for nearly a century, had raised barriers to trade by creating an imperial preference system that privileged the British Dominions—including Australia, Canada, New Zealand, South Africa, and other former colonies—as trading partners by agreeing to keep high tariff rates on "non-Empire" goods while keeping most "Dominion products on the free list."[38] The United States took the elimination of such barriers as its primary task: "the [U.S.] State Department hoped above all to shake the British loose from the imperial preference system . . . negotiated at Ottawa in 1932."[39] Britain and its Dominions, however, guarded imperial privilege throughout the postwar trade negotiations because of concerns that lowered trade barriers would slow their economic recovery.[40] In particular, "the southern dominions . . . worried about losing their British market for food."[41] When Britain became desperate for a loan from the United States in 1945, one provision of the loan required Britain to negotiate on its preferential trading system.[42] Nevertheless, preferences within the Commonwealth persisted through several more years and rounds of trade talks.[43]

Despite Britain's obstinance to relinquishing its system of trade preferences, the United States continued to push for the creation of a world economy based on free trade through GATT. Becoming effective in 1948, GATT aimed to reduce trade barriers in the world economy through multilateral trade agreements that rested on "two pillars: non-discrimination and reciprocity."[44] The key was most favored nation status, which required that all trade favors or preferences be given to all partners.[45] GATT was quite effective at reducing trade barriers in the world economy during the second half of the twentieth century: "the average tariff rate on dutiable imports fell from 40 percent in the 1940s to 5 percent in 1989."[46] Thus, the general trade regime under U.S. hegemony centered on reducing trade barriers and therefore expanding free trade—just as it had been previously under British hegemony, before the 1930s. Again, however, one point of distinction existed: agriculture.

The issue of agriculture shaped GATT in two important ways. First, GATT excluded agriculture from liberalization—the only economic sector left out of GATT's drive to eliminate trade barriers. Article XI of GATT prohibited quantitative restrictions, except when "used in support of certain domestic agricultural programs, particularly those which, by raising domestic prices above the world market price, tend to create an incentive for importation."[47] This exemption applied only when such barriers were needed to enforce state policies that impose limits on domestic sales or production, or "to remove a temporary surplus of the like domestic product."[48] In other words, GATT permitted supply management policy. This exemption matched an amendment to the AAA, Section 22 of that act, that "gives the President authority to impose import quotas or fees on commodities covered in the act if . . . he determines that the importation of these commodities is hindering . . . domestic agricultural programs."[49] In addition, Article XVI of GATT permitted export subsidies for agricultural products. These escape clauses in the agreement came at the request of the United States, specifically the USDA and Congress, and were tailored to fit U.S. agricultural policy. Consequently, the Farm Bureau, the NFU, and other U.S. farm organizations were supportive of expanding trade through GATT.[50]

Second, agriculture was a central issue in the struggle over the creation of an organization to oversee the trade rules set forth in the agreement. Participants of the Havana Conference in 1947 drafted a charter for the International Trade Organization (ITO), which was proposed to oversee the trade rules and regulations set forth in GATT. However, the United States failed to ratify the ITO charter, partly because it conflicted with U.S. domestic agricultural policy.[51] In hearings on the ITO charter, senators, particularly from the South and the Wheat Belt, expressed concern about the extent to which the ITO would limit the ability of the United States to continue using price supports, production controls, and export subsidies. For example, Walter George (D-GA) and Eugene Millikin (R-CO), who chaired the Senate Committee on Finance, gave these responses to Clair Wilcox of the U.S. State Department who appeared in support of the ITO:

SENATOR GEORGE: It looks to me like under these sections [of the ITO charter], that you are simply outlawing any subsidy, direct or indirect, on exportation, let us say, of cotton, as a particular product. . . . And, of course, there is a period in which you can have a stay of execution, but the day of execution is nevertheless fixed.

SENATOR MILLIKIN: And the extensions are in the hands of other countries.

SENATOR GEORGE: Yes.

SENATOR MILLIKIN: Taking that much of it, you again put the decision [affecting U.S. agricultural policy] in the hands of the Organization.[52]

Of some concern was the ITO's power to create intergovernmental commodity agreements that could involve export quotas, limiting the amount of a commodity that the United States and other producing nations could export. Such an agreement, for example, could limit the amount of cotton or wheat exported by the United States.[53] Senator Edwin Johnson (D-CO) received assurances that production controls would not be outlawed under the ITO charter.[54] Nonetheless, enough concern remained in the Senate that it failed to ratify the charter and allowed the ITO to die.[55] Without a formal organization governing it, GATT "began as an *ad hoc* negotiating forum."[56] GATT sponsored several rounds of trade and tariff negotiations, in 1947 (Geneva), 1949 (Annecy), 1951 (Torquay), 1956 (Geneva), 1960–1961 ("Dillon"), 1964–1967 ("Kennedy"), 1973–1979 (Tokyo), and 1986–1994 (Uruguay).[57] Despite the absence of the ITO, each of these rounds of trade talks gradually reduced trade barriers throughout the world economy.

Why did the United States fight to exempt agriculture from liberalization? Why did agriculture play such a central role in undermining the creation of the ITO? The position of U.S. agriculture on GATT was somewhat surprising from an historical viewpoint. U.S. agriculture had long relied on export markets, and therefore most segments of agriculture had historically been in favor of free-trade policies. U.S. wheat producers had dominated world markets since the 1860s, and cotton growers in the South had historically been strong advocates of free trade.[58]

Even though almost all segments of U.S. agriculture advocated expanding trade after World War II, opposition existed to the reinstitution of free market principles because of the fear that agricultural surpluses and falling prices would return.[59] As the previous chapters demonstrated, the cotton-wheat coalition fought to retain state intervention in agriculture markets. Again, this opposition to free trade was new for southern agriculture, which had traditionally supported it. The Southern Commissioners of Agriculture broke with their past in an historic pronouncement in 1947:

> The thirty seven millions of citizens of the great Southland and their duly elected state officials, the Southern Commissioners of Agriculture, are each one sprung from the loins of those who for more than one hundred years carried the standards of the Democratic Party in never-ending struggle and even on the field of battle . . . to support the economic theory and doctrine of "free trade" versus the "protective tariff." These stalwarts and Southern Democratic peoples, after long trials and due to the kaleidoscopic changes attending the national economy of the United States in a more modern world, are with reluctance compelled to burn all bridges behind them and to make prayer to the Chief Executive that he now retain on behalf of their agricultural products the vestiges of tariff protection which still remain in the [Smoot-Hawley] Act of 1930.[60]

Wheat producers likewise opposed liberalizing agriculture and supported state intervention. As already shown, the cotton-wheat coalition held substantial political power in both political parties and within Congress at this time. For example, for all but two years between 1940 and 1953, Sam Rayburn (D-TX) served as the speaker of the House, and Tom Connally (D-TX) was the chair of the Senate Committee on Foreign Relations.[61] Such political power allowed the cotton-wheat coalition to intimately shape GATT to reflect supply management policy.

In a fundamental way, supply management policy constrained free trade by raising domestic agricultural prices above world prices: "price supports . . . necessitate import restrictions in order to fend off imports attracted to the higher domestic prices; in addition, price supports require export subsidies in order to make possible, on the world market, sale of the surpluses created by the high domestic prices."[62] To protect the AAA programs, the cotton-wheat coalition influenced the negotiations creating GATT to permit a food regime based on national regulation rather than free trade. The political power of this agricultural coalition was such that it could maintain its trade barriers and intervention in the market even in the face of a widespread push for free trade. Thus, while Britain greatly limited the removal of trade barriers after the war, it certainly was not the only, or even the primary, hindrance to a free-trade–based world economy. The cotton-wheat coalition posed an even more insurmountable obstacle to a general free-trade regime.

### Spreading Supply Management Policy across the Globe

Exempting agriculture from GATT encouraged the spread of U.S.-style agricultural policies as other nations implemented (or continued to use) price supports, direct income supports to farmers, and export subsidies. This diffusion of national regulation stemmed partly from competition with U.S. agriculture. First, other nations had to focus on their domestic markets since the U.S. market was closed off because of price supports and restrictions on agricultural imports. Second, other nations needed to protect their farmers from U.S. agricultural commodities that were cheapened by export subsidies. Consequently, other nations also restricted agricultural imports. Third, to retain or expand export markets for their own agricultural products, these nations had to devise export subsidies to compete with U.S. exports. Much of the world economy, then, created policies that raised domestic farm income through price adjustments, raised import barriers, and used subsidies to export at lower than domestic prices—all in order to compete more effectively with U.S. agriculture. Each of these policies, of course, was perfectly legal under GATT. As GATT expanded, more nations adopted the U.S.-style national regulation of agriculture to make use of these tariff and subsidy exemptions. GATT consisted of nineteen member nations in 1948, thirty-five in 1955, sixty-three in 1965, and seventy-four in 1970.[63] Its membership surpassed one hundred nations in the 1970s, and each of these nations was subject to trade rules that allowed them to offer protections to their agricultural producers. Consequently, GATT encouraged the spread of national regulations for agriculture based on the model of supply management policy in the United States.

The CAP of the European Community (EC) provides an example of how supply management policy spread via GATT. In 1957, the Treaty of Rome outlined the objectives of an agricultural policy for EC members: increasing agricultural productivity, raising farm income, stabilizing markets, and creating "reasonable" food prices.[64] The CAP, formed a year later, employed several familiar policy devices to achieve these ends: government purchases of surplus commodities, target prices, import levies, and export subsidies. It aimed to increase the production of wheat, in particular. Importantly, the CAP exempted corn and soy products from import controls.[65] As a result, the United States lost the EC wheat market but became essentially the sole supplier of feed stuffs—corn and soybeans.

Some nations had adopted national policies supporting domestic agriculture during the economic crisis of the 1930s, but GATT prompted the retention and even the expansion of state intervention into agriculture. For example, Australia had tried to alleviate the plight of farmers during the Great Depression by devaluing its currency, reducing wages and interest rates, and imposing a moratorium on farm foreclosures, among other policies. However, the Australian government used subsidies only on an "ad hoc basis."[66] After World War II, Australia implemented price supports and similar mechanisms for wheat, cotton, tobacco, and a few other commodities in an explicit attempt to increase production. This policy was successful, and the country exported increasing amounts of wheat, especially during the 1960s. In Japan, the government likewise responded to the Great Depression by adopting policies to offer some protection from market vagaries. In 1929, the Japanese government created a price stabilization program to alleviate the sharp drop in prices that farmers experienced. As occurred in Australia, Japanese agricultural policy expanded substantially after the Second World War. In 1955, the Japanese government amended its agricultural policy to emphasize "a new politics of income support and parity between agriculture and the industrial sectors of the economy."[67] This policy was further reinforced by the passage of the Agricultural Basic Law in 1961.[68] Therefore, even though some nations adopted agricultural policies to raise prices or control production during the Great Depression, the rules set forth by GATT led to the continuation and expansion of these policies even after the world economic crisis had abated.[69]

This widespread use of national regulations for agriculture generated chronic surpluses in various nations, just as it did in the United States. This was especially true in Australia, Canada, and the EC. Overproduction, however, was not necessarily new because several countries, like the United States, had been confronting the problem of agricultural surplus for many years: "Countries like South Africa and Australia [had been] burdened with surpluses since WWI."[70] The EC, by contrast, had long been a net importer of wheat, but it became a net exporter by 1980.[71] Even Britain, which was the world's largest importer of grain in the early 1950s, became a "major net exporter" by 1985.[72] Therefore, surpluses gradually mounted with the spread of U.S.-style regulation throughout the world economy.

With such pervasive and widespread agricultural surpluses, nations faced a common dilemma: how to dispose of excess agricultural commodities. The answer was to expand markets through export subsidies in the form of food aid.

### International Food Aid

Subsidized agricultural exports to nations in "need" provided an outlet for the growing surpluses between 1945 and 1970.[73] Food aid was grounded in two major policies: the European Recovery Program, commonly called the Marshall Plan, and PL 480. Food aid originated with the Marshall Plan, created in 1948 to provide industrial and agricultural assistance to Europe after World War II. PL 480 was created in 1954 and was aimed primarily at poorer nations in the periphery. Though both policies tried to help nations feed their people, a key distinction existed between them: whereas the Marshall Plan sent resources, such as fertilizer and machinery, to reconstruct European agriculture, PL 480 centered on sending food, with little effort to build up agriculture.[74]

The first release for U.S. agricultural surpluses was to Europe through the Marshall Plan. This policy had two primary components: relief aid and reconstruction assistance. Initially, the United States sent shipments of wheat, corn, meat, and other commodities. Through this food aid, U.S. agricultural exports increased ninefold between 1945 and 1949, surpassing prewar levels.[75] Europe desperately needed this food aid because its "grain harvests in 1946 were expected to reach only 60% of pre-war levels."[76] This deficiency in production also signaled the need for reconstruction assistance, leading the Marshall Plan to center much of its agricultural assistance on feedstuffs and fertilizers to help rebuild European agriculture. Gradually, European agricultural production increased, and it was largely restored by 1954.[77] Thus, the Marshall Plan helped to reduce the European market for many U.S. agricultural exports. Figure 6.2 shows the decline in U.S. wheat exports going to Europe, which fell from 58 percent of all U.S. wheat exports in 1949 to just 17 percent in 1959. From 1945 to 1952, U.S. wheat exports to Europe averaged about 47 percent of total exports. Between 1957 and 1969, however, exports to Europe averaged less than 20 percent of total exports. As a result, the United States needed new markets for its agricultural surpluses, which were mounting again in the mid-1950s, especially for wheat and cotton. With the European market gone, wheat holdings of the CCC amounted to 850 million bushels in 1954—almost a year's worth of production.[78]

The second outlet for U.S. agricultural surpluses was the periphery of the world economy, especially newly independent nations undergoing state formation as European colonial empires collapsed. Between 1945 and 1965, more than forty-five new nations formed in Asia, Africa, and the Middle East out of this process of decolonization, and almost the entirety of the African continent became independent during this period.[79] Many of these new nations retained strong economic ties with their former colonizers, but they nevertheless represented potential new markets for U.S. exports. With European agricultural markets essentially closed off by the mid-1950s, the

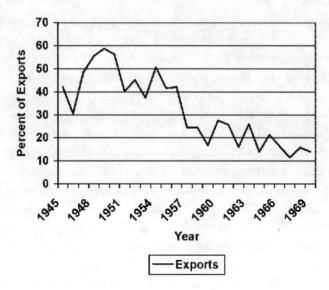

6.2. Percentage of U.S. wheat exports going to Europe, 1945–1969. *Source:* USDA (various years), *Agricultural Statistics.*

United States turned to Europe's former colonies to dispose of its agricultural surpluses—most notably, wheat. As a result, agricultural trade in the U.S. food regime flowed in the opposite direction (from core to periphery) of that of the British food regime (to the core). PL 480 was the cornerstone of this particular flow of agricultural goods.

PL 480 created a system through which the United States could provide economic assistance, in the form of agricultural commodities, to peripheral countries. The basic premise was to supply inexpensive food to aid in the economic development of nations. PL 480 consisted of three titles, but Title I was the core of the legislation. Administered by the USDA, this portion of the legislation provided for "concessional sales" of surplus agricultural commodities to "friendly" nations. As Friedmann explains, the U.S. government paid "private grain companies to ship the grain. The recipient countries in turn placed an equivalent amount of their national currencies at the disposal of the US government."[80] U.S. agencies within these nations could then use this noncontrovertible currency for "a range of development activities such as infrastructural projects, supplies for military bases, loans to U.S. companies (especially local agribusiness operations), locally produced goods and services, and trade fairs."[81] Title II allowed for disaster relief and similar aid, and Title III permitted foreign donations and barter trades. Title I sales, however, accounted for between about 50 and 90 percent of all commitments under PL 480.[82] Between 1958 and 1963, no less than 60 percent of PL 480 commitments were under Title I.

The USDA formulated PL 480 with the assistance of the Farm Bureau and the NFU.[83] Part of the stimulus for this legislation was the inability to reduce or eliminate price supports and the surpluses they encouraged. In 1955, a newly elected Democratic Congress expanded funding for Title I from $700 million to $1.5 billion "and stipulated that this . . . was 'an objective as well as a limitation, to be reached as rapidly as possible.'"[84] In 1956, Title I funding was raised to $3 billion.[85] At times, the distribution of these commodities through PL 480 conflicted with general U.S. trade policy as well as GATT because concessional sales closely resembled dumping and sometimes displaced the products of other nations, such as Australia and Canada.[86]

Perhaps the primary benefit of, and principal motivation for, PL 480 was that it allowed the government to dispose of the surplus agricultural commodities that accumulated through price support programs and CCC purchases.[87] This program allowed the state to continue supply management policy while averting crises of excess surplus stocks. In fact, PL 480 became a cornerstone of supply management because the program was so fundamental to U.S. agricultural exports: "At its peak [in 1965], U.S. aid accounted for 80 per cent of American wheat exports and more than 35 per cent of *world* wheat trade."[88] Therefore, PL 480 fueled U.S. exports of wheat as well as of other commodities, including rice, feed grains, cotton, oilseeds, and dairy products.

Just as supply management policy spread because of GATT rules, so too did the use of food aid spread as a means of disposing of surplus commodities, again primarily wheat. By the late 1960s, several other nations were also distributing food aid, including Argentina, Australia, Canada, the EC, and Japan.[89] By 1965, annual world food aid totaled more than $1 billion, with the vast majority coming from the United States.[90] One important effect of food aid was to build up potential commercial markets for agricultural goods in peripheral countries. In such countries, "per capita consumption of wheat rose by almost two-thirds . . . [meanwhile] per capita consumption of traditional root crops declined by more than 20 percent."[91] For example, "Iran, which spent only $15 million on American wheat ten years earlier, had become a $325 million customer by 1975."[92] In Tokyo and other urban areas in Japan, wheat consumption rose 300 percent between 1945 and 1958; mean-

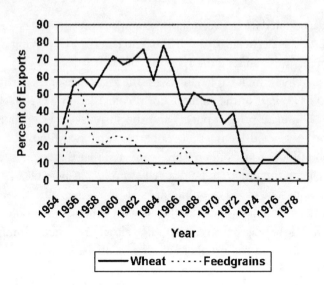

6.3. U.S. wheat and feed grain exports supported by PL 480, 1954–1978. *Source:*
U.S. Census Bureau (various years), *Statistical Abstract of the United States.*

while, the consumption of rice fell.[93] Countries in Latin America, Africa, and
Asia that had imported little wheat before 1954 came to account for almost
half of world imports by 1971 and received 78 percent of U.S. wheat exports
by 1978.[94] Food aid was central to the creation of these new markets.

Despite the world economic changes that PL 480 initiated, this program
was more important to some segments of agriculture than others. As Figure
6.3 demonstrates, PL 480 accounted for a very significant portion of U.S.
wheat exports between 1954 and 1971: no less than 33 percent of wheat exports were covered under PL 480 during this period. The peak period for PL
480 was 1959–1964, when this program accounted for 70 percent of annual
wheat exports, on average. By contrast, exports of feed grains, primarily
corn, relied much less on food aid. Fifty-eight percent of feed grain exports
were covered by PL 480 in 1955, and 47 percent were covered in 1956, but
use of PL 480 for feed grain exports declined quickly thereafter.

By 1958, the common divisions within agriculture emerged around PL
480. Though the Farm Bureau had helped to create the program, this organization expressed opposition to it just a few years later. John Lynn, the Farm
Bureau's legislative director, told the House Committee on Agriculture that
the Farm Bureau had "always considered Public Law 480 as a temporary
program, as one designed to help alleviate our surplus situation."[95] Lynn

repeatedly argued that PL 480 should not become a permanent program, in part because it failed to reduce surpluses even though exports expanded between 1954 and 1958. He claimed that expanding the program and making it permanent would hinder the expansion of commercial exports. Southern Democrats, who ran the House Committee on Agriculture, received Lynn's testimony cooly.[96] By contrast, the cotton-wheat coalition strongly advocated for making the program permanent. For instance, Read Dunn of the National Cotton Council (NCC) explained that PL 480 had been very effective at expanding markets for U.S. cotton in countries such as France, Germany, Italy, and Japan.[97] Floyd Root, the president of NAWG, not only recommended continuing PL 480 but urged "that it be adopted as a permanent part" of U.S. agricultural policy.[98] Similarly, Robert Downs of the NFU explicitly discussed the split in agriculture: the "Farmers Union does not concur with . . . the Farm Bureau . . . that the Public Law 480 program is only a temporary program. [The] Farmers Union feels that . . . Public Law 480 should be a permanent, long-term part of our Nation's foreign policy."[99] Downs argued that the United States had a moral obligation to share its agricultural surplus with the world, and he disagreed that food aid would undermine commercial exports. On this fundamental dimension of the U.S. food regime, then, the split between the cotton-wheat coalition and the corn segment was evident — just as it was regarding price supports and production controls.

This political battle within agriculture over export subsidies was largely due to differences in the segments' respective positions in the world economy. As Figure 6.4 shows, the corn segment dominated its world market: U.S. corn exports accounted for less than half of world corn exports only once between 1957 and 1980. In addition to dominating world corn markets, U.S. corn exports increased dramatically after 1945. Corn exports rarely rose above 3 MMT during the first third of the twentieth century (see Figure 2.4), and they were consistently about 3 MMT between 1948 and 1955. By 1961, however, U.S. corn exports rose to 13 MMT, and they reached 21 MMT by 1965 (see Figure 4.1). Most of this increase was done without the help of PL 480. Europe became an important destination for U.S. corn exports because the CAP did not raise significant trade barriers on feed grains. As Dan Morgan notes, "U.S. corn exports to Europe increased and soybean exports doubled after the advent of CAP."[100] This contrasts sharply with the situation for U.S. wheat, which lost access to the European market because of the CAP. In general, the expansion of U.S. corn exports was driven by

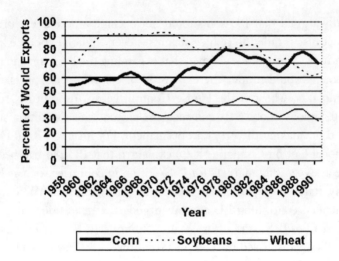

6.4. Dominance of U.S. agricultural exports in the world economy, 1958–1990 (three-year moving averages). *Source:* U.S. Census Bureau (various years), *Statistical Abstract of the United States.*

growing livestock industries in Europe, Japan, and other nations,[101] and this growing market reinforced the corn segment's preference for free trade. The Farm Bureau, in particular, called for expanding exports, increasing free trade, and limiting state intervention.

The U.S. wheat segment faced a much more competitive international market. Between 1960 and 1967, U.S. wheat exports accounted for approximately 39 percent of world exports. This was notably below the 60 percent of world corn exports accounted for by the United States during the same period. The wheat segment's reliance on export subsidies reflected its general support of state intervention into the economy, though as exports expanded wheat producers became less enamored of production controls (see Chapter 4). Correspondingly, the NFU not only favored supply management policy (including export subsidies), but it advocated extending such a policy to the world economy. The NFU supported expanding exports but favored doing so through international cooperation and coordination — not by simply liberalizing markets. The embodiment of this preference can be seen in the International Wheat Agreements from 1949 to 1956, which tried to stabilize the world wheat market by specifying "the basic maximum and minimum prices at which 'guaranteed quantities' of wheat [would] be offered by designated exporting countries or purchased by designated importing countries."[102] Thus, the wheat and corn segments followed distinct paths to expanding exports: one advocated government subsidies and coordination, and the other pursued free trade and liberalization. The greater degree of competition in the international wheat market and the access that U.S. feed grains had to the European market were the roots of this difference over the use of export subsidies.

The U.S. food regime that emerged after 1945 was based on GATT and food aid, and it was closely tied to supply management policy. The contours of this regime resulted from the political preferences of the cotton-wheat coalition in the United States, although this regime conflicted with the economic interests and political preferences of other segments of agriculture. Importantly, the proliferation of supply management policy and food aid throughout the world economy proved to be a fundamental contradiction that would eventually undermine the U.S. food regime—and threaten the viability of supply management policy, which depended on this particular food regime.

### The Crisis of Protection

By the early 1970s, the U.S. food regime began to show signs of breaking down, not the least of which was the disarray that emerged in the form of the food crisis. This regime's interventions into the market economy created conditions that eventually made the system unworkable.[103] Three inherent contradictions facilitated its collapse. First, national regulation continued to spread through much of the world economy, creating surpluses in several nations. Second, other nations began to subsidize their agricultural exports to dispose of their surpluses, leading to intensified competition for markets. Finally, the national regulation of agriculture and export subsidies built up a new actor for whom these features became limitations: transnational agribusiness. By the 1990s, supply management policy was threatened with retrenchment at least in part because these contradictions undermined the food regime upon which this policy rested.

### The Export Battles of the 1980s

Despite the food crisis from 1972 to 1974, world wheat production increased significantly during the 1970s and 1980s. In 1975, it equaled about 352 MMT and reached 534 MMT by 1986. The adoption of variations of supply management policy by Australia, Britain, Canada, France, Germany, and many other nations facilitated this increased production and helped to create widespread agricultural surpluses. Perhaps the most dramatic increase occurred in Europe, where wheat production rose from 51 MMT in 1975 to 83 MMT in 1985.[104] In Australia, Canada, and other wheat-exporting nations, production increased by more than 50 percent between 1974 and 1986, and this was in addition to the increase in U.S. wheat production from 48 MMT in 1974 to 76 MMT in 1982. This trend in world wheat production created problems in the food regime.

Like the United States, many nations began to face the dilemma of disposing of chronic agricultural surpluses. One popular solution followed the U.S. model of expanding markets by using export subsidies. At least eighteen countries besides the United States adopted food aid programs by 1980.[105] Consequently, the U.S. share of world wheat exports dropped precipitously from 48 percent in 1981 to 29 percent in 1985. During this same period, total U.S. wheat exports likewise fell from 48 MMT to 25 MMT. One source of this decline in the dominance of U.S. wheat was export subsidies created by Europe.[106] After being a net importer of wheat from 1965 to 1979, Europe became a net exporter in 1980.[107] Europe's wheat exports climbed from about 5 MMT in 1977 to 18 MMT in 1984, and wheat exports from Canada and Australia climbed similarly. Between 1970 and 1979, total exports for the United States averaged about 29 MMT annually, as did the combined exports of Australia, Canada, and the European Union (EU). But between 1980 and 1986, Australia, Canada, and the EU exported an average of 48 MMT annually compared with 37 MMT for the United States. In response to losing such a sizable share of world wheat markets, the United States created additional export subsidies with the Export Enhancement Program (EEP) in 1985. One important difference between PL 480 and the EEP was that the latter was devoid of the Cold War politics that often shaped the former. In addition, the EEP focused on commercial exports and was aimed directly at the EU's export markets. From 1986 to 1990, at least two-thirds of U.S. wheat exports were subsidized by the EEP, PL 480, or other programs. This led to a battle between Europe and the United States in which each used export subsidies to compete for markets, such as northern Africa. This competition using subsidies resulted in declining wheat prices, which hurt farmers in the United States, Europe, and other wheat-exporting countries, as well as farmers in nations receiving subsidized wheat.[108]

All of this suggests that the food regime was losing its ability to contain the secular problem of overproduction in agriculture. Nations around the world adopted surplus-inducing policies and then clogged world markets using export subsidies. For the United States, this situation strained the federal government's budget as the cost of price supports, production controls, export subsidies, and surplus storage all increased. As a result, the Reagan administration began pushing for greater liberalization of agriculture through the Uruguay Round of GATT, which began in 1986. That is, the United States advocated eliminating agriculture's special status in GATT despite being the nation that had won that status for agriculture five decades earlier. Other forces likewise pushed in this direction. In particular, a group of agricultural exporting nations formed the Cairns Group, which was led by Australia and included Canada, to work as a bloc in the Uruguay Round to win lower trade barriers and subsidies in agriculture.[109] These exporting nations could not afford to subsidize agriculture on par with the United States and the EU. And finally, additional pressure for liberalization came from transnational agribusiness corporations. Many of these calls for liberalization, of course, were aimed at the U.S. policy of supply management. Thus, a significant movement against regulation emerged and gained momentum after 1980. This is Karl Polanyi's double movement in motion.

### Agribusiness and National Policy

One notable element in the drive to liberalize agriculture was the increasing political influence of agribusiness. The food regime's focus on grain trade helped to build up agribusiness, especially agricultural transnational corporations (TNCs): "It was within the context of this food regime disbursing food at concessional—and later, commercial—prices that the huge grain traders, such as Cargill and Continental, prospered."[110] Export subsidies were especially lucrative for grain traders. After just the first five years of PL 480, "Anderson Clayton and Company exported nearly $60 million in cotton under . . . title I, $25 million more than the next largest exporter; title I grain exports flowed heavily through three major firms, Continental Grain Company ($385 million), Louis Dreyfus Corporation ($305 million), and Cargill, Incorporated ($264 million)."[111] Thus, export subsidies were often concentrated among a few companies and therefore contributed to increasing concentration in agribusiness. This was largely due to concentration within the grain trade: by the end of the 1970s, just six grain companies— Andre & Co., Bunge, Cargill, Continental, Dreyfus, and Mitsui/Cook—

accounted for more than 90 percent of the wheat and corn exports from the United States, as well as the vast majority of grain exports from Argentina, Australia, and Europe.[112]

The development of industrial agriculture, with its increasingly complex division of labor across nations and within commodity production, also spurred the growth of agribusiness corporations.[113] The livestock complex provides one example of how supply management policy broadened the scope of agribusiness: "Throughout the 1960s, the USDA worked closely with Cargill and other grain companies to establish Asian poultry industries, baking industries, cattle-fattening yards, and fast-food chains—all of which absorbed U.S. grains."[114] In general, trading companies such as these prospered and found expanded markets, with the help of U.S. agricultural programs, for their products in the world economy.

The barriers to agricultural trade permitted by GATT, however, impeded agribusiness regarding both commodity chains and trade flows.[115] Agribusiness corporations that operated in numerous nations advocated free trade and liberalization. One such example is Cargill, which had processing plants and operations that reached into Latin America, northern Africa, Asia, and Europe. The spread of tariffs and other trade barriers hindered the movement of Cargill's capital, resources, and products. In this way, then, national regulation became an obstacle to profit and capital accumulation for some agribusinesses.[116] Not all agribusiness TNCs had such global reach. For instance, Archer Daniels Midland was primarily concentrated in the U.S. market before 1990. As a result, it tended to be more supportive of supply management policy, especially export subsidies. The position of agribusiness corporations in the world economy, then, shaped their economic interests and policy preferences.

The food regime also drew agribusiness into the policy formation process. Chapter 3 showed that agribusiness—grain traders, processors, etc.— played little role in shaping the AAAs during the New Deal. Yet agribusiness did oppose particular elements of the AAA, most notably the processing tax. Although various agribusiness companies testified before Congress and lobbied against the legislation, they could not prevent the enactment of the policy—except through the U.S. courts. This marginal political position took a distinct turn as supply management policy expanded after World War II. Through PL 480, agribusiness corporations developed stronger ties with the USDA, the CCC, and political leaders. By the mid-1960s, for example, Senator Hubert Humphrey (D-MN) took Dwayne Andreas, the chairman of Archer Daniels Midland "on official foreign trips . . . billing his friend 'an advisor to the Department of Agriculture and specialist in the problems of Public Law 480.'"[117] Other agribusiness corporations entered the political process as a reaction against state regulations. For instance, Cargill created a policy task force to promote more favorable government policies after the Kennedy administration tried to expand supply management policy in the early 1960s.[118] This relationship was even closer in the 1980s with the Reagan administration. For example, Dan Amstutz was undersecretary for international affairs and commodity programs from 1983 to 1987, and he served as the chief negotiator for agriculture during the Uruguay Round of the GATT talks. Before his service in the Reagan administration, Amstutz was an executive for Cargill. In general, agribusiness became more involved in the development of national policy during the late twentieth century.

The very structure of the U.S. food regime strengthened a segment of agriculture, namely agribusiness, that would ultimately come to oppose the very policies upon which the regime rested. Consequently, a new push for free markets, led by agricultural TNCs and, paradoxically, the United States, resulted in the Uruguay Round of GATT negotiations, which concluded in 1994 with the first GATT agreement to include reductions in trade barriers and subsidies in agriculture. This change in the food regime undoubtedly threatened supply management policy.

From 1951 to 1954, more than three-quarters of the wheat consumed in Colombia was produced within that country.[119] After receiving U.S. food aid through the 1950s and 1960s, Colombia gradually became dependent on wheat imports: by the mid-1960s, more than two-thirds of the wheat consumed in that country came from imports. Other nations shared Colombia's fate of becoming reliant on grain imports. PL 480 did not emphasize building up agriculture in other nations, but instead centered almost entirely on supplying cheap agricultural imports. The consequence was essentially to destroy much local agriculture in the periphery because local producers could not compete with subsidized imports. As long as this food regime of low prices and abundant supply operated smoothly, then countries dependent on imported wheat were not threatened financially. But when the Soviet Union purchased record amounts of U.S. grain between 1972 and 1974, grain became less abundant and prices rose dramatically. The result was a financial squeeze that put many food-importing countries on the brink of starvation. Thus, Friedmann observes, "The crisis of the early 1970s . . .

was the collapse of the set of orderly international arrangements which had maintained grain surpluses and depressed prices."[120]

That the recipients of food aid in the 1950s and 1960s would become "some of our very best customers" of U.S. agricultural products in the 1990s shows the transformation created by the post–World War II food regime. The basis of this regime rested in the particular trade rules and regulations created under GATT, at the behest of the United States, as well as the trade flows developed through PL 480. Importantly, the dominant cotton-wheat coalition played a central role in shaping this particular food regime to protect supply management policy, which came to rest upon export subsidies. Previous chapters have left the world economy in the background, but this chapter has shown the important connection between national policy and the world economy. Supply management in the United States depended on the particular configuration of the food regime that emerged after 1945. The link between supply management policy and the international food regime is the dominant cotton-wheat coalition. In an ironic twist, however, the contradictions in this food regime ultimately altered the interests of segments of agriculture, including the cotton-wheat coalition, and undermined supply management policy.

The next chapter looks at the most significant retrenchment in twentieth-century agricultural policy: the FAIR Act of 1996. This policy shift rested in part on the contradictions that emerged out of the U.S. food regime. Both the regime and supply management policy itself transformed the political economy of U.S. agriculture: the structure of southern agriculture changed; the political power and economic interests within agriculture shifted; supply management policies spread throughout the world economy, hindering trade; and export subsidies became much less effective in disposing of agricultural surpluses. These developments culminated in an opportunity for U.S. agricultural policy to change in fundamental ways. Looking closely at the FAIR Act reveals how the same processes underlying the trajectory of supply management from its inception during the New Deal through 1990 also help to explain its ultimate retrenchment at the end of the century.

# CHAPTER 7

# The 1996 FAIR Act

## Changing U.S. Agricultural Policy

Producers will respond to market signals, and the market will manage supply.
—BILL NORTHEY, VICE PRESIDENT OF THE NATIONAL CORN GROWERS
ASSOCIATION, 1995

In 1996, the FAIR Act ended price supports and production controls. After about six decades of trying, opponents of supply management policy finally won a decisive victory: the federal government no
longer directly influenced either production decisions or market prices. This
legislation aimed for the market to be a greater influence in agriculture. But
why did supply management policy end at this historical moment? What
was so unique about the 1990s that would permit such a momentous policy
shift? These questions often elicit a particular response: partisan politics and
market prices. This is certainly a central part of most scholarly explanations
of the FAIR Act. However, as with previous shifts in agricultural policy,
partisan politics and market offer an incomplete answer. Instead, we need to
consider the political-economic context and historical trends that helped to
create particular divisions and coalitions within U.S. agriculture. The inadequacy of market prices and partisan politics to explain this retrenchment can
be seen with a quick look at the 1980s.

### Partisan Politics and Supply Management
### in the Late Twentieth Century

In 1980, Ronald Reagan won the Republican Party's presidential
nomination and then defeated Jimmy Carter, the Democratic incumbent. As
president, Reagan sought to reduce the size of the federal government, its
budget, and its reach into the market economy.[1] Agricultural policy was one

of the targets of his administration, which "proposed an outright elimination of income support through target prices and deficiency payments."[2] In part, the goal was to unleash market mechanisms in agriculture by limiting government's influence over production decisions and market prices.

Although Reagan was able to trim some government programs and spending, he was largely unsuccessful at reducing spending on agriculture or pulling the government out of the agricultural sector of the economy. He suspended production controls in 1981, but supply management policy remained in effect when Reagan left office in 1989. In fact, overall government spending on agricultural programs reached record heights—almost $26 billion in 1986. Direct payments to farmers also reached record levels at more than $16 billion in 1987.[3] Furthermore, supply management policy was bolstered by the expansion of export subsidies with the creation of the EEP in 1985. Finally, Reagan created the Payment-in-Kind (PIK) program in 1983. This was a new production control program that used government-held commodity surpluses to pay farmers to make cuts in acreage. Thus, Reagan's attempted retrenchment of supply management policy failed. In fact, during Reagan's presidency, supply management policy expanded notably, in terms of both spending and legislative initiatives.

Part of the reason for this failure may have been the strength of Democrats in the House, but Republicans controlled the Senate between 1981 and 1987—most of Reagan's two terms as president. Therefore, congressional Democrats were not the only, or even the primary, obstacle that Reagan encountered in his quest to alter agricultural policy and reduce spending; congressional Republicans were also wary of such changes. For instance, Jesse Helms (R-NC) chaired the Senate Agriculture Committee and showed little support for the administration's proposed farm bill in 1985, which would have repealed the permanent legislation of 1949 and reduced direct payments by about half.[4] The Republican majority leaders in the Senate were Howard Baker Jr. (1981–1985) and Bob Dole (1985–1987), from Tennessee and Kansas, respectively. Dole in particular was a strong proponent of supply management policy and government assistance to farmers. Therefore, Reagan faced resistance from his own party when he tried to change agricultural policy, just as Eisenhower had thirty years before.

Another factor helped to protect supply management policy: U.S. agriculture faced a devastating economic crisis in the 1980s. The export boom between 1970 and 1977 had encouraged many farmers to expand their operations by increasing their debt loads. In the late 1970s, however, world agricultural production recovered from the shortfalls seen earlier in that decade. This reduced the demand for U.S. agricultural exports, which fell in the early 1980s. Additionally, inflation was falling by 1982, making farm debts accumulated just a few years before more difficult to pay down. This situation was exacerbated by the Reagan administration's tight monetary policy, which drove up interest rates and further compounded the debt problem farmers faced. The final blow came as the value of the dollar increased relative to other currencies, which made U.S. farm products less competitive in world markets. Consequently, U.S. agricultural exports plummeted: wheat exports fell from 48 MMT in 1981 to 24 MMT in 1985, and corn exports from 76 MMT in 1980 to 39 MMT in 1985. Prices for agricultural commodities fell as exports declined. All of this contributed to the worst financial crisis in agriculture since the Great Depression.[5]

This crisis prompted more spending on farm programs and growing government-held stocks, and the Reagan administration ultimately reinstated production controls in 1983 after suspending them in 1981. The administration realized that its options for eliminating supply management policy were limited through domestic politics because of both resistance from congressional Republicans as well as Democrats and the economic crisis in agriculture. Consequently, the administration tried to change agricultural policy through a "back door": international trade talks. In particular, the administration used GATT talks to pressure U.S. policy-makers to reform supply management policy. Nonetheless, Reagan not only failed to reduce agricultural spending and change agricultural policy, he was also unable to prevent the expansion of supply management policy and spending on farm programs.

Almost a decade later, by contrast, Bill Clinton, a southern Democratic president, signed the FAIR Act.[6] Under this act, "farmers . . . would receive fixed, but declining, payments every year, regardless of market prices or their planting decisions. Furthermore, the government could no longer require subsidized farmers to take cropland out of production for economic reasons."[7] The FAIR Act ended price supports and production controls for most agricultural commodities, including corn, wheat, and cotton. In doing so, this legislation achieved the goal that had eluded presidents Eisenhower, Nixon, and Reagan: ending supply management policy. In place of price supports, farmers received fixed payments, known as Production Flexibility Contract (PFC) payments, that decreased gradually between 1996 and 2002. Unlike price supports, PFC payments were not tied to market prices or production decisions. In this way, the FAIR Act decoupled income supports by "providing support to farmers in ways that [did] not distort production, consumption or trade."[8] The FAIR Act ended production controls completely by eliminating acreage allotments tied to price supports and the Acreage Reduction Program (ARP), which administered set-asides.[9] Thus, two pillars of supply management policy were gone.

The FAIR Act clearly changed the fundamental basis of U.S. agricultural policy, but it fell short of complete retrenchment of supply management policy on three counts. First, it continued price supports and production controls for a few commodities, such as tobacco and peanuts. Second, the FAIR Act did not end export subsidies, continuing both PL 480 and the EEP. Third, it did not repeal the Agricultural Act of 1949, which therefore remained permanent farm legislation.[10] Instead, the FAIR Act was set to expire in 2002. Despite these exceptions—the retention of price supports and production controls for a few commodities, the continuation of export subsidies, and the temporary nature of this policy—the FAIR Act was a significant departure from the supply management policy of the previous six decades. Its aim was to gradually eliminate all income support so that agricultural prices were dictated by the market. And with production controls eliminated as well, farm income would no longer be boosted by controlling supply. Proponents of the FAIR Act promoted it as giving farmers the "freedom to farm" because it removed the government from decisions related to production by ending production controls. This was a fundamental change in U.S. agricultural policy.

How can we explain the timing and substance of this historic policy shift? Why did the political-economic context of the 1990s allow for this policy retrenchment? And why did this policy shift take the particular shape that it did—eliminating production controls, decoupling price supports, and retaining export subsidies? Answers to these questions rest on the analytical pillars of class, state, and market. Before delving into this explanation, however, we should first look at how most scholars explain this historic turn in U.S. agricultural policy—the end of supply management.

## Partisan Politics, Market Prices, and the FAIR Act

Most analyses of the FAIR Act argue that the political and economic context of the mid-1990s facilitated the shift in agricultural policy in two ways: Republicans gained control of Congress, and commodity prices rose significantly. Such explanations concentrate on the surface of politics and the market economy during one snapshot of the trajectory of agricultural policy, and they fail to capture completely the complex and secular relations between class, state, and market. Nonetheless, this focus on partisan politics and market prices seems to be the most commonly accepted explanation for the retrenchment of supply management policy.

Several scholars explain the 1996 FAIR Act by stressing party control of Congress.[11] In 1994, the Republican Party won majorities in both the House and Senate for the first time since 1954. Though Republicans were somewhat divided over agricultural policy, this change in partisan control of Congress facilitated the shift in agricultural policy. Robert Paarlberg and David Orden assert that "Democrats . . . are prone to support intrusive price support and supply-control policies. Republicans . . . more often favor benefit programs that do not raise market prices or discourage full production."[12] Adam Sheingate makes a similar observation, stating that "commodity programs . . . provided an opportunity for the Republicans to illustrate their commitment to free-market principles."[13] From this perspective, then, the mere shift in partisan control of Congress contributed to the passage of the FAIR Act.

For some scholars, budget politics, which became increasingly important during the 1980s and 1990s, are a central aspect of how partisan politics facilitates policy retrenchment.[14] In fact, Wayne Moyer and Tim Josling argue, "Perhaps the most important economic trend at the time of the 1995–6 Farm Bill debate was the chronic federal budget deficit."[15] After campaigning on their "Contract with America" in 1994, Republicans believed that their election victory gave them a mandate to reduce the size of government.[16] Congressional Republicans linked agricultural policy directly to the budget debate by putting the original "Freedom to Farm" bill in their 1995 budget reconciliation bill.[17] Under Republicans, then, agricultural policy became a primary target for reductions to achieve a balanced federal budget. Notably, a balanced budget was a higher priority for Republicans than for Democrats. In the end, a shift in policy such as the FAIR Act would have been less likely had Democrats retained control of Congress.[18]

In addition to this historic shift in partisan politics, economic conditions for agriculture improved significantly leading up to the passage of the FAIR Act in April 1996. Market prices for wheat rose from $3.25 a bushel in August 1994 to more than $5.30 a bushel in April 1996. Market prices for corn increased from about $2.16 a bushel to $3.85 a bushel during the same period.[19]

Price support levels were set at $4.00 for wheat and $2.75 for corn. When market prices rose above these support levels, farmers received fewer subsidies from the government. Consequently, the increase in commodity prices between 1994 and 1996 "weakened the short-term attraction of traditional deficiency payments."[20] By decoupling income supports from market prices, the FAIR Act actually increased government payments to farmers relative to what they would have received under supply management policy. At least in the short term, then, the FAIR Act benefited farmers' pocketbooks. High market prices, then, created an economic context in which eliminating price supports was possible.

Most explanations of the FAIR Act follow this focus on partisan politics and market prices relative to support levels. The 1994 Republican congressional victory and high market prices no doubt facilitated this historic retrenchment of agricultural policy, yet we should carefully consider how well these two factors explain (1) the retrenchment of supply management in general, and (2) the substance of this particular instance of retrenchment in 1996.

## Politics, Prices, and Retrenchment in Historical Perspective

Partisan politics and market prices likely played some role in the retrenchment of supply management policy in 1996, but placing the FAIR Act in historical perspective makes it clear that some other underlying factors have been overlooked. We might consider, again, the three important policy shifts before the FAIR Act: 1954, when price support levels were reduced and made flexible; 1964, when production controls were weakened; and 1973, when parity was removed from the price support formula and production controls were suspended. A focus only on partisan politics and market prices fails to explain these policy shifts.

As Table 7.1 shows, no clear relationship exists between partisan politics and retrenchment in supply management policy. In 1954, a Republican president (Eisenhower) and a Republican-controlled House and Senate reduced price support levels and made them flexible.[21] In 1964, production controls were weakened under a Democratic president (Johnson) and Democrat-controlled House and Senate. Then, in 1973, a Republican president (Nixon) suspended production controls and fundamentally changed price supports with Democratic majorities in the House and Senate. And, in 1996, a Democratic president (Clinton) and a Republican-controlled House and Senate

**Table 7.1.** Market prices, partisan politics, and retrenchment of agricultural policy, 1954–1996

| Year | Market prices above support levels | | | Control of Congress | Presidential administration |
|------|------|-------|--------|---------|---------------|
|      | Corn | Wheat | Cotton |         |               |
| 1954 | No   | No    | Yes    | Republican | Republican |
| 1964 | No   | No    | No     | Democrat   | Democrat   |
| 1973 | Yes  | No    | No     | Democrat   | Republican |
| 1996 | Yes  | Yes   | Yes    | Republican | Democrat   |

finally ended supply management policy. Since 1945, then, each political party has overseen retrenchment in supply management policy. Democrats indeed seem less likely than Republicans to move agricultural policy away from supply management, but agricultural retrenchment has nonetheless occurred when Democrats were firmly in control of Congress and the presidency. Perhaps most notably, the instances of the most extensive retrenchment, in 1973 and 1996, occurred when Republicans were not in full control of the federal government. Thus, the role of partisan politics becomes less clear in a historical perspective.

We find this same murkiness when considering the expansion, rather than the retrenchment, of agricultural policy. Agricultural policy expanded during the 1980s when Republicans controlled the presidency and the Senate. Republicans also controlled the presidency and the House in 2002 when a version of price supports was reinstituted after the FAIR Act expired. Therefore, we should be careful not to overstate the connection between partisanship and policy retrenchment. Instead, we need to consider why such a connection, however strong or clear, exists between political parties and agricultural retrenchment and expansion. In other words, why have Democrats been more likely than Republicans to favor supply management policy? Is it simply partisan ideology? Furthermore, why have Democrats supported the retrenchment of agricultural policy at times when they were politically dominant, such as 1964?

Placing the relationship between partisanship and policy trajectory in this historical perspective also brings into question the importance of budget politics in leading to the FAIR Act. Sheingate argues that in the 1980s and 1990s, "the congressional budget process became an effective mechanism for agricultural retrenchment."[22] Again, President Reagan and congressional Republicans certainly gave high priority to reducing and balancing the budget, as well as cutting back government regulations and other interventions into the economy. Spending on farm programs was a primary target of such retrenchment. However, budget politics were almost entirely unsuccessful at even containing supply management policy, much less retrenching it. Whether we measure the trajectory of supply management policy in terms of government spending or legislative action, there is little ground for asserting that agricultural retrenchment occurred in the 1980s. First, new programs were created to expand supply management policy: the PIK program expanded production controls in 1983, and the EEP expanded export subsidies in 1985. Second, government spending on farm programs reached record heights. Finally, more land was removed from production (through production controls) in the late 1980s than ever before.[23] Therefore, we should not overstate the effect of budget politics during this period.

Table 7.1 also demonstrates that market prices have not played a determining role in the retrenchment of agricultural policy since 1945. The argument found in most analyses of the FAIR Act suggests that retrenchment in supply management policy occurs when market prices are high and price support levels are therefore largely irrelevant. That is, farmers' attachment to supply management policy fades when market prices are high. As with a focus on partisan politics, this argument based on market prices fails to explain earlier episodes of retrenchment.

When price support levels were changed and lowered in 1954, wheat and cotton prices were higher than the average for the previous ten years, but corn prices were lower.[24] Additionally, whereas cotton prices were above price support levels, wheat and corn prices were below their support levels.[25] Most importantly, as Chapter 4 demonstrated, dominant corn producers, who faced market prices that were below the ten-year average and below price support levels, called for severely curtailing supply management policies in 1954. If market prices were the primary explanation, then we should have seen cotton farmers, who had high market prices above support levels, push for changes in price supports. In 1964, market prices were down for wheat and cotton, and market prices for all three commodities were below support levels.[26] This time, wheat and cotton producers called for less rigid production controls despite low market prices. Then in 1973, the market price for corn was high and above support levels, but cotton and wheat prices were below support levels.[27] Nonetheless, price supports and production controls for each commodity were weakened significantly. Only in 1996 were market prices high and above support levels for all three commodities. Previous instances of retrenchment in supply management policy, by contrast, occurred when commodity prices were below support levels. High market prices, then, do not explain the retrenchment of agricultural policy, in general.

Although market conditions and partisan politics likely have some influence, Table 7.1 shows that there is no clear pattern between market prices, partisan politics, and retrenchment in agricultural policy. Retrenchment has occurred under Democrats as well as Republicans, and it has occurred when market prices were lower than support levels as well as when they were higher than support levels. In fact, the retrenchment of supply management policy in 1964 occurred when market prices were low and Democrats controlled Congress and the presidency. Focusing on the FAIR Act in 1996, then, produces an incomplete picture of retrenchment in agriculture: this was the only major retrenchment of supply management policy to fit the common explanation based on partisan politics and market prices. Clearly, other factors must be at work in the process of retrenchment.

### The Substance of the FAIR Act

Just as a focus on partisan politics and market prices fails to explain previous shifts in agricultural policy, so too does this perspective leave an important question about the 1996 retrenchment unaddressed: why did the FAIR Act take the shape that it did? In particular, why were price supports replaced with income supports, production controls eliminated entirely, and export subsidies left intact? Existing analyses of the FAIR Act are frequently silent on this fundamental issue. Explaining the timing of retrenchment is not enough. How can we explain the contours of the new policy?

Clearly, market prices and partisan politics do not adequately explain these contours. High market prices could be as conducive to the elimination of all income supports as they are to shifting from price supports to income supports decoupled from market prices. Some observers suggest that the shift to income supports served to entice support from farmers, who would receive no federal subsidies under the existing price support system.[28] Although the increased subsidies under the FAIR Act no doubt garnered support from some farmers, this explanation of the substance of the shift to some extent undermines the central importance of high market prices. That is, even with high market prices, farmers needed significant monetary incentive to accept a change in subsidies. Perhaps more accurately, these high prices prompted a shift away from price supports because farmers could not take advantage of the prices. High market prices were not sufficiently conducive for farmers to shake off government support. Market prices, high or low, likely matter only in particular political-economic contexts. Therefore, even with high market prices in 1995–1996, farmers had to be bought out.

The specific shape of the FAIR Act is perhaps even more noteworthy when we consider the elimination of production controls: why did farmers not require a buyout to forego production controls? Was it simply the fact that production controls were more onerous than price supports? Some farmers favored production controls even more adamantly than they did price supports. So why did the latter require a cash payoff but not the former?

Similar questions emerge regarding the continuation of export subsidies. Why were export subsidies not eliminated like production controls? Or why were export subsidies not replaced with a program that minimized market interference (for example, promotion and advertisement), as with income supports replacing price supports? Why did Republicans not buy off farmers on export subsidies as they did with price supports? Again, some farmers were much more adamantly opposed to export subsidies than they were to price supports. Why, then, were export subsidies left unaltered?

The FAIR Act affected the trajectories of these three principle programs of supply management policy differently, but market prices and partisan politics, either independently or together, fail to adequately explain these different paths. Even if the explanation of this particular policy trajectory rests on political compromises and deals, then we need to explain why these particular compromises occurred. The previous chapters have demonstrated that we must look beyond partisan politics and market prices to understand significant shifts in agricultural policy. In part, research focused on partisan politics generally fails to ask why Democrats might be less likely to roll back supply management policy; instead, this policy position is taken for granted. Recognizing Democrats' role in previous instances of retrenchment reveals that partisan ideology is not the key to Democrats' support for supply management policy.[29] Similarly, scholars focused on market prices often overlook the myriad of economic factors that influence farmers' interests. The economic interests of farmers are often less influenced by market prices than by production and trade dynamics in the world economy, position in the production process (such as income from livestock versus from field crops), and existing government policy. Finally, these analyses fail to examine the political power of competing agricultural coalitions. As seen with previous shifts in agricultural policy, competing coalitions within agriculture are especially important. The economic interests and political power of segments of agriculture have an important effect on national policy.

How does the historical analysis presented in the previous chapters help us understand why agricultural policy shifted so dramatically in 1996? Is it possible to explain this policy retrenchment in a manner similar to past retrenchments? Is there a common explanation for the retrenchment of agricultural policy throughout the twentieth century that furthers our understanding of the FAIR Act?

Beneath the battles between political parties lie the coalitions of segments of agriculture, which are fundamental to explaining agricultural policy. Agricultural policy is likely to change when these coalitions shift. That is, political forces within agriculture contributed to the significant changes in supply management policy, including retrenchment. This focus, explains both the timing and the substance of the FAIR Act in a manner that accounts for previous shifts in agricultural policy as well.[30] Consequently, the perspective developed here moves beyond analyses focused on partisan politics and market prices.

### Beneath the Surface of Partisan Politics

Why, after about sixty years, were price supports and production controls finally eliminated? Why were price supports changed to income supports instead of being eliminated altogether, as happened with production controls? Why did export subsidies, a contentious policy for four decades, survive the assault on agricultural policy? The answers to these questions are found, at least in part, in the coalitions within agriculture supporting and opposing production controls, price supports, and export subsidies. First, some segments of agriculture advocated increasing flexibility by ending production controls, arguing that this would enhance U.S. farmers' economic position. Second, some segments proposed ending price supports for a variety of reasons, including to expand export markets or lower the costs of inputs, such as livestock feed. Third, some segments wanted to end export subsidies, in part to increase free trade in the world economy. The politics of the FAIR Act were not merely about battles between groups inside and outside of agriculture; rather, this policy was intimately shaped by political battles and competing interests within agriculture.

### Eliminating Production Controls

The political battle over production controls was really at the heart of the FAIR Act. This battle was the most contentious of the three programs, and the political divisions within agriculture were particularly clear. The continuation of production controls faced far more opposition than did either price supports or export subsidies. Calls to eliminate production controls so that farmers could "produce for the market instead of producing for the government" pervaded the debate over agricultural policy in 1995. Several proposals aimed to "increase flexibility" through two means: ending production requirements tied to price supports, and eliminating the ARP. Farmers had to follow production restrictions, including growing particular program commodities, with supply management policy. Created by the 1985 Food Security Act, the ARP was the primary form of production control in the 1990s and allowed the secretary of agriculture to require farmers to set aside a certain percentage of program acres (for example, 8 percent of corn acres). Notably, the ARP did not pay farmers for land left idle. Thus, it was also a budget saving device. The FAIR Act eliminated the ARP and created full flexibility since PFC payments contained no production requirements tied to income subsidies and no set-aside requirements. Importantly, this shift from supply management policy was not entirely imposed upon agriculture.

A familiar regional split, reflecting the primary division in agriculture throughout much of the twentieth century, occurred in agriculture with the Corn Belt on one side and the Wheat Belt and South on the other. The corn segment was part of a coalition that also included livestock and agribusiness segments, and this coalition favored more flexible production and the elimination of production controls.[31] The key for the corn segment was the flexibility to plant "fence row to fence row" to escape the production restrictions imposed by the traditional programs. The core organizations of the corn segment—the Farm Bureau, the National Corn Growers Association (NCGA), and the American Soybean Association (ASA)—each supported eliminating the ARP and other production requirements.[32] State farm bureaus in the Corn Belt, especially the Iowa Farm Bureau, likewise tended to favor such full flexibility.[33] Although farmers in the Corn Belt could produce a wide variety of crops if given the flexibility, the elimination of production controls would also allow them to expand their corn and soybean production.

The livestock segment aligned with the corn segment on the issue of flexibility. For instance, the National Cattlemen's Association expressed opposition to production controls.[34] The livestock segment favored greater flexibility because it would allow farmers already producing corn or other feed grains to produce more, and it would allow producers of other commodities to switch to various feed grains.[35] This would increase the supply of feed grains and reduce the price of the primary input for livestock producers.[36]

The agribusiness segment, not surprisingly, also favored eliminating production controls. Both input suppliers and purchasers of farm products argued that supply management policies were harmful. A representative for the Kansas Fertilizer and Chemical Association stated, "we do, however, believe that acreage idling programs other than [for] true environmental purposes have outlived their usefulness as a tool of U.S. farm policy."[37] This sentiment was likewise expressed by other trade associations representing agribusiness suppliers, such as the Agribusiness Association of Iowa, the Idaho Fertilizer and Chemical Association, and the Agricultural Retailers Association.[38] Agribusinesses that purchased agricultural commodities also expressed opposition to production controls. A representative of the Louis Dreyfus Corporation, a major grain company, argued that supply management programs reduced the competitiveness of U.S. agriculture and distorted markets.[39] The Coalition for a Competitive Food and Agricultural System (CCFAS), "a newly formed coalition of agricultural processors," also advocated for eliminating the ARP.[40] A representative of the National Grain and Feed Association stated that "land-idling and land-retirement programs are the most harmful aspect of current farm programs. . . . Policies that restrict the supply of grains hurt cattlemen, hog, poultry, and dairy producers."[41] Production controls limited the use of inputs (such as fertilizer) and distorted the price of commodities by restricting supply. As Lyle Schertz and Otto Doering state, "the elimination of the ARP . . . made it possible for the agribusiness interests to attain their goal of increased volumes of inputs and products to handle . . . without appearing to be in conflict with the financial interests of producers."[42] Consequently, the agribusiness segment was relatively united in its opposition to production controls.

By contrast, organizations representing wheat and cotton producers tended to oppose proposals to weaken production controls.[43] For example,

John Whitaker of the NFU stated, "Supply stabilization is one of the most important aspects of federal farm policies."[44] The organizations representing these segments of agriculture suggested that they had little to gain from increasing flexibility in production and that the existing commodity programs already offered enough flexibility.[45] As NAWG's president, Ross Hansen, pointed out, "For the majority of wheat growers, especially through the high plains, from Texas through Montana, you'd plant wheat [even with increased flexibility]. We have a very limited amount of alternative crops that are viable."[46] Many of the southern state farm bureau federations contradicted their national organization by opposing increased flexibility. For example, Don Waller, president of the Mississippi Farm Bureau, stated that "in Mississippi . . . and I think in the entire Southeast, really, we do not need to rotate . . . nearly as much as some of the Midwestern crops and other crops do. So flexibility is something that is not nearly as important to the state of Mississippi."[47] Other state farm bureaus in the South and the Wheat Belt favored retaining production controls, but the Corn Belt federations were more influential in the policy proposals of the national Farm Bureau. The coalition anchored by wheat and cotton generally opposed increasing flexibility and favored retaining the ARP.

The political lines between supporting and opposing production controls were much clearer than those around either price supports or export subsidies. The issue of production controls required no compromise on the part of the corn segment, which was as opposed to production controls as were the agribusiness and livestock segments. The FAIR Act eliminated production controls cleanly, without any compromise, buyout, or phasing out. The ARP was dropped, and base acres no longer restricted acres eligible for program benefits or required the production of program crops. This represented the most significant retrenchment in the FAIR Act as well as a fundamental turn in agricultural policy. The attempts to eliminate price supports and export subsidies fell short of this standard.

## Changing Price Supports

Existing analyses of the FAIR Act emphasizing market prices are most effective at accounting for the elimination of price supports.[48] Three options were before Congress in formulating the 1996 farm bill: (1) retain the traditional price support structure of existing farm policy (possibly reducing target price levels), (2) phase out price supports gradually over a number of years, or (3) eliminate price supports immediately.[49] Ending price supports did not require eliminating all income subsidies for farmers, as long as the subsidies were not tied to market prices or production decisions. Decoupling income supports in this manner would end traditional price support policy.

The FAIR Act did exactly this: it ended price supports by eliminating target prices and deficiency payments. PFC payments, which offered producers fixed payments that were not contingent upon prices or supply management principles, replaced price supports and were computed for each former program commodity as a percentage of overall expenditures.[50] Regardless of what crops they actually produced, farmers received payments based on their historical base acreage. Therefore, they could grow almost any crop they chose and still remain eligible for income supports.[51] Additionally, farmers would receive PFC payments regardless of how high commodity prices were. Therefore, income supports remained, but they were decoupled from market prices and production decisions.

Within agriculture, political support for retaining traditional price supports was surprisingly fragmented by 1996.[52] Most segments of agriculture favored some sort of income supports for farmers, but there was actually less support for retaining price supports and deficiency payments per se. Organizations that favored maintaining the target price system tended to represent the wheat segment: the Idaho Grain Producers Association, the Oregon Wheat Growers League, the Texas Wheat Producers Association, the Kansas Association of Wheat Growers, and the Washington Association of Wheat Growers, among others.[53] The NFU was perhaps the largest farm organization that favored retaining traditional price supports without reductions in target prices.[54] Democrats from the Wheat belt, including Senate minority leader Tom Daschle (D-ND), also tended to favor retaining traditional price supports without significant reductions in support levels. Yet other representatives of the Wheat Belt took a different position. In particular, Pat Roberts (R-KS) chaired the House Committee on Agriculture and proposed the "Freedom to Farm" bill, the precursor to the FAIR Act, but he "opposed cutting farm program spending sharply."[55] Senate majority leader Bob Dole (R-KS), however, was less enthusiastic about the changes Roberts proposed.[56] Thus, the wheat segment showed a fairly strong tendency toward favoring the retention of price supports, but there was some division.

Initially, the cotton segment joined much of the wheat segment in favoring the continuation of existing price support programs. In 1995, Senator Thad Cochran (R-MS) introduced a bill that retained target prices and de-

ficiency payments, gaining the support of other southern Republican senators, including Jesse Helms (R–NC) and John Warner (R–VA).[57] That same
year, some House Republicans, including Larry Combest (R–TX), proposed
continuing the "existing support mechanisms for the deficiency payment
crops."[58] Ultimately, however, cotton producers, who had been among the
most important advocates for price supports in previous decades, were more
wedded to marketing loans than to target prices.[59] Marketing loans were created in 1985 and permit producers to repay loans "at less than the announced
loan rates whenever the world market price or posted county price for the
commodity is less than the commodity loan rate."[60] According to the NCC,
these loans allow producers to respond more effectively to shifts in the market.[61] As long as the FAIR Act retained marketing loans, organizations and
politicians representing the cotton segment would not necessarily oppose a
change in price support policy.

The corn segment, which had historically opposed supply management
policy, was clearly less favorable toward retaining target prices and deficiency
payments. Senator Richard Lugar (R–IN) proposed reducing target prices by
3 percent a year for five years for corn, wheat, cotton, and rice.[62] In contrast
to the NFU, the Farm Bureau and the NCGA were open to changes in price
supports and advocated marketing loans for corn and soybeans. This helped
to facilitate a compromise with cotton producers who already relied on marketing loans. In the end, the Farm Bureau and the NCGA both "endorsed
decoupled farm payments."[63] The primary concern of these organizations
was not protecting the price support system but maintaining sufficient income support for farmers.

The compromise of decoupled income supports encouraged many segments of agriculture to abandon price supports for another important reason:
the change from price supports to income supports decoupled from market
prices was tied to the battle over production controls.[64] Within agriculture,
the opposition to production controls, especially the ARP, was far greater
than the opposition to price supports. But eliminating production controls
significantly increased the danger that the cost of price supports would rise.
As farmers expanded production after the elimination of production controls, market prices would likely fall. This would lead to greater subsidies
through deficiency payments, thereby increasing the budget costs of the
farm program. Decoupling subsidy payments offered a way of eliminating
production controls without breaking the budget. This connection gave fur-

ther incentive to segments opposed to production controls, in particular the corn segment, to abandon price supports for income supports.

Similarly, agribusiness generally favored income supports decoupled from production and market prices over price supports. A representative of the CCFAS, for example, argued that existing programs hurt food processors.[65] Nevertheless, the option of eliminating all farm subsidies received relatively thin support.[66] A representative of the National Grain and Feed Association stated that this organization "support[s] an income safety net for farmers, provided that it does not distort markets."[67] Tom Tunnell, president of the Kansas Fertilizer and Chemical Association, stated that "our foremost hope is that however the 1995 Farm Bill is structured it will still provide an income safety net adequate to help farmers maintain a reasonable return on their assets."[68] This position was echoed by other agribusiness trade associations, such as the Idaho Fertilizer and Chemical Association.[69] The same was true of nonprogram commodities, such as the livestock segment: a primary complaint was that supports interfered with prices or production.[70] Therefore, although these segments of agriculture opposed price supports, they did not object to income supports for farmers that were not tied to market prices or production decisions; that is, decoupled income supports were preferable to price supports.

Scholars, such as Orden and his colleagues, are correct that high market prices made farmers less likely to favor traditional price supports and target prices.[71] Such prices made a shift away from price supports more attractive to farmers. By replacing price supports with fixed payments decoupled from market prices, farmers would actually receive greater subsidies from the government. Furthermore, the temporary nature of the FAIR Act reduced the risk of moving away from a system of government support that increased during market downturns.

These studies, however, understate the opposition to price supports and target prices that existed within agriculture. Some segments of agriculture opposed these policies, irrespective of market prices. That the NFU and other Wheat Belt organizations continued to favor retaining price supports made little difference in the absence of a broader political coalition. But there was much broader support for income supports than for price supports; most commodity organizations, and farm state representatives and senators, favored retaining some kind of safety net for farmers. Even the agribusiness and livestock segments did not strongly object to decoupled income supports; these segments objected to the distortions price supports created. Thus, if the proposal had been to eliminate all income supports, then the coalition supporting target prices would likely have been stronger, especially if the final outcome included reductions in support levels. In addition, the cotton segment supported the FAIR Act partly because it retained marketing loans for these commodities.

### Continuing Export Subsidies

Calls came for cuts not only in price supports and production controls but also in export subsidies. Representative Bill Barrett (R-NE), for example, noted, "Unfortunately, just like the domestic commodity programs, the agricultural trade programs are part of the Government's mandatory spending programs which of course, must be reduced in order for us to meet the House-passed budget resolution."[72] As with production controls and price supports, the traditional division between the wheat and corn segments was at the core of the political battle over export subsidies. Yet in contrast to the battle over price supports, the most significant cracks occurred in the corn segment's political coalition: agribusiness was somewhat split over the EEP, and soybean organizations supported the export subsidies.

Some corn organizations opposed the EEP. For example, Tom Sleight, executive director of the U.S. Feed Grains Council stated, "officially our membership has adopted a policy of not supporting EEP."[73] Such opposition to export subsidies was based in part on the EEP's potential to distort world production and prices of feed grains. As Senator Lugar pointed out, the EEP might encourage producers in other nations to compete with U.S. corn, soybeans, or other feed grains: "For example, the export enhancement program is supposed to promote wheat exports. By keeping wheat prices low, however, it may also encourage other countries to shift acreage into feed grains, soybeans, and other crops whose prices are not so depressed. That is hardly a benefit to United States corn and soybean growers."[74] The livestock industry aligned with the corn segment over the issue of subsidies. A representative of the U.S. Meat Export Federation stated, "The beef industry of the United States has not advocated the use of EEP and the beef industry has never used EEP."[75] Providing other nations with subsidized grain that might be used as feed presented the possibility of putting the U.S. livestock industry at a disadvantage by raising the cost of U.S. meat, which does not use subsidized feed. Yet even this opposition was limited to the EEP, as such organizations tended to support more market-oriented programs, such as the Marketing Promotion Program and the Foreign Market Development Program.[76] These programs subsidized product promotion, advertising, and the like, thereby aiming to expand markets without interfering with commodity prices.

By contrast, some organizations representing the corn segment supported export subsidies. In particular, the Farm Bureau expressed support for the EEP. Perhaps more importantly, the ASA also supported continuing the EEP, in part because oilseeds benefited from the program. John Long, the vice president of the ASA, stated that his organization "oppose[d] making any additional substantial cuts in the export enhancement program."[77] This split meant that any opposition by the corn segment to the EEP was necessarily tempered. Such divisions in the political coalition anchored by the corn segment did not occur over production controls.

Agribusiness was likewise somewhat divided over the issue of export subsidies. The CCFAS did not advocate retaining the EEP; two representatives of the organization gave testimony supporting numerous export programs, but they did not mention subsidies as found in the EEP.[78] Although these organizations did not explicitly oppose or support the EEP, some corporations, including Cargill, did express opposition.[79] This is initially surprising given that through 1991, Cargill was the leading recipient of EEP bonuses at $688 million.[80] In part, this position reflects the traditional resistance of grain companies to government regulation of the grain trade.[81] Additionally, Cargill employs a more global strategy than some other agribusiness corporations, with soy and wheat processing plants in several nations (including the United States).[82] A representative of the Louis Dreyfus Corporation expressed opposition to export subsidies because they hurt grain exports by causing price distortions.[83] Yet other corporations supported the EEP. Dwayne Andreas, president of Archer Daniels Midland, argued that export subsidies were necessary for U.S. wheat to compete with other nations — including Canada, Australia, and the EU — that subsidize their wheat producers: "I do not advocate export subsidies just to make things cheap. I advocate them because if you do not meet the European prices, you will lose all of your business, all of it."[84] Some of the world's leading grain trading companies, then, expressed opposing viewpoints on retaining export subsidies.

The coalition anchored by the wheat and cotton segments was largely unified in its support of the EEP. The NCC and NAWG expressed strong support for export subsidies, and many other cotton and wheat organizations

echoed this support. The wheat segment, however, was one of the most ada-
mant supporters of continuing the EEP. As Don Ball of the Idaho Wheat
Commission testified: "The wheat producers would like to live in a utopia
where we don't have export subsidies, we don't have a subsidy program at all.
But wheat is not quite the same as corn and soybeans where we do have competition around the world, very severe competition—as you see, the European Union is highly subsidized; and we would wholly support no subsidies
if we could live with it, but we cannot produce wheat, at least I can't produce
wheat below the cost of production. Growers cannot afford to do that."[85]
Ross Hansen, president of NAWG, echoed this sentiment: "I appear before
you today as a strong advocate of USDA's export programs, particularly the
export enhancement program (EEP) and the foreign market development
program. . . . The continuation of an aggressive, more market-sensitive EEP
will be critical to our success in the post-GATT period."[86] Clearly, the wheat
segment favored the continuation of export subsidies. This economic interest
derived not from the level of market prices but rather, as I discuss shortly,
from this segment's position in the world economy.

The FAIR Act continued the EEP and even increased the level of funding from $350 million in 1996 to $478 million in 2002. Again, the coalitions
supporting and opposing the EEP were anchored by wheat and corn, respectively. Most notably, the corn and agribusiness segments split over the
retention of the EEP. Therefore, although these segments were central to the
changes in production controls and price supports, the divisions within this
coalition prevented the elimination of the EEP.

## Political Coalitions and the FAIR Act

The makeup of coalitions that formed around the issues of production controls, price supports, and export subsidies varied in important ways.
Table 7.2 shows the basic coalitions. The political battle over production
controls stands apart from the clashes over price supports and export subsidies in three important ways: the fight over production controls was the
most contentious of the three programs, the divisions were particularly clear,
and no compromise policy was pursued.[87] Opposition to production controls was much more solid than opposition to either price supports or export
subsidies. The coalitions around production controls were clearly drawn: a
corn-agribusiness coalition against production controls, and a cotton-wheat

**Table 7.2.** Positions of primary agricultural class segments on agricultural policy, 1996

| Position | Production controls | Target prices | Export Enhancement Program |
|---|---|---|---|
| Supporting | Wheat, cotton | Wheat | Wheat, cotton, soybeans, agribusiness (split) |
| Opposing | Corn, livestock, agribusiness | Corn,* livestock, agribusiness, cotton* | Corn (split), Livestock, agribusiness (split) |

*Segments' position was dependent on a compromise.

coalition in favor of production controls. Only the livestock segment wavered in its opposition to production controls. Nonetheless, the corn-agribusiness coalition was amply strong and stable in its desire to end production controls.

The coalitions around price supports were more contingent. The cotton-wheat coalition supported target prices and deficiency payments, but cracks existed in this support. First, the NFU favored limits on deficiency payments, but the NCC opposed such proposals, in part because southern producers tended to reap a disproportionate share of farm payments. Second, cotton organizations voiced more support for marketing loans, which are slightly different from traditional price supports. Thus, the cotton segment was not as solidly behind the target price system. Third, high commodity prices made the prospect of subsidies decoupled from market prices more attractive, especially in the Wheat Belt where drought conditions threatened farmers.[88] Many southern farmers were likewise unable to take advantage of high market prices because yields were down.[89] In this way, the cotton-wheat coalition still preferred to retain price supports, but income supports decoupled from market prices were attractive for some at the moment.

The corn-agribusiness coalition was similarly contingent on the issue of price supports. First, the corn segment's preference was for some income support, even if it was decoupled from market prices and production. Thus, this segment tended to oppose proposals calling for the end of all income supports. Second, the agribusiness segment would accept income supports decoupled from market prices, so this option did not break the coalition. As a result, price supports were ended, but income supports remained.

Whereas the cotton-wheat coalition provided fairly strong support for retaining the EEP, the corn-agribusiness coalition was more splintered and weakened in opposing export subsidies than it was on production controls or even on price supports. Some corporations, such as Archer Daniels Midland, advocated for the retention of export subsidies. Since soybean exports were often helped by export subsidies, organizations generally associated with the corn segment, such as the ASA, also supported continuing the EEP. With such divisions within the corn-agribusiness coalition, export subsidies were retained in the FAIR Act.

One key to the end of price supports and production controls, then, was the strength of opposition within agriculture to these policies. The competing agricultural coalitions underlie the partisan divisions. Because the corn segment had long been aligned with the Republican Party, its policy preferences were privileged when that party gained control of Congress. However, the growing strength of the South and traditional place of the Wheat Belt in the Republican Party necessarily tempered the Republican opposition to income supports and export subsidies.

## The Political Economy of the FAIR Act

We can see, then, the different alignments of class segments behind each of these policies. Why did these particular coalitions form? Why did they differ across the three dimensions of supply management policy? That is, how can we explain these economic interests? And, perhaps more importantly, how can we explain why particular coalitions were successful? If the divisions within agriculture were almost identical to past divisions (cotton-wheat versus corn), then why was agricultural policy changed so fundamentally in 1996? To answer these questions, we need to examine the several changes in the world economy regarding agriculture as well as changes in the structure of U.S. agriculture. These changes contributed to shifts in the economic interests and political power of competing segments of agriculture.

## The World-Economic Context of the FAIR Act

In the world economy, agriculture became both more liberalized and more competitive in the last two decades of the twentieth century. The ratification of several trade agreements, in particular the North American Free Trade Agreement (NAFTA) (1994) and the Uruguay Round of GATT (1994), and the creation of the World Trade Organization in 1995 signaled a fundamental structural change in the international food regime: the reduction of state influence in agricultural production and trade. An important impetus for eliminating price supports and production controls in 1996 came from the attraction of greater liberalization in the world economy and the potential for expanding U.S. exports. This liberalization, however, exacerbated the intense competition in the international food regime that emerged from the adoption of supply management policy by many national governments, as Chapter 6 demonstrated. As the agricultural sector of the world economy liberalized, competition increased not only between agricultural producers in different nations but also between different segments of U.S. agriculture. These two trends of increased liberalization and heightened competition for expanding markets created tensions and opportunities that influenced the economic interests, and hence the policy preferences, of segments of agriculture in the United States.

### Expanding Markets through Liberalization

U.S. corn producers had long argued that expanding markets and consumption was the key to controlling supply and keeping market prices at acceptable levels. This is why the Farm Bureau opposed supply management policy from the late-1940s onward. At that time, the biggest potential market was within expanding meat consumption. In the 1990s, however, the corn segment primarily focused on expanding export markets and liberalizing trade. With the intensified competition in the international food regime due to expanding government intervention in agriculture through the 1970s, some segments of U.S. agriculture saw liberalization as increasingly beneficial. Just as wheat producers became less supportive of production controls as wheat exports increased during the 1960s, the new opportunities for exporting corn, soybeans, and other feed grains during the 1990s strengthened the opposition of the corn segment to production controls. Three new markets for U.S. agricultural exports emerged in the 1990s: former socialist nations, including Cuba and those in Eastern Europe; China and other nations in East Asia; and Mexico. Various agricultural organizations and agribusiness corporations became some of the leading political advocates for free trade in the 1990s. They were among those calling for reopening economic relations with Cuba, strengthening trade relations with China, and supporting NAFTA.

Perhaps the most significant expansion came in corn exports to Mexico following the beginning of NAFTA in 1994 — only about two years before the passage of the FAIR Act. Before the 1990s, Mexico maintained trade barriers to protect its domestic production of corn, a central component of the Mexican diet.[90] NAFTA, however, liberalized Mexico's corn market. In addition, income growth in Mexico before 1996 suggested that the potential for increased exports existed in that nation.[91] Consequently, farm organizations that made up the core of the corn segment emerged as proponents of NAFTA: the Farm Bureau, the ASA, and the NCGA.[92] In addition to these organizations, several livestock organizations likewise supported NAFTA with expectations of expanding exports. In contrast, however, organizations tied to the wheat segment, the NFU and NAWG in particular, opposed NAFTA out of concerns over competition from Canadian wheat.[93] For U.S. corn producers, NAFTA was indeed a boon. Between 1980 and 1993, annual U.S. corn exports to Mexico averaged about 2.3 MMT. After NAFTA passed, corn exports to Mexico increased sharply, averaging almost 4.8 MMT per year between 1995 and 2003. On the effect of NAFTA on corn exports, Vic Riddle, vice president of the Illinois Corn Growers Association, stated: "Before NAFTA went into effect, I think we were exporting around 25 million bushels of corn [to Mexico] and the first year it jumped to almost 100 million bushels nationwide. . . . So I think it showed us that NAFTA was a good idea and a good program, and it is working and . . . benefiting us."[94] Notably, most of this exported corn was used in Mexico's growing livestock industry.[95]

Another potential export market made expanding production especially attractive to the corn segment: new major markets emerging in Asia. Asia had long been an important export market for U.S. corn, importing more than 20 MMT annually and accounting for more than one-third of annual corn exports since 1986. More than half of this corn went to Japan for its livestock industry, but the potential for increased corn exports to Asia rested in other nations expanding their livestock industries. In particular, China represented a potential new export market. China had been a net exporter of corn through the 1980s but became a net importer of corn in the early 1990s as its domestic production dropped. Like Mexico, income growth in China suggested that exports might be expanded. Furthermore, China began expanding its livestock industry in the 1990s. U.S. producers were in a position to control this potentially tremendous market since they dominated world corn markets. Consequently, U.S. agriculture was an important advocate of China receiving most favored nation trading status with the United States as well as admission to the World Trade Organization.[96]

Other markets likewise seemed ripe for expansion. U.S. farm organizations called for normalizing trade relations with Cuba, and new democracies in Eastern Europe and the former Soviet Union presented potential export recipients. These formerly socialist nations expressed interest in expanding their livestock industries and, like China and Mexico, were experiencing some degree of income growth. Although not all of these potential markets were realized, they nonetheless reinforced the perception that supply management policy was increasingly unnecessary—an antiquated policy hindering the possible capture of new markets for U.S. agricultural commodities. Expanding agricultural exports once again became an important alternative to supply management policy and its emphasis on government regulation of production and market prices. Daniel Amstutz, representing the CCFAS and the North American Export Grain Association, summed up this position well: "on the prospects for American farm product exports . . . I think there is tremendous growth potential in all areas, from bulk grains and oil seeds to high value to value-added products, and that is why I think it is so important that we give our farmers freedom to produce for these growing markets."[97] Consequently, the potential for expanding exports shaped the economic interests and the policy preferences of the corn segment, as well as the livestock and agribusiness segments, which could also benefit from these new markets. This led the Farm Bureau, ASA, and NCGA to propose eliminating production controls and significantly weakening supply management policy. These expanding markets would manage supply—for corn, if not for wheat and other commodities as well.

### Competition in the International Food Regime

As markets gradually liberalized and expanded, competition for new markets increased. During the 1980s, competition within the international food regime intensified. This increased competition existed not only between

nations but also between different segments of U.S. agriculture, thereby reinforcing divisions within U.S. agriculture on important policy issues.

The dominance of U.S. agriculture in the world economy, for some agricultural commodities, slowly eroded during the last two decades of the twentieth century. U.S. wheat and soybean exports declined as a percentage of
world exports beginning in the 1980s. Between 1957 and 1979, U.S. wheat
and soybean exports accounted for about 39 percent and 85 percent of world
exports, respectively (see Figure 6.4). U.S. wheat exports dropped slightly to
an average of 35 percent of world exports between 1980 and 1995, but U.S.
soybean exports declined significantly, accounting for about 71 percent of
world exports during this later period. By contrast, U.S. corn exports became
more dominant in the world economy: the United States accounted for about
62 percent of world corn exports between 1957 and 1979, but this figure rose
to about 71 percent for the period 1980 to 1995. The world economy became
more competitive in wheat and soybean markets, but this was not true for
corn.

The increased competition in wheat markets in particular led to the creation of the EEP in 1985. Notably, U.S. corn exports did not rely on export
subsidies to dominate the world market. The different degrees of competition that segments of agriculture faced was at the heart of the debates over
the EEP. The debates that focused on budgetary constraints merely masked
the underlying and ongoing conflict between these two segments of agriculture. The corn segment did not use export subsidies, but the wheat segment
depended on them. This was the root of the conflict, and the different positions of these segments in the world economy influenced this divergence of
economic interest. U.S. corn exports dominated the world market for much
of the latter half of the 1900s, but the world wheat market was more competitive.

In the 1980s, wheat producers faced growing competition from Australia, Canada, and the EU (especially France), which each held significant
shares of the world wheat market. This flow of wheat out of the EU as well as
other regions displaced U.S. wheat exports to important markets, including
Eastern Europe, the former Soviet Union, and China to a lesser extent.[98] Importantly, these major competitors of U.S. wheat also used export subsidies.
The United States created the EEP in response to other nations' export
subsidies, the loss of markets, and increased competition. Between 1987 and
1995, no less than 67 percent of annual U.S. wheat exports relied on some
form of export subsidy, primarily from the EEP. Therefore, wheat producers

faced a world economy in which export subsidies were used to compete for markets. Increasing flexibility to allow more wheat production in the United States was less than appealing in such a competitive market.

U.S. corn producers did not confront such increased competition from Europe but nonetheless faced different problems with Europe. Primarily, the corn segment had to contend with Europe's Common Agricultural Policy. Before the 1980s, U.S. corn and soybean exports had a relatively secure market in Europe; however, trade barriers emerged on corn and soybean imports into Europe during the 1980s.[99] As a result, U.S. corn exports to Europe fell dramatically: 42 percent of all U.S. corn exports went to Europe in 1975, but only 5 percent went there in 1986.[100] Export subsidies would not necessarily help the corn segment win back the European market, but they might help the wheat segment increase its share of the world market. Liberalizing trade and reducing barriers were more appealing to the corn segment.

Another point of contention emerged between the wheat and corn segments regarding the EEP: export subsidies sometimes put U.S. corn in unfair competition with U.S. wheat exports. As noted earlier, the U.S. Feed Grains Council expressed concern about "the substitution issue [in] countries . . . where you see wheat coming in at levels that go beyond the milling capacity . . . that grain is ending up in feed channels."[101] And Senator Lugar pointed out that the EEP might also encourage producers in other nations to grow corn, soybeans, or other feed grains "whose prices are not so depressed."[102] Thus, the EEP put the wheat and corn segments at odds with one another as they each tried to capture greater shares of the world market. The EEP also posed the danger of encouraging an increase in the world supply of corn. Consequently, the corn segment split over the continuation of export subsidies.

We need to consider the world economic context of the FAIR Act. In particular, some segments of agriculture saw significant possibilities for expanding exports due to the general process of liberalization in the 1980s and 1990s. GATT and NAFTA were especially beneficial for the corn segment and presented an opportunity for reducing reliance on production controls. Yet the competition that accompanied this liberalization also shaped the economic interests of segments of agriculture, notably the wheat segment. Unlike corn producers, U.S. wheat producers faced a competitive world market in which export subsidies were the norm. High market prices are therefore an insufficient explanation for the timing of the FAIR Act. With this position in the world economy, the wheat segment was more supportive of production controls and export subsidies even when market prices were high. By contrast, we might assert that the corn segment would favor ending production controls and reducing price supports even with lower market prices given the potential to expand its market. This was precisely the larger context in 1954 when the corn segment pushed for significant reductions in supply management policy (see Table 7.1 and Chapter 4).

## The Changing Political and Economic Structure of Agriculture

In previous political battles over supply management, the cotton-wheat coalition was able to prevail and protect its economic interests through state policy. This coalition, however, lost the battle over the 1996 farm bill. In particular, it was unable to protect its economic interests by retaining production controls. Why was this coalition, which was so politically successful in the past, unable to do this during the 1990s? This is really the key question underlying the FAIR Act. What had changed in the political power of this coalition? How did the overall political-economic context of U.S. agriculture change to increase the influence of opponents of supply management? Two important trends during the last quarter of the twentieth century help to answer these questions: the livestock segment continued to grow in importance in U.S. agriculture, and the South's position on supply management changed.

### The Expanding Livestock Sector

The importance of livestock production increased dramatically during the twentieth century, as both the qualitative characteristics and the size of the livestock sector changed. This affected the economic interests found in agriculture in two ways. First, many farmers, especially corn and soybean producers, found themselves selling to the growing intensive livestock industry. Second, the livestock industry itself became more assertive in the policy formation process, and its economic interests did not necessarily coincide with those of farmers. In general, the livestock segment tended to oppose various elements, if not all, of supply management policy. These trends were particularly evident in the South, the region most supportive of supply management policy, during the last third of the twentieth century.

Figure 7.1 shows the growth in the livestock complex since 1930. Total

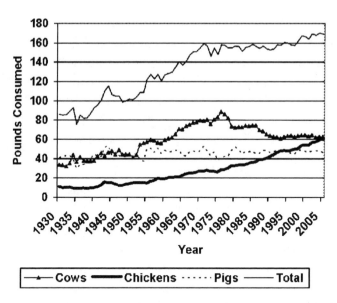

7.1. U.S. per capita meat consumption, 1930–2005. *Source:* USDA, Economic
Research Service, "Food Availability (Per Capita) Data System."

per capita meat consumption increased gradually from 102 pounds in 1950
to 153 pounds in 1990. This understates the growth in the livestock complex, however, because the U.S. population grew substantially during this
period. Even if per capita meat consumption had stayed constant, the livestock complex would have grown in size because the total meat consumption
would have increased as the population grew in size. Thus, an increasing per
capita consumption coupled with growth in the overall population meant
that the livestock complex increased significantly in size. Although the per
capita consumption of hogs stayed relatively constant through this period,
the consumption of cows increased after World War II and peaked in the
mid-1970s. The per capita consumption of chickens stands out: it increased
steadily between 1945 and the mid-1970s, and then increased faster through
the end of the century.

The increased size of the livestock complex was accompanied by a qualitative change. "Factory farms" replaced family farms as the primary source
of livestock, especially for hogs and chickens. Intensive production measures, such as concentrated animal feeding operations, became widespread.[103]
Within the past twenty years, contract farming has also become more prevalent among farmers raising livestock. With these changes came increasing

concentration within the livestock complex. Consequently, a reliable supply of cheap feed grains became essential. In this way, the livestock complex was built upon supply management policy, which encouraged farmers to increase both their productivity and their production. The expanding livestock complex became an important outlet for the growing supply of feed grains, including corn and soybeans. Nonetheless, the livestock complex had less economic interest in maintaining production controls and price supports, each of which distorted the market for their primary input: feed grains.

These trends in economic interests were especially evident in the South, where poultry production became prevalent. Figure 7.2 shows the growth in the southern poultry industry, which expanded in two notable spurts: 1955 to 1970 and 1975 to 1995. This corresponds with the South's shift to soybean production after World War II (see Figure 4.2). During the initial formation and expansion of supply management policy from the New Deal to 1950, the livestock industry was largely absent from the South. Certainly, chickens, hogs, and other animals were raised on southern farms, but the livestock industry was not an independent economic and political force in the region. This changed during the postwar period as the South became more integrated into the national livestock complex by shifting its primary production to feed grains and significantly expanding regional poultry production. The value of poultry production in the South became more important as well. By 1960, poultry was one of the three most valuable commodities in the region, alternating in various years with cotton, tobacco, and soybeans. From 1980 onward, however, poultry production created more value than any other agricultural commodity. When the FAIR Act was passed in 1996, the poultry industry in the South produced about $8.7 billion, which was nearly as much as the value of cotton, tobacco, and soybeans combined.[104] Thus, the face of southern agriculture changed significantly during the twentieth century. Whereas planters who produced cotton and depended on production controls and price supports dominated southern agriculture until the late 1960s, the livestock complex grew increasingly important in the region's agriculture thereafter. The demise of southern planters some twenty years before weakened the political coalition favoring supply management and changed the structure of power in U.S. agriculture. The FAIR Act is partly a legacy of this historic shift.

The expansion of the livestock complex also fundamentally changed the structure of agriculture, both nationally and within the South. Importantly, the livestock complex, of which corn is an integral part, is closely tied to the

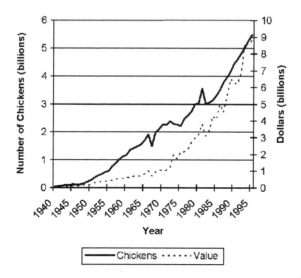

7.2. Expansion of the "broiler" chicken industry in the South, 1940–1995. *Source:* USDA (various years), *Agricultural Statistics.*

larger food system that relies on high value and high-profit commodities.[105] This change influenced the economic interests that were voiced as well as the strength of competing political coalitions within agriculture. Again, supply management policy, which keeps the supply of feed grains low and prices high, has not been the preferred policy of the livestock segment.

### The South and Supply Management Policy

During the second half of the twentieth century, the relationship between southern agriculture, partisan politics, and agricultural policy changed in important ways. The South made a partisan shift away from the Democratic Party, and the region also shifted away from cotton production. Chapters 4 and 5 discussed these shifts in detail, but how did these secular trends influence the passage and substance of the FAIR Act?

Part of the explanation for the act has to do with the South's gradual shift to the Republican Party. The FAIR Act passed the Senate by a vote 74 to 26 and the House by a vote of 270 to 155. Most of those voting in favor of the bill were Republicans, and most voting against it were Democrats. Thus, it appears that the Republican shift of 1994 was key, and it certainly played a role. The southern shift to the Republican Party facilitated the FAIR Act's

**Table 7.3.** The anatomy of the South's vote on the FAIR Act

|  | Senate | | | | House | | | |
|---|---|---|---|---|---|---|---|---|
|  | Yea | Nay | No vote | Total | Yea | Nay | No vote | Total |
| Democrats | 6 | 3 | 0 | 9 | 32 | 21 | 3 | 56 |
| Republicans | 12 | 0 | 1 | 13 | 63 | 4 | 1 | 68 |
| Total | 18 | 3 | 1 | 22 | 95 | 25 | 4 | 124 |

passage as well. However, we might take a closer look at the South's vote on this legislation. Table 7.3 outlines how southern senators and representatives voted on the FAIR Act. In 1996, thirteen of the South's twenty-two senators were Republicans and nine were Democrats; in the House, the South had sixty-eight Republicans and fifty-six Democrats. All twelve Republican senators who voted on the FAIR Act voted in favor of it.[106] Sixty-three of the sixty-eight southern Republicans in the House voted in favor of the bill. So southern Republicans were important to the passage of the FAIR Act. Yet six of the nine southern Democratic senators voted for it.[107] Likewise, thirty-two southern Democratic representatives voted for this policy that would significantly weaken supply management policy. Well over half of southern Democrats voted for the FAIR Act. Therefore, support for supply management policy seems to have weakened even among southern Democrats. Why? We might also ask why southern Republicans were willing to oppose supply management policy in 1996 but not in the 1980s, when they controlled the Senate and a Republican president was intent on cutting it.

Understanding this shift away from supply management by both Republicans and Democrats in the South requires moving beyond mere partisan politics. The Republican congressional victory in 1994 gave the corn-agribusiness-livestock coalition much more influence over agricultural policy. As we have seen, this coalition opposed key elements of supply management policy and therefore did not share the preferences of much of the South regarding agricultural policy. In this way, the rise of southern Republicanism necessarily tempered the party's stance against supply management policy. When the South became Republican, that party was influenced by the preferences of the cotton segment in a way that Republicans had not been in the past. Just as the Republican Party had to contend and compromise with

7.3. U.S. cotton exports (three-year average), 1930–1995. *Source:* USDA (various years), *Agricultural Statistics.*

a strong party faction from the Wheat Belt in the mid-twentieth century, southern Republicans were in a position to win concessions on important policy issues. The exemption of tobacco and peanuts from the FAIR Act are examples of such compromises won by southern senators and representatives.[108] Furthermore, the cotton segment was content with marketing loans, which were also left intact. By retaining elements of supply management that were particularly important to the South, the FAIR Act was more palatable to both southern Republicans and Democrats.

In addition to such political compromises, the economic context was conducive to the South favoring retrenchment in supply management policy: cotton exports had generally been trending upward since about 1970 (see Figure 7.3). In fact, they increased significantly leading up to 1996. Cotton exports reached almost 9.2 million bales in 1994 — the largest export of cotton since 1931. By contrast, cotton exports were steadily declining in the early 1980s. As with corn, the growth in cotton exports was partly due to liberalization in the world economy, particularly as markets opened in Mexico and China.

We also need to consider that the predominant agricultural commodities in the South during the mid-1900s were cotton, tobacco, and corn, and they relied heavily on supply management. By the 1990s, this was no longer the case. Again, poultry was the top agricultural commodity in terms of value, and producers in this industry had far less interest in continuing supply management policy than producers of traditional southern commodities. As poultry production became more important in the region's economy, southern politicians became increasingly likely to consider this industry's interests in forming agricultural policy.

Several concessions made the FAIR Act acceptable to the South, and the economic conditions were more favorable for cotton in some respects. These two factors help to explain the bipartisan southern shift away from supply management. The economic interests and the political power of southern agriculture had changed significantly since the mid-1900s. Such a vote against supply management policy was not possible when the southern planters had dominated southern politics—unless their economic interests began to conflict with the policy, as happened in 1964. The transformation of this region, which had protected New Deal agricultural policies for decades, was fundamental to the passage of the FAIR Act. Part of the difficulty in retaining the policy of supply management forged during the New Deal was the absence of an agricultural coalition with adequate political power or economic interest to do so.

Agricultural policy followed a different trajectory under President Reagan than under President Clinton: supply management expanded under Reagan, a Republican, but it was retrenched under Clinton, a southern Democrat. At least initially, this comparison seems to undermine an argument focused on partisan politics, even if partisan control of Congress was split during Reagan's terms and was Republican during Clinton's. Yet another important difference existed between these two presidencies: a crisis affected agriculture during Reagan's terms but not Clinton's. Perhaps, then, the key is the conjuncture of partisan politics and market prices. Although this explanation for the retrenchment of supply management policy appears to fit fairly well with the 1990s, we must look beyond these surface-level factors to truly understand the secular trajectory of this policy.

Political coalitions within agriculture are a central part of the explanation of this retrenchment of supply management policy—just as they were in the policy's formation during the 1930s, in its expansion during the next two decades, and in its gradual retrenchment that began in the mid-1950s. Since political coalitions change over time, we need to examine what factors alter the economic interests of segments of agriculture. We also must examine how the political power of competing coalitions and various segments of agriculture change over time. Republican control of Congress in the 1990s, for example, occurred when particular agriculture segments—namely, agribusiness and livestock—had become more important economically and politically. Agribusiness, for example, was largely excluded from agricultural policy formation between 1933 and 1975, but it was much more visible and active in the process by 1996. These political-economic shifts underlie the contours of twentieth-century agricultural policy. Market prices and partisan politics are just part of the general context that affects these underlying coalitions within agriculture. And these coalitions are the link between the FAIR Act of 1996 and previous instances of agricultural retrenchment.

# Epilogue

## After FAIR: A New Departure?

I don't think we'll ever end [our farm programs]. . . . They may look different
next time around, but I don't think we'll ever end them.
—SAXBY CHAMBLISS (R-GA), CHAIR OF THE SENATE AGRICULTURE
COMMITTEE, 2005

Policy trajectories are not generally straight lines; instead, policies experience periods of expansion, stagnation, and retrenchment. Trajectories can be long or short, and the patterns can be cyclical.
What happened after the historic retrenchment seen in the FAIR Act? Did
agricultural policy continue on the same trajectory set forth by FAIR? In
brief, agricultural policy expanded again, but supply management policy did
not return in its pre-1996 form. The Farm Security and Rural Investment
(FSRI) Act of 2002 reintroduced a version of price supports, called countercyclical payments. Yet production controls, such as the ARP and allotments
tied to price supports, did not return. Thus, the elimination of production
controls, which was the primary retrenchment of the FAIR Act, remained
intact. In this way, the FSRI Act was a relatively minor shift in the ongoing
ebb and flow of agricultural policy. How can we explain this turn in agricultural policy? Why did a version of price supports return while production
controls remained largely absent?

The same processes that were important in shaping agricultural policy
throughout most of the twentieth century also underlie its recent trajectory.
In part, the strength of political coalitions at the time of policy formation or
retrenchment is important for understanding the subsequent policy trajectory.[1] Yet the political-economic context created by the FAIR Act also facilitated this turn in agricultural policy. Furthermore, dynamics in the world
economy influenced the economic interests and policy preferences of seg-

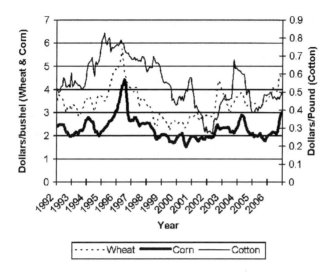

8.1. Monthly prices for wheat, corn, and cotton, 1992–2006. *Source:* USDA, National Agricultural Statistics Service, "Quick Stats: Agricultural Statistics Data Base."

ments of agriculture. This overarching context facilitated agricultural coalitions that favored expanding agricultural policy to bring back one important element of supply management—price supports.

### The FAIR Act in Action

Since the FAIR Act replaced price supports with decoupled PFC payments and eliminated production controls, farmers had almost total flexibility in what commodities they produced and in what quantities. The act became law amid high agricultural prices, but this prosperous period proved to be very short-lived.[2]

Market prices for cotton, wheat, and corn began to decline by the fall of 1996, but this slide did not reach alarming levels until 1997 and 1998. Figure 8.1 shows the trends of monthly prices for these commodities from 1992 to 2006. Wheat prices peaked at $5.75 per bushel in May 1996; corn prices peaked at $4.43 per bushel in July; and cotton prices reached about 79 cents per pound in July. Although prices declined throughout the remainder of that year, they did not fall to alarming levels. In January 1997, wheat and corn prices were still higher than they had been before July 1995, at the beginning of the steep rise in prices. And cotton prices remained above the average price of the early 1990s. In essence, then, market prices fell from the near-record highs in 1995–1996 to "average highs" shortly thereafter. The real trouble was still to come.

Wheat and corn prices continued to decline and hit bottom in 1998 and 1999. Cotton prices, however, had their most notable decline between 1998 and 2002. For each commodity, prices fell markedly below their pre-1995 levels. Wheat prices fell to $2.22 per bushel in mid-1999—a decline of 62 percent from their peak in 1996. Corn prices fell to about $1.75 in mid-1999, which represented a drop of about 60 percent. And finally, cotton prices fell below 43 cents per pound in late 1999—a decline of about 47 percent. By early 2002, cotton prices hit bottom at about 28 cents per pound. This decline in prices contributed to falling farm income, which dropped from $62.8 billion in 1996 to $48.7 billion in 1999—a decrease of about 23 percent. Perhaps even more significant, government payments increased as a percentage of net farm income, from 12 percent to 45 percent. Finally, market prices for these commodities remained below the pre-1995 average until the last half of 2002. Thus, the market became much more hostile to farmers for the duration of the FAIR Act.

The decline in agricultural prices was due to a couple of factors. First, production for some commodities increased because the FAIR Act removed production controls. Corn production in particular increased by almost 18 percent after this policy shift. Figure 8.2 shows this increase. The three-year average smoothes out the year-to-year fluctuations in production, helping to demonstrate that production remained consistently higher after 1996: annual corn production averaged 257 MMT between 1990 and 1995, but this rose to 302 MMT between 1996 and 2001. Partly underlying this increase was an expansion of national corn acreage, which rose from an average of about 75.5 million acres from 1990 to 1995 to about 78.6 million acres from 1996 to 2001. Average yields also increased from an annual average of about 119 bushels per acre in the earlier period to 133 bushels per acre after the FAIR Act. Wheat production increased at a similar rate (about 17 percent), from 59 MMT in 1995 to 69 MMT in 1998. And soybean production likewise increased: from an annual average 78 MMT from 1990 to 1995, up to an average of 99 MMT from 1996 to 2001 (an increase of about 26 percent). Such increases in agricultural production helped to drive supply up and prices down.

Second, agricultural prices fell as exports declined with the onset of the East Asian financial crisis in 1997. The crisis involved the deflation of na-

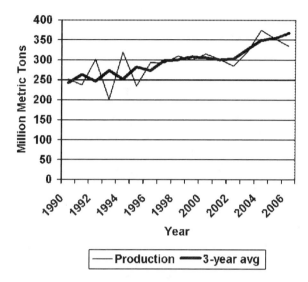

8.2. U.S. corn production, 1990–2006. *Source:* USDA, National Agricultural Statistics Service, "Quick Stats: Agricultural Statistics Data Base."

tional currencies in countries such as Japan, South Korea, Taiwan, and Thailand, and it engulfed much of the region, which was a primary importer of some U.S. agricultural commodities. One consequence of this crisis was that the purchasing power of these countries, and therefore their ability to import goods, declined significantly. Consequently, U.S. agricultural exports to East Asia (especially China, Japan, Taiwan, and South Korea) began to decline. For example, corn exports to the region declined by almost 23 percent between 1996 and 1998.[3] Soybean exports to Asia also declined by about 25 percent during the same period. Importantly, East Asia was the top destination for U.S. corn and soybean exports. This drop in consumption and exports, coupled with the increased production of some agricultural commodities, contributed to the drop in market prices during the late 1990s.

The federal government responded to this market downturn by expanding agricultural policy to offer greater support to farmers. In 1998, Congress passed an emergency spending bill to increase direct payments to farmers. This bill made up for declining commodity prices with Market Loss Assistance (MLA) payments, which again tied income support to market prices. As market prices remained low in 1999, Congress passed another emergency spending bill that again increased payments to farmers. In all, "Congress enacted . . . five supplemental emergency assistance packages" between October 1998 and 2002.[4] These bills provided more than $25 billion to farmers in addition to the fixed PFC payments under the FAIR Act. Government subsidies rose from less than $8 billion annually between 1994 and 1997 up to $12.4 billion in 1998, $21.5 billion in 1999, $23.2 billion in 2000, and $22.4 billion in 2001.[5] Consequently, income subsidies increased to record levels under the FAIR Act despite the declining PFC payments.

Shortly after the passage of the FAIR Act, then, some shortcomings of the policy became clear. Most importantly, the act ultimately left farmers vulnerable to market fluctuations; price supports no longer protected farmers from significant declines in market prices. When market prices declined after 1997, Congress passed legislation in several years that gave farmers emergency assistance to help make up for the decline. This led farm subsidies to rise dramatically between 1998 and 2001, despite the FAIR Act's aim to reduce government spending in agriculture. In effect, these emergency assistance bills reaffirmed the government's willingness to subsidize farm income during market downturns—the precise purpose of price supports dating back to the New Deal. Therefore, even before the FAIR Act expired, some of the retrenchment brought by this policy was reversed.

Given this political-economic context—the decline in market prices, the increase in production, the decline in exports, and the increase in government subsidies—a complete return to supply management policy might have been expected. Price supports and production controls might have returned to stabilize prices and manage production. Yet only part of this happened. How can we explain why some policy retrenchment became permanent or long-term policy while other reforms were simply reversed after a short period?

### Beyond FAIR: Understanding Recent Agricultural Policy

In 2002, Congress passed the FSRI Act to replace the expiring FAIR Act. This new farm legislation expanded agricultural policy in terms of income supports, which had three components under the FSRI Act: marketing loans, direct (fixed) payments, and countercyclical payments. Both marketing loans and direct payments were continued from the FAIR Act, and the countercyclical payments reflected the MLA payments of the emergency assistance packages. The FSRI Act also continued to subsidize exports by reauthorizing the EEP. Importantly, however, the FSRI Act did not revive production controls. Under this legislation, the ARP was not brought back nor did farmers have to adhere to federal production requirements regarding the commodities they could produce and in what quantities to be eligible for government subsidies. Although some land could be taken out of production for environmental reasons, farmers could grow almost any commodity on their land and in any amounts without penalty or loss of their eligibility for subsidies. Thus, the program that was the pillar of supply management policy remained absent. How can we explain these short-term policy trajectories? Why were income supports expanded while production controls were not revived?

One explanation might focus on the same factors that many scholars use to explain the FAIR Act: market prices, partisan politics, and federal budget politics. In explaining the emergency bills, for example, Sheingate argues that declining market prices and the return of budget surpluses after 1997 permitted this reexpansion of income supports.[6] Although this is true, the expansion of income supports under the FSRI Act occurred as large budget deficits were looming under the George W. Bush administration. Though budget politics might have played some role in the FAIR Act, the sense of impending deficits in 2001 seemed to encourage a quick expansion of income supports.[7] Therefore, the effect of budget politics on agricultural policy seems inconsistent during this short time period, just as it was during the 1980s. Furthermore, a focus on budget politics does not explain why production controls were not revived during this period, especially in 2002.

Regarding partisan politics as a primary explanation for the expansion of agricultural policy, we should remember that Republicans controlled the House and Senate when the emergency spending bills were passed and thereby increased farm subsidies. Still, some observers might point out that Democrats, who tend to favor "intrusive support and supply-control policies," regained control of the Senate in 2001 before the passage of the FSRI Act.[8] Therefore, this shift in partisan politics might be offered as the reason for the expansion in agricultural policy. Nevertheless, a Republican House and administration oversaw this expansion in income supports, undermining the argument that partisan politics is fundamental to explaining retrenchment and expansion in agricultural policy. It is difficult to believe that the Democratic Senate overwhelmed Republicans in the House and the Bush administration, especially given the fact that Senate Democrats had a very thin, one-seat 50–49–1 majority thanks to Vermont Republican Jim Jeffords, who left the Republican Party to become an independent and voted with the Democratic caucus. Finally, in the House, the proportions of Democrats and Republicans voting for the FSRI Act were almost identical: 65.8 percent of Republicans and 66.8 percent of Democrats voted in favor of this expansion of agricultural policy.[9] Support from Republicans from the South and Wheat Belt was even higher—68 percent and 72 percent, respectively. Consequently, the one-seat Democratic majority in the Senate seems much less important than the support of many Republicans. In this light, partisan politics do not seem to explain this expansion of agricultural policy very well.

Lastly, market prices remained relatively low in 2001–2002 (see Figure 8.1) and likely did play a role in this policy shift. As I have argued throughout this book, however, we should be careful not to place too much emphasis on prices themselves. Instead, we should look at how market prices contribute to a larger political-economic context that affects the divisions and coalitions within agriculture.

## Agricultural Divisions and Coalitions in 2002

To explain the expansion of agricultural policy at the turn of the century, we need to return to the strength of the agricultural coalitions in the policy formation process. We should begin by looking at what happened to the coalitions that won the FAIR Act. The 2002 shift in agricultural policy was possible only with a change in the agricultural coalitions underlying the retrenchment seen in the FAIR Act. The coalition that advocated ending production controls in 1996 remained intact and strong in 2002, but the coalition favoring the end of price supports was much more tenuous and changed a few years after 1996.

We will look at price supports first. With the decline of commodity prices in the late 1990s, flat and declining PFC payments became less appealing to producers, including those in the corn segment. As a result, the corn segment left the coalition opposing price supports, as evident from the congressional testimony leading up to the FSRI Act in 2002. Bob Stallman, president of the Farm Bureau, argued for price supports but envisioned them as eventually fading: "we will continue to need income support consistent with our international trade obligations. Part of this new spending authority would be countercyclical and, therefore, would decline as opportunities for market growth are realized."[10] Lee Kline, president of the NCGA, reflected on the primary weakness of the FAIR Act: "In hindsight, the 1996 FAIR Act provided farmers with many of the tools we are looking for, but it was shortsighted in its ability to provide a safety net that would be sufficient in times of sustained low farm income. . . . After three years of low prices and needed bailouts by the U.S. Congress totaling over $19 billion, we now know that an additional component is vitally needed. . . . NCGA has surfaced as committed to a comprehensive, countercyclical income support proposal."[11]

Even in the heart of the Corn Belt, many farmers, politicians, and others advocated greater protection from the market regarding prices. Senator Tom Harkin (D-IA), who had opposed the FAIR Act, led the fight to expand agricultural policy: "Fundamentally, we must seek to help agricultural producers earn a better return and a better return of the consumer dollar in the market. . . . The planting flexibility and increased support for conservation in the last Farm bill were successes. The bill's income enhancement was not, so we need to improve the system of farm income enhancement, I believe, in the next Farm bill."[12] The *Des Moines Register* praised the FSRI Act saying, "It should bring more stability to the farm economy by making government payments predictable, instead of relying on periodic emergency bailouts from Congress as in the last several years."[13] And many Iowa corn farmers themselves changed their opinion of the FAIR Act: about "64% support among Iowans for the government's move toward elimination of subsidies" in 1996, but by 2001 less than half "agreed that 'the basic directions of the 1996 Freedom to Farm bill should be continued in the 2002 farm bill.'"[14] Thus, sentiment in the Corn Belt seemed to have changed since 1996.

Others also saw the failure to protect farmers from swings in market prices as the primary failing of the FAIR Act, especially those segments of agriculture that had favored price supports in 1996. Leland Swanson, president of the NFU, suggested in a Senate hearing that the 2002 farm bill should allow farmers "to achieve 100 percent of full cost of production and a reasonable profit from the marketplace" in part through a "countercyclical safety net."[15] James Echols, chairman of the NCC, stated, "Our members prefer crop-specific payments that are triggered when the price of a covered commodity falls below a specified threshold, similar to the target price concept in the 1990 farm law."[16] And finally, Dusty Tallman, president of NAWG, recommended "the creation of counter-cyclical payments that would be made only when prices fall so low as to create real need across the agricultural economy."[17] The core of the cotton-wheat coalition, then, continued to favor income supports tied to market prices. In all, the agricultural coalition advocating a version of price supports was quite broad, including the cotton and wheat segments as well as portions of the corn segment.

By contrast, the agricultural coalition that had opposed production controls in 1996 remained strong in 2002. This coalition — which included the corn, livestock, and agribusiness segments — opposed production controls in 1996 not because market prices were high or because the budget deficit was a salient political issue. Rather, this coalition opposed production controls based on economic interests that derived from the respective positions of the segments in the overall production process and within the world economy. Although market prices, partisan politics, and budget deficits may have changed between 1996 and 2002, neither the fundamental class position nor the economic interests of these segments of agriculture changed during that brief period. As a result, this coalition in 2002 remained nearly identical to the coalition in 1996. Production controls were not reinstituted because the opposition to this aspect of supply management remained.

In particular, the Farm Bureau continued to "oppose new supply management programs" that would regulate or control agricultural production.[18] Tony Anderson, president of the ASA, expressed opposition to reviving production controls: "oil seed organizations support maintaining key elements of the FAIR Act in the next Farm bill [including] full and unrestricted planning flexibility; continuation of non-recourse marketing loans; no statutory authority to impose setasides and no authority to establish Government or farmer-owned reserves for oil seeds."[19] John Miller, a milling company executive, stated his opposition to any supply management policy: "We oppose the inclusion of the following features: do not add any supply management features in any form to current policy. Do not create new inventory management programs such as a farmer-owned reserve, energy reserves or hunger reserves, and do not add any new countercyclical payment program."[20]

Other segments of agriculture, however, continued to call for production controls. Both the American Corn Growers Association and the NFU advocated creating a set-aside program to help prevent overproduction.[21] Yet NAWG recommended keeping the production flexibility of the FAIR Act. Likewise, the NCC favored retaining "full production" programs, in contrast to its 1996 support for production controls. Therefore, the coalition in favor of production controls was weaker than in 1996 and simply too weak to bring back supply management policy in 2002.

Given the broader political-economic context discussed earlier, the coalitions around price supports and production controls in 2002 make sense. Though the financial crisis in East Asia reminded farmers and others in agriculture that market volatility is not terribly uncommon, the reexpansion of exports to East Asia reaffirmed the possibility of an expanding world market for many U.S. producers. The collapse of market prices broadened the coalition favoring a version of price supports. In addition, some organizations that had favored production controls in 1996, such as NAWG and the NCC, changed their positions after six years of production flexibility. By 2002, the agricultural coalition opposing the return of production controls was formidable. In this light, the return of price supports and continued absence of production controls should not have been unexpected. Ultimately, this expansion reflects the dynamics behind the ebb and flow of agricultural policy throughout the twentieth century.

Although these recent instances of retrenchment and expansion—the FAIR and FSRI acts, respectively—are important, we need to recognize that they are but individual moments in the secular trajectory of agricultural policy. The 2002 FSRI Act departed from the path set forth by the FAIR Act, but the dynamics behind each policy shift reflect the dynamics behind the contours of agricultural policy since the New Deal. Therefore, we need to ask how these recent shifts fit within the long-term trajectory of agricultural policy rather than analyzing them as isolated snapshots of policy change. How can we account for the various instances of policy shifts between 1920 and today? What factors help to explain historic shifts such as the AAA and the FAIR Act? Why did supply management policy end in 1996? Why did supply management last as long as it did instead of ending much earlier? I have tried to answer such questions in a way that moves beyond the extant literature by emphasizing the intertwined relations between class, state, and market.

From beginning to end, supply management policy was not merely a function of market prices or partisan politics. Rather, regional divisions and coalitions within agriculture were fundamental influences on the contours of agricultural policy for the past century—and they remain so today. Although some scholars acknowledge regional divisions, they generally leave these divisions out of their theoretical explanations for why this policy changes. One region in particular has stood out as politically important and economically distinct: the South. This region played a central role in the creation, expansion, and retrenchment of supply management policy, but few studies of retrenchment in agricultural policy emphasize its influence. Finally, existing analyses of twentieth-century agricultural policy pay surprisingly little attention to the world economy.[22] Not only are the regional divisions in U.S. agriculture to some degree a function of the world economy, but U.S. agricultural policy has had a profound effect on the organization of agricultural production, trade, and consumption around the globe. The adoption of supply management policy and the U.S. model of intensive agricultural production by other nations eventually led to changes in the world economy: greater competition within commodity markets, more barriers to the flow of agricultural trade, and shifts in nations' agricultural production. These world economic changes facilitated changes in U.S. agricultural policy, in part by exacerbating some divisions within agriculture while easing others. In the end, U.S. agricultural policy was intimately tied to the organization of agriculture in the world economy. A complete understanding of the "life" of supply management policy, then, is possible only by exploring how class, state, and market influence one another.

## Cultivating Conflict and Change

So exactly what is it that facilitates change and promotes conflict in agriculture? Is it class, state, or market? It should be clear by now that each of these social forces has promoted conflicts and changes in agriculture. The market crisis beginning in the 1920s prompted some segments of agriculture to fight for state protection from market vagaries, resulting in the creation of supply management. As this policy became firmly entrenched, it encouraged shifts in regional production—most notably from cotton to soybeans in the South—and expansion of the livestock complex as a means for consuming chronic surpluses. This policy also became the model for agricultural policy throughout the world economy. In these ways, supply management policy changed the very economic and political structures of agriculture that had given rise to it in the first place. Agribusiness corporations became more active in policy formation; the livestock complex grew in size and changed qualitatively; the class structure of southern agriculture changed; the world economic context of agriculture shifted; and finally, the relationship between political parties and agriculture changed as the South became Republican. Caught up in this double movement were southern blacks: supply management policy led many planters to cast aside black (and white) tenant farmers and sharecroppers, which thereby freed the forces of production as planters mechanized. This process, in turn, freed blacks from the repressive plantation system and allowed them to challenge the planters' political dominance. Class, state, and market each played a part in driving these changes and conflicts in agriculture, which in turn resulted in a particular trajectory for supply management policy from the 1930s through the turn of the century.

Behind all of this change and conflict lies the double movement—of forces simultaneously pushing for and against state regulation of the market. As Karl Polanyi argued, the market operates in such a way that it promotes continual change and conflict through the process of the double movement.[23] This movement is the essence of the relationship between class, state, and market that a class segment perspective tries to capture. Since a market system is inherently dynamic, policies that benefit segments at one time can become impediments to those same segments at a later time because of how those policies reshape the interests of segments. Polanyi described this oscillation between nonmarket and market policies as a basic process of markets: some economic interests seek policies that regulate the market, but this state involvement eventually leads to problems in the market and to attempts to free the "normal operation" of the market without regulation. Free markets eventually wreak social havoc and foster movements for state regulation. This ebb and flow is the double movement of class, state, and market.

Analyzing supply management policy from beginning to its near end captures almost an entire cycle of Polanyi's double movement: in response to market vagaries, a movement for state intervention into the economy emerges; yet state policies regulating the market eventually become a hindrance to profits and bring forth contradictions that make continued intervention unpopular; consequently, a new movement emerges to "free" market forces. Twentieth-century agricultural policy ebbed and flowed between free market principles and state intervention into the economy. Importantly, this double movement *is* capitalism, as opposed to being a struggle of "state versus market." The free market does not exist without its counterpart of state intervention. Beyond establishing how well Polanyi's insights fit with the rise and fall of supply management policy, this analysis has demonstrated how class conflicts underlie this double movement. The shifts in the economic interests and political power of various class segments were the motor driving the double movement in agriculture during the twentieth century.

# Appendix
## Notes on Methods and Data

This book follows in the comparative-historical tradition within political sociology. The FAIR Act is the centerpiece of the analysis, but the material in the chapters leading up to the 1996 legislation is more than mere background. Rather, the whole of twentieth-century agricultural policy is a fundamental part of the analysis of recent retrenchment in two ways. First, this history contains the elemental processes that shape agricultural policy—past, present, and future. The emergence and evolution of supply management policy is crucial to understanding the retrenchment of this policy. Trying to understand the FAIR Act outside of this historical development is simply too narrow in scope.

Second, the history of twentieth-century agricultural policy contains key moments: the McNary-Haugen bills of the 1920s, the AAAs of 1933 and 1938, the Brannan Plan of 1949, the Agricultural Acts of 1949 and 1954, the Cotton-Wheat Act of 1964, the Agriculture and Consumer Protection Act of 1973, the FAIR Act of 1996, and the FSRI Act of 2002. These key historical moments provide important points of comparison that help to explain the long-term trajectory of agricultural policy. Each historical moment falls into one of three possible outcomes: policy expansion, contraction, or stasis. Comparing the political-economic context of these moments illuminates the importance of divisions and coalitions within agriculture. And in comparing these various policy shifts or attempted shifts, we gain a better understanding of how policy expands or contracts, and why it fails to change, at certain times.

At the core of these comparisons, I have focused on political coalitions of class segments. Given the importance of "class segments" to this analysis, we should take a moment to consider this concept more closely. What exactly are "class segments"? And, perhaps more importantly, how can we identify them? Chapter 1 addresses the idea of class segments in discussing theoretical perspectives on national policy. This appendix, however, offers a brief discussion focused more closely on the concept itself. It also briefly explains how I collected, organized, and analyzed data—primarily, statistics, congressional roll-call votes, and congressional hearing testimony. These three types of evidence provide various vantage points for identifying class segments and discerning the underlying relations between class, state, and market.

## Conceptualizing Class Segments

The idea of class rests on a Marxist understanding, in which "class" is defined through relations to the means of production. The two basic classes in capitalism are capital (the owners of the means of production) and labor (workers who own only their labor power to sell in the market). Yet Marx clearly recognized other classes, including the landed elite, peasants, and petite bourgeoisie (small capital). One example can be found in *The 18th Brumaire of Louis Bonaparte*, in which Marx examined political struggles in France between 1848 and 1851 by analyzing the rise and fall of various political coalitions of class segments.[1] Because most conflict is within rather than between classes, the focus is on class segments. Thus, capitalism is not a simplistic bifurcated society, and tracing coalitions within and between classes is a central part of this perspective.

Importantly, classes typically are fractured or segmented. For example, the working class is often divided in various ways: race, gender, skill, organization (union versus nonunion), and industry, among others. Similarly, divisions abound within the capitalist class, in part because of competition inherent within the market. These divisions frequently become meaningful enough to pit segments of a single class against one another. Chapter 1 details the processes through which classes become divided. The question becomes, then, how can we identify such divisions within a class?

In this analysis, I have used two measures to identify class segments: political parties and farm organizations. These two measures provide insight into political coalitions by shedding light on the economic interests, political power, and policy preferences of farmers in various regions. Here, "class segment" (or just "segment") refers to the organizations and political representatives of regional producers of different commodities. Specifically, I use cotton segment, wheat segment, and corn segment to refer to farmers of these commodities in particular regions—the South, the Wheat Belt, and the Corn Belt, respectively. Notably, the relationships between segments and political parties change over time, such as when the South shifted from being solidly Democratic to heavily Republican. And a great diversity of farm organizations emerged as the twentieth century progressed. For example, the cotton segment includes southern Democrats as well as various organizations: the National Cotton Council, southern farm bureaus and farmers unions, and other cotton organizations. The corn segment generally includes the national Farm Bureau, many Republicans, and congressional representatives and senators from the Corn Belt. The wheat segment was most identified with the NFU, but other organizations emerged, such as NAWG. This segment tended to be more divided in its political ties: whereas the Wheat Belt tended to be heavily Republican, the NFU had its strongest ties with the Democratic Party.

We should avoid the mistake of assuming that these organizations and political representatives protect and advocate the interests of all or even most farmers in a region. Certainly, southern Democrats frequently countered the interests of many tenant farmers and croppers. In general, agricultural policy has tended to benefit larger farms the most. This is in part due to how well economically dominant farmers—farmers who produce a disproportionate amount of agricultural production and value and often hold farms much larger than average in acreage—have had their interests represented in the policy formation process. The interests of these farmers have tended to be represented by farm organizations, such as the Farm Bureau. These are the farmers, then, who tend to make up the agricultural class segments that influenced agricultural policy.

### Data Sources

In identifying the economic interests and political power of class segments, this analysis relies on statistics, congressional roll-call votes, and congressional hearing testimony.

#### Statistics

I use statistics on agricultural production, trade, and so forth to effectively demonstrate the general political-economic context in which class segments form their economic interests. Many of the statistics used in this book come from two sources: *Agricultural Statistics* and the *Census of Agriculture.* Since 1936, the USDA has published *Agricultural Statistics* annually. From 1926 to 1935, this publication was titled the *Agricultural Yearbook. Agricultural Statistics* holds a wealth of information about most aspects of U.S. agriculture: production, acreage, productivity, prices, farm income, exports, government expenditures, the use of hybrid seeds and machinery, and so on. Importantly, much of this information is available for individual states as well as the entire nation. One minor inconvenience with this source, however, is that studying a longer period of time—say, 1930 to 1995—often requires compiling statistics from several volumes. This is particularly the case with state-level data. The USDA now posts recent additions of *Agricultural Statistics* on its website at http://www.usda.gov. At the present time, however, these electronic versions go back only to about 1992. Most of the statistics that I use in this book come from *Agricultural Statistics.* Because of the compiling that is frequently required, I often do not provide citations for specific tables, pages, or volumes. This is particularly true for most of the figures in this book. Instead, most figures designate only the general source.

The *Census of Agriculture* is published roughly every five years by the Census Bureau. The *Census of Agriculture* overlaps with *Agricultural Statistics* in some regards. Both provide information on production levels, for instance. The difference between these two sources is that the *Census of Agriculture* breaks down and organizes all statistics by state and county. Thus, the information it provides is much more specific and localized than the statistics appearing in *Agricultural Statistics.* Another difference is that the *Census of Agriculture* does not provide annual statistics, sometimes making trends shorter than five years more difficult to observe. I used this source extensively in my discussion in Chapter 5 of the changes in southern agriculture.

In a few chapters, I discussed market prices for various agricultural commodities. The USDA's National Agricultural Statistics Service (NASS) provides data on market prices by month and by year for various commodities. The discussion of price supports and market prices for wheat, corn, and cotton in Chapter 7 for 1954, 1964, 1973, and 1994–1996 relies on monthly data from Quick Stats (Agricultural Statistics Data Base).[2] For these discussions, I also obtained price support levels and the ten-year average price from *Agricultural Statistics*. In Chapter 3, the discussion of market prices from 1914 to 1940 relies on annual price data.[3]

For statistics on agricultural production and trade in the world economy, I used several sources. In addition to *Agricultural Statistics*, I used the "Production, Supply, and Distribution Database" which is online at the website for the USDA's Foreign Agricultural Service (FAS). This electronic database provides statistics on agricultural production and trade for most countries from 1960 to the present. In some instances (such as statistics related to PL 480 or demographic shifts), I used the *Statistical Abstract of the United States.*

More and more agricultural statistics are available from various Internet sources. Several agencies within the USDA—in particular NASS, the Economic Research Service (ERS), and FAS—have made much of their data available on the Web. However, the farther one goes back in time, even to just before 1960, the more difficult some statistics are to find. Most university libraries have printed copies of the *Census of Agriculture, Agricultural Statistics,* and the *Statistical Abstract of the United States,* so historical tables and graphs can always be compiled from these sources if the particular information is not available on the Web. These statistics help to illuminate the political-economic context that shaped economic interests and political power.

## Roll-Call Votes

Ultimately, statistics are generally not people; that is, they do not capture the precise actions or interpretations of people in different events. I used roll-call votes in Congress as one source to help bring individuals into the analysis. A number of scholars have used congressional votes in identifying coalitions. In particular, Richard Bensel uses votes in the U.S. House of Representatives to identify sectional and regional coalitions.[4] T. J. McKeown analyzes votes in the British Parliament to discern support from different groups in ending the Corn Laws, which protected British agriculture from imports, in the 1840s.[5] Because geographic region is closely tied to commodity production, it plays a central role in the formation of class segments within agriculture. Using roll-call call votes thus provides an effective way of demonstrating the existence of political coalitions of agricultural commodities.

In contrast to some other analyses using roll-call votes, I often focus on votes in the Senate because the Senate appears more likely to hold true "roll-call votes," in which the vote of each senator is recorded. By contrast, the House seems more likely than the Senate to hold "voice votes," in which individual votes are not recorded. Nonetheless, I analyze House votes in instances where other scholars do so and I directly examine their arguments. The main instance of this is in Chapter 4 with the discussion of the Agriculture and Consumer Protection Act of 1973.

In roll-call votes, many representatives and senators frequently miss the vote for various reasons. On some votes, a large number of senators may not vote. This appears to occur sometimes when the outcome of a vote seems a foregone conclusion. For example, forty-three of ninety-six senators did not vote on the Agricultural Act of 1949, which passed by a vote of forty-six to seven. In such instances, I discern the intentions of many nonvoting senators from their pairings as expressed in the *Congressional Record*. That is, when the roll call is taken, a senator may speak up for an absent senator and express the latter's wishes regarding the vote. Although these votes do not count in the final outcome, they do lend insight into the extent of support that existed among the forty-three senators who did not vote for the Agricultural Act. In this instance, twenty senators expressed support and five expressed opposition, changing the vote total to sixty-six to twelve, with eighteen senators refraining from either support or opposition. In analyzing roll-call votes, I consistently use the announcement of pairings to discern the preferences of absent senators. In stating the final vote on any policy, however, I always use the actual roll-call results, which exclude pairings.

The Inter-University Consortium for Political Science Research (ICPSR) maintains a database that contains all congressional roll-call votes since the late 1700s. This database can be very beneficial for this kind of research; however, not every university is an ICPSR member with access to this data set. Unfortunately for me, Georgia Tech is not an ICPSR member university. This meant finding individual roll-call votes in one of two sources. Votes after 1945 are generally available in the *Congressional Quarterly Weekly Report* or the *Congressional Quarterly Almanac*. I used the latter source to find the roll-call vote on the Agricultural Act of 1954, and I used the former for votes on agricultural legislation in 1973 and 1996. For earlier legislation (from 1924 to 1949), I used the *Congressional Record*, which records all debates, statements, proposals, votes, and other discussions on the House and Senate floors. Roll-call votes help to illuminate regional political coalitions in the policy formation process.

### Congressional Hearings

Examining the political positions various organizations espouse also provides insight into the interests of class segments. Such positions are available in congressional hearings held in forming the various policies. A number of scholars use congressional hearing testimony because representatives of organizations give the perspective of organizations such as labor unions, industry trade associations, business organizations such as chambers of commerce, and farm organizations.[6] In addition to testimony by representatives and officials from organizations, congressional hearings often include policy statements by the organizations that provide further evidence of segments' interests. These hearings also reveal instances in which disagreement over a policy is evident within an organization. This situation has been relatively common for federations, such as the Farm Bureau, where state-level organizations have regularly opposed the policy position of the national federation. Testimony at these hearings help to provide insight into the economic interests and policy preferences of organizations and class segments.

I blend evidence and information from these sources into the preceding history to demonstrate the political coalitions behind the formation, expansion, and retrenchment of supply management policy. Examining statistics, congressional votes, and the policy preferences of organizations for various national policies over time also allows for some insight into how policy shifts alter political coalitions, class structures, and the market.

# Notes

## Chapter 1. Introduction

Epigraph. Bryce Neidig quotation from U.S. House, "Formulation (Part III)," 32.

1. A few restrictions remained. First, farmers could not grow fruits, vegetables, or other commodities that were traditionally excluded from supply management programs (that is, nonprogram commodities). Second, farmers could not grow crops on land deemed environmentally fragile. Despite these restrictions, the FAIR Act remains a dramatic shift in agricultural policy.

2. Agriculture in the Northeast and West was much less influential in the formation and development of supply management policy than in the South, Corn Belt, and Wheat Belt. The South includes Alabama, Arkansas, Florida, Georgia, Louisiana, Mississippi, North Carolina, South Carolina, Virginia, Tennessee, and Texas. The Corn Belt includes Illinois, Indiana, Iowa, Michigan, Minnesota, Missouri, Ohio, and Wisconsin. The Wheat Belt includes Colorado, Idaho, Kansas, Montana, Nebraska, North Dakota, Oregon, South Dakota, and Washington.

3. U.S. House, "Program Proposals." At this time, corn was the primary feed grain used for livestock. Other feed grains included oats, barley, grain sorghum, and rye. Soybeans were increasingly used in feed, as was wheat in times of surplus. Ibid., 21.

4. Ibid., 1.

5. Ibid., 24–25.

6. Ibid., 22.

7. Ibid., 30–31.

8. Ibid., 45–46.

9. Ibid., 46.

10. Ibid., 47–48.

11. See *Wall Street Journal*, "House Committee," 8; Warden, "House Group," B5; and *Washington Post and Times Herald*, "Bid to End," B4.

12. *Wall Street Journal,* "House Committee," 8. Philip Warden reported: "With the meeting adjourned, the committee members and spectators jumped to their feet and began milling about the room. Poage stalked out of the room and went to his office." Warden, "House Group," B5. Woolley left the room a few minutes after Poage. *Washington Post,* "Bid to End," B4.

13. Milk and sugar also had price supports and production controls, though the programs for these commodities operated independently of the programs for the basic commodities.

14. Hallberg, *Policy for American Agriculture,* 345.

15. When price supports were variable, the secretary of agriculture had discretion in setting supports according to commodity supply.

16. Harriet Friedmann notes, "As a portion of US exports, US aid fell from 71 percent in the early 1960s . . . to 13 percent . . . [in the early 1970s]." Friedmann, "The Origins," 22–23.

17. Hansen, *Gaining Access,* 109.

18. The FAIR Act ended the long-standing supply management programs, but it did not repeal the permanent legislation of 1938 and 1949. Therefore, it had to be replaced in 2002, though the new legislation did not reintroduce supply management policy. Additionally, supply management programs for all commodities except peanuts and tobacco were ended in 1996. Despite these exceptions—the temporary nature of the FAIR Act and the retention of programs for two commodities—the act represented a significant departure from previous legislation.

19. Programs to protect the environment, such as the Conservation Reserve Program, remained. Such programs idle the most environmentally fragile farmland (such as land susceptible to soil erosion) but without the explicit goal of managing supply as found in the Acreage Reduction Program.

20. See, for example, Hansen, *Gaining Access;* and Sheingate, *Agricultural Welfare State.*

21. A smaller farm population need not "be a disadvantage in the struggle to form effective political organizations . . . [because] narrow-based coalitions tend to face lower organization costs." Orden, Paarlberg, and Roe, *Policy Reform,* 49. See also Browne, *Cultivating Congress.*

22. Bonnen, Browne, and Schweikhardt, "Further Observations"; and Hansen, *Gaining Access;* Lyons and Taylor, "Farm Politics."

23. Friedmann, "Distance and Durability."

24. Polanyi also argued that the state is integral to the market economy, including its creation: "Regulation and the market, in effect, grew up together." *Great Transformation,* 68; see also 62–67.

25. Polanyi stated that the social history of our time is "the result of a double movement: . . . The one [is] the principle of economic liberalism, aiming at the establishment of a self-regulating market, . . . the other [is] the principle of social protection aiming at the conservation of man and nature as well as productive organization." *Great Transformation,* 76, 132.

26. One of the best contemporary discussions of how political-economic contexts

may prompt capitalists to favor state regulation of the market can be found in Swenson, *Capitalists.*

27. Moore, *Social Origins.*

28. Bonnen, Browne, and Schweikhardt, "Further Observations"; Hansen, *Gaining Access;* Lowi, *End of Liberalism;* Lyons and Taylor, "Farm Politics"; McConnell, *Decline of Agrarian;* Orden, Paarlberg, and Roe, *Policy Reform;* and Schertz and Doering, *Making the 1996 Farm Act.* Other scholars stress the role of political institutions and policy experts within government. This state-centered perspective, however, is rarely used to explain the retrenchment of supply management policy. See Finegold, "From Agrarianism"; and Finegold and Skocpol, *State and Party.* Sheingate argues that institutional processes, such as partisan control and budget politics, explain the 1996 FAIR Act. Sheingate, *Agricultural Welfare State.*

29. Hansen, *Gaining Access,* especially Chapter 6.

30. Bonnen, Browne, and Schweikhardt, "Further Observations"; Hansen, *Gaining Access;* and Lyons and Taylor, "Farm Politics."

31. See, for example, Grubbs, *Cry from the Cotton;* Heffernan, "Agriculture"; and Wells, *Strawberry Fields.*

32. See Marx, *18th Brumaire.*

33. Rubinson and Sokolovsky, "Patterns of Industrial Regulation"; Wallerstein, *Modern World-System.* A class segment perspective stands in contrast to perspectives focused almost entirely upon *inter*class conflict, usually between labor and capital. For example, Finegold and Skocpol focus entirely upon conflicts between farmworkers and landowners. Finegold and Skocpol, *State and Party,* 140–150. By contrast, much of my analysis emphasizes conflicts between dominant farmers in various regions (for example, the South versus the Corn Belt) as well as between farmers and agribusiness corporations. Focusing on class segments is much more fruitful in understanding the contours of twentieth-century agricultural policy.

34. Prechel, "Steel and the State"; Swenson, *Capitalists;* and Winders, "Maintaining."

35. Gourevitch, *Politics;* Rubinson, "Political Transformation"; and Wallerstein, *Modern World-System.*

36. For example, the structure of the labor market can shape the interests of segments of capital to favor policies such as multiemployer collective bargaining, which other segments of capital might oppose. In the textile industry in the Northeast and the coal industry in the Midwest, companies favored such collective bargaining and unions—an interest that directly conflicted with the other preferences of other segments of capital regarding unions. Swenson, *Capitalists.*

37. Yet as Swenson deftly shows, specific historical contexts might prompt capitalists to try to overcome the competition inherent in capitalism, as in Sweden. Swenson, ibid.

38. Although the divisions within agriculture may seem obvious, not all scholars acknowledge this point. Take this statement, for example: "during the depression years of the 1930s, . . . farmers were a relatively *homogenous,* numerous, and conspicuously disadvantaged segment of the population." Orden, Paarlberg, and Roe, *Policy Reform,*

24, emphasis added. Max Pfeffer demonstrates that the South, Midwest, and West each developed particular rural class structures that prevented the formation of such a homogenous class of farmers. Pfeffer, "Social Origins." On the importance of divisions within agriculture, see also Gilbert and Howe, "Beyond"; Moore, *Social Origins,* Chapter 3; and Rubinson, "Political Transformation."

39. Rubinson, "Political Transformation."

40. Pfeffer, "Social Origins."

41. Pfeffer, "Social Origins"; and Winders, "Roller Coaster."

42. Mooney, "Toward a Class Analysis."

43. Heffernan, "Agriculture."

44. Morgan, *Merchants of Grain.*

45. To the extent that class segment analyses consider "state autonomy," this is the point at which it becomes salient. The state's autonomy emanates not from its bureaucratic strength, but from its position as the mediator of conflicting class segments. For example, during the 1930s, social movements, especially those of labor and farmers, compelled politicians and policy experts to create various New Deal policies. These state actors tried to reduce the class conflict and social unrest created by the worldwide depression. While the state acted as a mediator of class conflict, segments of capital, agriculture, and labor heavily influenced the policies that the state ultimately developed. From this perspective, then, the state was not autonomous in that it saw social disruption and addressed it in a manner of its own (independent) choosing; its decisions were not made in isolation from social actors. See, for example, Gilbert and Howe, "Beyond"; Jenkins and Brents, "Social Protest"; and Winders, "Maintaining."

46. Steinmo, "Political Institutions"; and Werum and Winders, "'In' and 'Out.'"

47. This is, in part, why pluralist analyses of U.S. politics are often accurate. Rubinson, "Class Formation"; and Steinmo, "Political Institutions."

48. Rather than referring to "southern planters," a surprising number of scholars refer to "southern interests," "southern politicians," simply "farmers," or even "southern employers." This portrays planters as nonclass interests or as part of a larger, homogenous class (farmers or business). Neither is accurate, however, as the South had a class structure distinct from both the Midwest and the Northeast. Recognizing a landed elite as a class (or class segment) is not new. Marx suggested that capitalism had "three great classes": "Capital, landed property, [and] wage labor." Marx, *A Contribution,* 9. Marx applied this directly in *The 18th Brumaire of Louis Bonaparte.*

49. See Quadagno, "Welfare Capitalism." Chapter 5 discusses this in detail.

50. The relationship of class segments to political parties and organizations is not one of overt control. First, parties and organizations may have functions that go well beyond the concerns of class segments (for instance, selling life insurance or coordinating community events). Segments exert their influence on issues related to their economic interests (for instance, trade policy). Second, conflicts over policy often exist within organizations and parties. Thus, organizations and parties do not act only in the interests of class segments nor does everyone within them share the same interests. In addition, we should not make the mistake of assuming that these organizations and political representatives protect and advocate the interests of all or even most farmers in a region.

Certainly, southern Democrats frequently countered the interests of tenant farmers and croppers. Agricultural policy tended to benefit economically dominant farmers the most. That is, farmers who accounted for a disproportionate amount of overall agricultural production and value and often held farms much larger than average in acreage generally had their interests well-represented in U.S. agricultural policy. The interests of these farmers also tended to be well-represented in farm organizations, such as the Farm Bureau. These are the farmers, then, who tend to make up the agricultural class segments that influenced agricultural policy.

51. Gilbert and Howe, "Beyond."

52. Gourevitch, *Politics;* and Moore, *Social Origins.*

53. Moore, *Social Origins.*

54. Winders, "Maintaining" and "Roller Coaster."

55. Peter Swenson clearly demonstrates that political-economic contexts shape the economic interests of class segments. Swenson, "Varieties."

56. Winders, "Maintaining."

57. Gourevitch, *Politics;* Polanyi, *Great Transformation;* Rubinson, "Political Transformation"; and Wallerstein, *Modern World-System.*

58. Wallerstein, *Modern World-System.*

59. Conze, "Effects"; Coppa "Italian Tariff"; and Kindleberger, *World in Depression.*

60. Friedmann, "Political Economy (1982)"; and Friedmann and McMichael, "Agriculture and the State."

61. See, for example, Lipson, "Transformation of Trade."

62. Kindleberger, *World in Depression;* and Wallerstein, *Modern World-System.* Some scholars emphasize other factors in regime stability, continuity, and change. One such alternative can be found in the "world polity" perspective, which emphasizes global culture in its analyses. See Boli and Thomas, "World Culture."

63. For example, see Silver and Arrighi, "Polanyi's 'Double Movement.'" They discuss how Polanyi's double movement helps to explain the ebb and flow of hegemony within the world economy.

64. One notable example is Hansen, *Gaining Access.*

65. Sheingate, *Agricultural Welfare State,* 20.

66. Polanyi, *Great Transformation;* Swenson, *Capitalists;* and Wallerstein, *Modern World-System.*

67. Among others, see Moore, *Social Origins.*


## Chapter 2. The Early Battles Lost

1. The USDA was established by *12 Stat. 387,* and the Morrill Act of 1862 created the land-grant university system.

2. Campbell, *The Farm Bureau,* 5.

3. Werum, "Sectionalism."

4. Benedict, *Farm Policies,* 57.

5. Rubinson, "Political Transformation."

6. Hurt, *Problems,* 25.

7. The Fordney-McCumber Tariff of 1922 raised tariff rates "higher than those of 1913 but not so high as the Republican tariffs of 1883 to 1909." Benedict, *Farm Policies,* 204.

8. Hurt, *Problems,* 34.

9. The Cotton Futures Act also "restricted speculation and market manipulation, and helped end fraudulent practices on the New York Cotton Exchange." Ibid., 28.

10. The "Farm Bloc" refers to a specific organization formed by representatives and senators from farm states. Over the years, the term "farm bloc" (without capital letters) has come to refer to "informal alliances of farm state lawmakers" and sometimes farm organizations. See Hansen, *Gaining Access,* 31.

11. USDA, *Agricultural Statistics, 1942,* 662, Table 736.

12. A debate exists as to whether a depression actually hit agriculture during the 1920s. For a brief discussion of this debate, see Hamilton, *From New Day,* 9–10. Interestingly, gross farm income did not fall between 1925 and 1929 even though market prices fell during this period. Although I focus here on falling prices, this farm crisis was also linked to issues such as overcapitalization and overinvestment in new equipment and land between 1914 and 1919. This left farmers particularly vulnerable even to slightly declining prices. One indicator of this is the numbers of foreclosures during the early 1920s. See Clarke, *Regulation,* 208, Figure 7.1.

13. See, for example, Daniel, *Breaking the Land;* and Hansen, *Gaining Access.*

14. USDA, *Agricultural Statistics, 1957,* 579, Table 683.

15. U.S. Census Bureau, *Statistical Abstract, 1933,* 566, Table 538.

16. Shover, *Cornbelt Rebellion,* 16. Gilbert and Howe state that "in late 1932, about half of midwestern farms were threatened by foreclosure." Gilbert and Howe, "Beyond," 209.

17. Calculated from USDA, *Agricultural Statistics, 1941,* 123, Table 155. Between 1929 and 1938, cotton carry-over averaged 6.5 million bales a year—nearly three times that of the period 1921–1925. Carry-over stock reached 9.7 million bales in 1931 before falling to 4.4 million in 1936.

18. Cotton exports accounted for 59 percent of cotton produced between 1921 and 1925. However, between 1926 and 1931, cotton exports accounted for only 56 percent of overall production, falling to just 48 percent in 1929.

19. Hamilton, *From New Day,* 11.

20. Paarlberg, "Tarnished Gold," 40.

21. Henry C. Wallace served as secretary of agriculture from 1921 until his death on October 25, 1924. Wallace did not always agree with Coolidge or Hoover about the problems farmers faced or the political solutions. After Wallace's death, President Coolidge appointed William Jardine as secretary of agriculture. Jardine was a friend of Hoover and shared the president's opposition to policies that would regulate market prices or production. See Fite, *George N. Peek,* 83, 116.

22. Cooperatives are organizations that allow farmers to pool resources to more efficiently distribute, market, and sometimes process agricultural commodities such as

grains, cotton, fruits, and vegetables. Cooperatives can also help to control the supply of agricultural commodities. See Hurt, *Problems*, 18–22; and Fite, *George N. Peek*.

23. For a detailed history of the development of Peek's proposal and its legislative journey through Congress, see Fite, *George N. Peek*.

24. Ibid., 87.

25. Hansen, *Gaining Access*, 39; and Sheingate, *Agricultural Welfare State*, 102.

26. Hurt, *Problems*, 59.

27. Fite, *George N. Peek*, 85.

28. Ibid., 65.

29. Porter, "Pluralist Perspective."

30. Fite, *George N. Peek*, 77–84, 91.

31. U.S. Congress, *Congressional Record* (1924), 10340–10341.

32. Fite, *George N. Peek*, 93.

33. The McNary-Haugen bill seemed headed for a tie vote in the Senate, which would have meant that Coolidge's vice president, Charles Dawes, would cast the deciding vote. Ibid., 165.

34. U.S. Congress, *Congressional Record* (1926), 9862–9863, 11872.

35. Fite, *George N. Peek*, 173.

36. U.S. Congress, *Congressional Record* (1927), 3518, 4098–4099.

37. U.S. Congress, *Congressional Record* (1928), 6283, 8647.

38. Outright opposition declined markedly: of twenty-two southern Democratic senators, eleven voted against the McNary-Haugen bill in 1926, nine voted against it in 1927, but only three did so in 1928.

39. For Coolidge's veto message in 1928, see U.S. Congress, *Congressional Record* (1928), 9524–9527. Senate reaction to the president's message follows immediately after Coolidge's veto message. For the vote to override Coolidge's veto, see ibid., 9879–9880. The vote was fifty to thirty-one, well short of the necessary sixty-four votes to attain a two-thirds majority.

40. Again, the Coolidge administration's position against the McNary-Haugen bill tended to reflect the interests of grain traders, millers, and the U.S. Chamber of Commerce—all of whom were well-connected to the Republican Party. See Fite, *George N. Peek*, 77–84, 91.

41. Porter, "Pluralist Perspective," 390.

42. After Coolidge's 1928 veto of the McNary-Haugen bill, Lowden "immediately . . . reiterated his devotion to surplus-control legislation." Fite, *George N. Peek*, 203.

43. Hamilton, *From New Day*, 41.

44. Porter, "Pluralist Perspective," 391.

45. Fite, *George N. Peek*, 216.

46. Ibid., 218–219.

47. Quoted in Hamilton, *From New Day*, 42.

48. The reaction of farm leaders, who still believed such proposals to be sorely deficient, was to let the new president try his policy. Fite, *George N. Peek*, 224.

49. Ibid., 224.

50. Hamilton, *From New Day*, 53.

51. Ibid., 63.

52. Hurt, *Problems*, 62.

53. Fite, *George N. Peek*, 227; and Hurt, *Problems*, 63.

54. Hamilton, *From New Day*, 122–123.

55. If some farmers reduced production, then market prices would increase. The biggest beneficiaries of higher prices, however, would be those farmers who did not reduce production because they would receive higher prices for their full crop. Thus, the social organization of agriculture made "cheating" the rational action. Hoover failed to grasp the inadequacy of voluntary reductions in production.

56. Hamilton, *From New Day*, 121–122. The Farm Board canceled this deal with Germany under the pressure of cotton exporters.

57. Hurt, *Problems*, 62.

58. Hamilton, *From New Day*, 122.

59. Hoover had already created southern antagonism by nominating Carl Williams as the cotton representative on the Farm Board. Williams was the founder of the Oklahoma Cotton Growers Cooperative and had been a livestock, corn, and wheat farmer in Colorado. Because he was neither a cotton farmer nor from the South (by most definitions), many southern cotton producers felt particularly snubbed by Hoover. See Snyder, *Cotton Crisis*, 20.

60. Ibid., 27.

61. Fite, *George N. Peek*, 230–233.

62. Snyder, *Cotton Crisis*, 24.

63. Regarding cotton production, the United States was in a strong position to influence world cotton production and prices as between 1925 and 1931, it accounted for 57 percent of world cotton production.

64. Snyder, *Cotton Crisis*, 118.

65. Hansen, *Gaining Access*, 70.

66. Long rescinded Louisiana's holiday legislation; legislation in other states (for example, Mississippi and South Carolina) expired because of sunset clauses that rested on other southern states passing reduction laws (which did not happen); and state courts declared Texas's reduction legislation unconstitutional. Snyder, *Cotton Crisis*, 126.

67. Hansen, *Gaining Access*, 64–67.

68. Snyder, *Cotton Crisis*, 132.

## Chapter 3. Winning Supply Management

1. Calculated from tables in Hosen, *Great Depression*, 257, 258, 268, 270.

2. *Chicago Daily Tribune*, "U.S. to Kill More Bonus Pigs," 35.

3. *New York Times*, "Hog Plan Dooms 5,000,000 Animals," 22.

4. *Chicago Daily Tribune*, "U.S. to Kill More Bonus Pigs," 35.

5. *Chicago Daily Tribune*, "Butter—Millions of Pounds," 11.

6. *Chicago Daily Tribune*, "Packers Pile Up Fertilizer," 32. On the number of pigs killed, see *Chicago Daily Tribune*, "Farmers Say," 25. Most criticism aimed at the fed-

eral government for its pig purchase program focused on the withholding of millions of young pigs from the market during a period of hunger, but outrage was also expressed at the mass slaughter of animals to correct for an economic mistake. In response to those opposed to the slaughter of baby pigs, Secretary of Agriculture Henry A. Wallace stated: "I suppose it is a marvelous tribute to the humanitarian instincts of the American people that they sympathize more with little pigs which are killed than with full-grown hogs. Some people may object to killing pigs at any age. Perhaps they think that farmers should run a sort of old-folks home for hogs and keep them around indefinitely as barnyard pets." Quoted in Leuchtenburg, *Franklin D. Roosevelt*, 73. Despite Wallace's quip, we should recognize that millions of young pigs and pregnant sows were sacrificed to raise prices for farmers and meatpackers. This same tragedy and commodification of pigs and other "livestock" continues today. As later chapters demonstrate, expanding livestock production, and hence the exploitation and slaughter of animals, was one part of the solution to the problem of surplus grains. Not only did this solution mean tougher times for animals in the form of greater numbers slaughtered and worsened living conditions, but it also meant more dangerous conditions for slaughterhouse workers and less healthy diets for consumers. See Nibert, *Animal Rights;* and Winders and Nibert, "Consuming." In a market economy, the central concern is not with the morality or ethics of consuming animals, the health of workers, or even the health of consumers; the primary concern is profitability.

7. *Chicago Daily Tribune,* "U.S. Will Spend," 4.

8. Hurt, *Problems,* 77.

9. *Chicago Daily Tribune,* "Little Pigs Go to Market," 24.

10. Cheever, *House of Morrell,* 221. John Morrell & Co., a major meatpacking company, "destroyed" 86,785 pigs and slaughtered 20,312 pigs for food. Ibid., 221.

11. *Chicago Daily Tribune,* "Butter—Millions of Pounds," 11.

12. *Chicago Daily Tribune,* "Packers Pile Up Fertilizer," 32.

13. Tesche, "Stabilize or Agonize," H3. John Steinbeck writes of "mountains of oranges slop[ping] down to a putrefying ooze" after being doused with kerosene to dispose of excess supply. Steinbeck, *Grapes of Wrath,* 385. One source reported the "dumping of large quantities of vegetables into the ocean." *Los Angeles Times,* "California Vegetables," 18.

14. *New York Times,* "$246,000,000 Rise Given to Cotton," 12.

15. Ibid.

16. Hurt, *Problems,* 77.

17. Quoted in Choate, *Disputed Ground,* 134. Secretary Wallace's response to such criticisms was candidly insightful: "The people who raise the cry about the last hungry Chinamen are not really criticizing the farmers or the AAA, but the profit system." Quoted in Schlesinger, *Coming of the New Deal,* 63.

18. *Chicago Tribune,* "Butter—Millions of Pounds," 11.

19. For example, "The butter purchasing program . . . is designed to cut into an existing surplus estimated at about 70,000,000 pounds." *Chicago Daily Tribune,* "Butter and Beef," 26.

20. The "alphabet programs" were often known by their bureaucratic administra-

tions: the Agricultural Adjustment Administration, National Recovery Administration (NRA), Security and Exchange Commission (SEC), Works Progress Administration (WPA), Civilian Conservation Corps (CCC), and Federal Depository Insurance Corporation (FDIC), among many others.

21. Hallberg, *Policy for American Agriculture*, 345.

22. Since the AAA was not enacted until March of 1933, the acreage restrictions could have little immediate effect on many agricultural commodities, particularly wheat and cotton, because the planting season had already passed. Therefore, the AAA paid farmers in the South to plow under portions of their cotton crop to reduce production.

23. Hansen, *Gaining Access*, 78; and Murphy, "The New Deal," 165.

24. Conrad, *Forgotten Farmers*, 23.

25. Among others, see Campbell, *Farm Bureau;* Conrad, *Forgotten Farmers;* Domhoff, *State Autonomy;* Finegold, "From Agrarianism"; Finegold and Skocpol, *State and Party;* Gilbert and Howe, "Beyond"; and McConnell, *Decline of Agrarian.*

26. Fite states that "it was only a short step away from Peek's equalization fee to the processing tax incorporated in the AAA." Fite, *George N. Peek*, 223.

27. Campbell, *Farm Bureau*, 61–62.

28. Conrad, *Forgotten Farmers*, 21.

29. Ibid., 21; and Murphy, "The New Deal," 160.

30. In addition, Senator McNary (R-OR) served as the Senate's minority leader and favored government support for farmers.

31. See Katznelson, *When Affirmative;* and Winders, "Maintaining."

32. Furthermore, legislation, such as antilynching bills, that directly aimed to reshape southern race relations often did not receive serious consideration. Katznelson, Geiger, and Kryder, "Limiting Liberalism."

33. Weller, *Joe T. Robinson*, 140–145. Of course, support for the AAA was unanimous among neither southern Democrats nor southern landowners. For instance, "Cotton Ed" Smith (D-SC) chaired the Senate Agriculture Committee for a time during the New Deal but opposed the original AAA. Hansen, *Gaining Access*, 87.

34. Calculated from U.S. Congress, *Congressional Record* (1933), 3121.

35. Nelson, *King Cotton's.*

36. Schlesinger, *Coming of the New Deal*, 61.

37. Ibid., 61. Notably, Jesse Jones was a Texas banker who "converted the RFC into a vastly different organization from what it had been under Hoover." Leuchtenburg, *Franklin D. Roosevelt*, 71. The RFC was created in 1932 under Hoover and made loans to support business and farmers.

38. Kirby, "Transformation," 263–264.

39. Conrad, *Forgotten Farmers*, 43.

40. Corn was also an important agricultural commodity in the South, with about as many southern acres devoted to corn production as to cotton production. Behind cotton and tobacco, corn was the most valuable southern crop in the 1930s. Winders, "Welcome," 255, Table 2.3, 274, Figure 2.1.

41. Conrad, *Forgotten Farmers*, 52–53; and Gilbert and Howe, "Beyond," 212–213.

42. Hansen, *Gaining Access*, 87.

43. USDA, *Agricultural Statistics, 1957,* 597, Table 683. The improved economic health of agriculture helped to bolster the entire economy: "Government payments to farmers benefited merchants and mail order houses. Even the staunchly conservative Sewell Avery, head of Montgomery Ward, conceded that the AAA had been the single greatest cause in the improvement of Ward's position." Leuchtenburg, *Franklin D. Roosevelt,* 77. Nonetheless, farm income in 1936 was still below what it was in 1929. Some scholars argue that the U.S. state was too weak to produce an effective solution to the depression. See, for example, Finegold and Skocpol, *State and Party.* We need to acknowledge, however, that this was a world economic depression that could not be solved by policy changes within one nation. This fact made many New Deal policies relatively ineffective and played a role in the limitations of the AAA.

44. Jean Choate offers an important history of seven farm organizations that opposed Roosevelt's agricultural policy. Choate, *Disputed Ground.*

45. A cost-of-production formula would be based on the cost of farm inputs including the price of land, seed, machinery, fertilizer, and so on.

46. Ibid., Chapter 2; and Conrad, *Forgotten Farmers,* 28.

47. Choate, *Disputed Ground,* 134.

48. Ibid., 89.

49. *New York Times,* "6,000,000 Total," 25.

50. For example, Choate notes that the leaders of the Macomb (Illinois) Corn Belt Liberty League received letters of support "from farmers in Iowa, Missouri, Indiana, Ohio, Minnesota and Wisconsin"—all of which are in the Corn Belt, as I have defined it. Choate, *Disputed Ground,* 168. Nonetheless, a few similar organizations, such as the Grain Belt Liberty League, emerged in the Wheat Belt. In addition, some southern Democrats, planters, and farmers opposed the expansion of the federal government in agriculture through the AAA, but few organizations emerged in the South in opposition to price supports or production controls. Still, as I discuss shortly, southern Democrats and planters did oppose particular elements of the AAA.

51. Choate, *Disputed Ground,* 84, 100–102.

52. Gilbert and Howe examine three policy themes in the AAA: supply management (based on production controls), land-use planning (based in the Bureau of Agricultural Economics), and rural social reform (for example, addressing rural inequality). Gilbert and Howe, "Beyond," 212. My analysis here concentrates on supply management and social reform, which I refer to as rural reform. For a thorough discussion of land-use planning, see Gilbert and Howe, "Beyond"; or Gilbert, "Eastern Urban."

53. Conrad, *Forgotten Farmers,* 52.

54. Gilbert, "Eastern Urban."

55. Grubbs, *Cry from the Cotton,* 34. Grubbs notes that Chester Davis "in matters affecting the cotton reduction program . . . consulted, naturally enough, with men who 'knew' the South: men like the county agents. Officials, in other words, who represented the planters." Ibid., 33.

56. Gilbert and Howe, "Beyond," 212–213.

57. Baldwin, *Poverty and Politics,* 81.

58. Gilbert and Howe, "Beyond," 213.

59. Baldwin, *Poverty and Politics*, 82.

60. Gilbert, "Eastern Urban," 179.

61. U.S. House, "Agricultural Adjustment Program," 282–283.

62. Ibid., 283, 290–291.

63. For example, see U.S. Senate, "Agricultural Adjustment Relief," 241–244. Much disagreement existed between farmers, farm organizations, and Congress, on the one hand, and agricultural processors, on the other hand. Hansen notes the House Agriculture Committee's "ecumenical contempt" for agricultural processors and traders. Hansen, *Gaining Access*, 94.

64. Hoover appointed Charles Hughes Chief Justice in 1930, and he also appointed Benjamin Cardozo and Owen Roberts to the Court in 1932 and 1930, respectively. President Coolidge appointed Harlan Stone in 1925. President Harding appointed George Sutherland and Pierce Butler in 1922 and 1923, respectively. One appointee to the Court by Republican president Howard Taft remained: Willis Van Devanter, who joined the Court in 1911. Finally, two appointees by Democratic president Woodrow Wilson remained on the Court in 1936: James McReynolds and Louis Brandeis, who joined the Court in 1914 and 1916, respectively.

65. Black, *Franklin Delano Roosevelt*, 377.

66. See, for example, *Chicago Daily Tribune*, "Process Taxes," 2.

67. Murphy, "The New Deal," 160–161.

68. This would all change beginning in the 1960s. As Chapter 6 details, supply management policy, particularly export subsidy programs, slowly brought important segments of agribusiness (that is, grain traders and processors) into the policy formation process.

69. Approximately fifty meatpacking companies filed lawsuits against the AAA. Cheever, *House of Morrell*, 223.

70. Hoosac Mills was bankrupt at the time of the Supreme Court hearing. Benedict, *Farm Policies*, 348.

71. Before its hearing in front of the Supreme Court, a district court found the processing tax in the AAA to be valid and ordered that Hoosac Mills pay it. Upon appeal, however, a circuit court of appeals reversed the order.

72. Roberts, "Opinion of the Court," 61.

73. Ibid., 59.

74. Justice Roberts dismissed using the commerce clause as justification for the regulation of production under the AAA: "the act under review does not purport to regulate transactions in interstate or foreign commerce." Ibid., 63. Roberts's majority opinion also refused to consider the amendments to the AAA after the Court ruled the NIRA unconstitutional, stating that the case concerned only the AAA as originally passed and when the suit was filed.

75. Ibid., 69.

76. Ibid., 71–72.

77. Ibid., 75. Hurt states, "The Court did not rule specifically that federal regula-

tion of the agricultural economy was unconstitutional, only that Congress could not do so under the taxing power granted by the Constitution." Hurt, *Problems*, 80–81.

78. Schlesinger, *Politics of Upheaval*, 473.

79. Stone, "Dissenting Opinion," 81.

80. Black, *Franklin Delano Roosevelt*, 377; and Schlesinger, *Politics of Upheaval*, 470. Butler was also "an associate of Frederick H. Prince, one of the nation's greatest financiers and a substantial shareholder in the largest meatpacking businesses, Swift and Armour." Black, *Franklin Delano Roosevelt*, 377.

81. Calculated from U.S. Congress, *Congressional Record* (1938), 1881–1882.

82. Hooks, "From an Autonomous," 34.

83. Benedict, *Farm Policies*, 415; and Hansen, *Gaining Access*, 112. The Steagall Amendment, as it is commonly called, was attached to a bill (*55 Stat. 498*) in July 1941 to continue the CCC. Benedict, *Farm Policies*, 415. This legislation is PL 77-144. Becker, "Farm Commodity," 2.

84. Becker, "Farm Commodity." These fourteen commodities came to be known as the "Steagall commodities" and held the status of "nonbasic" commodities. Thus, under supply management policy, the Steagall commodities were not seen as having equal status relative to the basic commodities.

85. Tweeten, *Foundations*, 306.

86. Wilcox, *The Farmer*, 246.

87. McConnell, *Decline of Agrarian*, 111.

88. Hurt, *Problems*, 98.

89. Wilcox, *The Farmer*, 51.

90. Cotton production averaged 13.1 million bales between 1920 and 1929, and 13.2 million bales between 1930 and 1939. Between 1935 and 1940, it averaged 13.1 million bales. Cotton production failed to reach 13 million bales in any year during the war.

91. Bensel, *Sectionalism*, 192.

92. Baker, *Wartime Food*, 134.

93. Wilcox, *The Farmer*, 64.

94. In 1942, 1943, and 1944, the carry-over cotton (12.8, 11.4, and 12.2 million bales, respectively) was larger than the amount produced in those years (10.6, 10.6, and 10.7 million bales, respectively).

95. The war effort called for longer staple length cotton "partly because of army specifications," but "the annual carryover from year to year became increasingly a stock of short staple length cotton and of inferior grades." Thus, the carry-over stock was less in demand. Nonetheless, the short staple length cotton tended to be grown in certain geographic areas that could have been shifted to different agricultural production to reduce the cotton surplus. Wilcox, *The Farmer*, 64, see also 65–67.

96. Schapsmeier and Schapsmeier, "Farm Policy," 361.

97. Benedict, *Farm Policies*, 405, 427n., 445; and McConnell, *Decline of Agrarian*, 110, 122.

98. Benedict writes of Marvin Jones, "His leadership in the War Food Administration was not strong, and he tended to concur with the views of Congress and the farm

organizations. He did not see eye to eye with the OPA administrators." When the OPA attempted to roll back some agricultural prices, Jones fought the move. Benedict, *Farm Policies*, 427, n.76.

99. Hooks, "From an Autonomous," 38.

100. Gilbert and Howe, "Beyond," 218. Gilbert writes, "An anti–New Deal Congress, aided by large-farm organizations and interdepartmental enemies, gutted the BAE and FSA in 1942 and 1943, and later finished off both agencies." Gilbert, "Eastern Urban," 180.

101. Winders, "Maintaining," 397, Table 2. Using constant dollars to control for inflation (and deflation), the increase is even larger: from $1,219 in 1938, to $7,027 in 1952.

102. Clarke, *Regulation*, 207.

103. Marx and Engels, *Communist Manifesto*, 29.

## Chapter 4. Shifting Agricultural Coalitions

Epigraph. Allan Kline quotation from U.S. House, "General Farm Program (1949)," 434; and Theodore Steed quotation from ibid., 394.

1. This was not always the case. From 1860 to 1900, the Republican Party advocated government intervention in various facets of the economy, most notably tariffs and trade protections for industry. By contrast, the Democratic Party promoted free trade and battled against trade barriers. Thus, Democrats were more "promarket" in this regard. In the early 1900s, a faction of the Republican Party favored "progressive" government policies that promoted government regulation of business, markets, and labor. Thus, the relationship between the market economy and political parties has been fluid over time. Furthermore, partisan differences should be viewed as disagreements over the *type* of government intervention into the economy. This is all evident in agricultural policy.

2. By the late 1960s, a common Republican campaign theme was to "get government off our backs." Social policies were a frequent target of Republicans: Nixon sharply criticized the Great Society programs in his 1968 presidential campaign, and Reagan made significant budget cuts for many social programs. Yet the partisan divide was at times a façade: "Contrary to the popular perception of Nixon as a tough-minded conservative, his social policy record was one of almost unparalleled willingness to support new federal spending and regulation." Hacker, *Divided Welfare*, 254.

3. Additionally, some of the most ardent opposition to social support policies (for example, "welfare") came from rural Democrats and Republicans. Thus, support for supply management policy was not usually based on a general antimarket ideology.

4. U.S. House, "Long Range," 2736.

5. Hansen, *Gaining Access*, 127.

6. Benson, *Freedom to Farm*, 23.

7. Peterson, *Agricultural Exports*.

8. Hadwiger and Talbot, *Pressures and Protests*. In a 1958 referendum, corn farmers rejected production controls and the parity price formula in favor of a more market-

oriented policy "to discontinue . . . acreage allotments . . . and receive supports at 90 percent of the average farm price for the preceding 3 years." Rasmussen and Baker, "Price-Support," 21.

9. Rasmussen and Baker, "Price-Support."

10. Congressional Quarterly, *Congressional Quarterly* (1973), 1549.

11. Gilmore, *Poor Harvest*, 76.

12. Constance, Gilles, and Heffernan, "Agrarian Policies," 39.

13. Hansen, *Gaining Access*, 109.

14. Benedict, *Farm Policies*, 484.

15. Dean, *Opportunity Lost*, 137.

16. Benedict, *Farm Policies*, 485; and Hurt, *Problems*, 108.

17. Dean, *Opportunity Lost*, 138.

18. Ibid., 140. "A 'unit' was defined as the equivalent of 10 bushels of corn, about 8 bushels of wheat or about 50 pounds of cotton." Benedict, *Farm Policies*, 487.

19. Jim Patton, president of the NFU, was friends with Secretary Brannan; both were from Colorado and became friends when Brannan had "directed the regional office of the Farm Security Administration." Hansen, *Gaining Access*, 120, n.19; see also Dean, *Opportunity Lost*, 129–130.

20. Dean, *Opportunity Lost*, 130.

21. Benedict, *Farm Policies*, 488–489.

22. Farmers in the South relied more heavily on government payments than did farmers in the Corn or Wheat Belts. In 1949, for example, southern farmers received $65.1 million in government payments, whereas farmers in the Corn and Wheat Belts received $39.5 million and $37.3 million, respectively. Calculated from U.S. Census Bureau, *Statistical Abstract* (1951), 579, table 679.

23. Senator Olin Johnston (D-SC) introduced bill S. 1671; Representative Harold Cooley (D-NC) introduced bill H.R. 4753; Representative Stephen Pace (D-GA) introduced bill H.R. 5345; and Representative Albert A. Gore (D-TN) introduced H.R. 5617. Dean, *Opportunity Lost*, 173, 176–178. In addition, Senator Richard B. Russell (D-GA) had introduced bill S. 367 before Brannan even presented his proposal. Ibid., 173, n.6. The Pace bill incorporated some elements of the Brannan Plan.

24. Ibid., 177.

25. Hansen, *Gaining Access*, 123.

26. U.S. House, "General Farm Program (1949)," 433.

27. Alternatively, flexible price supports could fluctuate inversely with market prices. In this situation, price support levels would be reduced as market prices rose, making supports almost irrelevant in a strong market. But support levels would increase as market prices fell, thereby providing a safety net if prices collapsed. The Farm Bureau was not advocating flexible price supports of this type.

28. U.S. House, "General Farm Program (1949)," 433.

29. Ibid., 433, 435, 440.

30. Ibid., 438.

31. U.S. House, "Long Range," 2733.

32. Ibid., 2747.

33. Ibid., 2731.

34. U.S. House, "General Farm Program (1949)," 361.

35. In fact, Patton and the NFU advocated for the Brannan Plan. See Dean, *Opportunity Lost*.

36. U.S. Senate, "Farm Price Supports," 95.

37. Ibid., 98.

38. U.S. House, "Long Range," 4217.

39. Ibid., 3277.

40. U.S. House, "General Farm Program (1949), 445–446.

41. Ibid., 487–488.

42. Ibid., 506. By contrast, Hassil Schenck, president of the Indiana Farm Bureau in the Corn Belt, stated: "I wholeheartedly endorse the statement presented by President Kline. . . . [There] are a few things that I think are . . . much more important than . . . to give a farmer 100 percent of parity." Ibid., 452.

43. Hansen, *Gaining Access*, 130–131, 168; and Schapsmeier and Schapsmeier, "Farm Policy," 368.

44. Ten of the eleven Wheat Belt senators who voted in favor of the Agricultural Act of 1949, which maintained high levels of price supports, were Republicans. In fact, more than half of all Republican senators voted for this act.

45. I explain how support in Senate and House votes is calculated in the Appendix.

46. Quoted from Allan Kline's testimony. U.S. House, "General Farm Program (1949), 438.

47. Matusow, *Farm Policies*, 136.

48. Ibid., 136; and U.S. House, "Long Range," 2731.

49. Gilmore, *Poor Harvest;* and U.S. House, "Long Range," 4220.

50. See, for example, U.S. House, "General Farm Program (1949)," 491–497.

51. Bonnen, Browne, and Schweikhardt, "Further Observations," 138.

52. U.S. House, "General Farm Program (1949)," 493.

53. Hardin, "The Republican."

54. Half of the thirty members of the House Committee on Agriculture were from the South or Wheat Belt, with southern representatives accounting for more than a third of the committee.

55. Hansen (*Gaining Access*) argues that the Farm Bureau lost access to the policy formation process in Congress. Yet his analysis seems to overlook the fact that this loss of access coincided with the Farm Bureau adopting the policy preferences of the corn segment, which clashed with the interests of the cotton and wheat segments, both of which were amply represented on the agriculture committees of the House and Senate.

56. Cochrane and Ryan, *American Farm*, 229; and Hallberg, *Policy for American Agriculture*, 48.

57. Rasmussen and Baker, "Price-Support," 22.

58. Congressional Quarterly, *Congressional Quarterly* (1962), 1089. See also, Hadwiger and Talbot, *Pressures and Protests*.

59. Congressional Quarterly, *Congressional Quarterly* (1962), 1090. This reflects the

split in the South, which was in the midst of shifting from cotton to soybean production.

60. Hansen, *Gaining Access,* 148.

61. Cochrane and Ryan, *American Farm,* 220.

62. On the NFU's support, see U.S. Senate, "Wheat Programs," 105–108. For a detailed discussion of the wheat referendum, see Hadwiger and Talbot, *Pressures and Protests.*

63. U.S. House, "Wheat Legislation," 134.

64. On the NFU, see U.S. Senate, "Wheat Programs," 106. On the Farm Bureau, see ibid., 120–140.

65. See Friedmann, "Political Economy (1993)"; and Peterson, *Agricultural Exports.*

66. U.S. House, "Extension of Public," 115.

67. Friedmann, "Political Economy (1993)."

68. For example, see U.S. Senate, "Wheat Programs," 106. PL 480 also strength-ened agribusiness corporations (for example, Cargill, Continental, and Archer Daniels Midland) by infusing them with millions of dollars and bringing them into the policy formation process. Portions of agribusiness opposed supply management policies and gained increasing influence over agricultural policy during the 1960s and 1970s. Fried-mann, "Political Economy (1993)"; Gilmore, *Poor Harvest;* Morgan, *Merchants of Grain;* and Winders, "Welcome."

69. Winders, "Welcome," 255, Table 2.3.

70. Hansen, *Gaining Access,* 148.

71. Hallberg, *Policy for American Agriculture,* 41.

72. Cochrane and Ryan, *American Farm,* 172.

73. For example, see Bonnen, Browne, and Schweikhardt, "Further Observations"; Browne, *Cultivating Congress,* 23; Hansen, *Gaining Access;* Lyons and Taylor, "Farm Politics"; and Sheingate, *Agricultural Welfare State.*

74. Hansen, *Gaining Access,* 193; and Lyons and Taylor, "Farm Politics," 137.

75. Barton, "Coalition-Building."

76. Even Barton's own analysis offers little indication that a rural-urban coalition led to the passage of the 1973 farm bill. Ibid., 158–159.

77. In contrast to other legislation, I focus on the bill's passage in the House rather than the Senate for two reasons. First, Barton and others focus on the House vote, so it is appropriate to examine their claims using the same data. Second, the Senate passed this bill by a vote of 78 to 9. Such a margin yields fewer insights than does the House vote, which was 226 to 182.

78. Congressional Quarterly, *Congressional Quarterly* (1973), 2021–2022.

79. Ibid., 2314.

80. U.S. House, "General Farm Program (1973)," 41.

81. Congressional Quarterly, *Congressional Quarterly* (1973), 2314.

82. Morgan, *Merchants;* and U.S. House, "General Farm Program (1973)," 42.

83. Congressional Quarterly, *Congressional Quarterly* (1973)," 1149; and U.S. House, "General Farm Program (1973)," 39–44.

84. U.S. House, "General Farm Program (1973)," 121.

85. Ibid., 154.

86. Congressional Quarterly, *Congressional Quarterly* (1973), 2219, 2314–2315.

87. Gilmore, *Poor Harvest*, 117, Table 7.2.

88. On high wheat prices, see U.S. House, "General Farm Program (1973)," 168. On the perceived necessity of price supports, see Lyons and Taylor, "Farm Politics," 129; and Morgan, *Merchants*, 215.

89. On the wheat segment's view, see U.S. House, "General Farm Program (1973)," 130.

90. Mann, "Rise of Wage Labor," 239.

91. These figures are calculated from Congressional Quarterly, *Congressional Quarterly* (1973), 1147.

92. Ibid., 1153.

93. Winders, "Welcome," 255, Table 2.3.

94. For example, Bonnen, Browne, and Schweikhardt, "Further Observations"; and Hansen, *Gaining Access*.

95. Congressional Quarterly, *Congressional Quarterly* (1973), 2010.

96. Five Wheat Belt states—Colorado, Kansas, Nebraska, North Dakota, and South Dakota (the core states of the Wheat Belt)—went for the Republican candidate in almost every presidential election between 1940 and 1972. And at least half of the Senate delegation from the Wheat Belt was Republican during each year in which major agricultural legislation was passed after 1945.

97. For example, almost every senator from the Wheat Belt who voted for the Agricultural Act of 1949 was Republican, and they teamed with the all-Democratic delegation from the South.

## Chapter 5. The Decline of the South

Epigraph. Norman Thomas quotation from Kester, *Revolt*, 85.

1. Chaney was black and from Mississippi, and Schwerner and Goodman were both white and native New Yorkers. For a detailed history of this tragedy, see Cagin and Dray, *We Are Not Afraid*.

2. For a summary of such incidents during Freedom Summer, see McAdam, *Freedom Summer*, 257–282.

3. Educating black children per se was not necessarily an affront to Jim Crow. But the substance taught in Freedom Schools, subjects such as black history and even community organizing, certainly was. Even the housing conditions during Freedom Summer challenged southern race relations: many white volunteers stayed in the homes of local blacks.

4. Only 34 percent of Mississippi's voting-age population voted in the 1964 presidential election. The national voter turnout rate was about 62 percent. U.S. Census Bureau, *Historical Statistics*, 1071–1072, Series Y 27–78.

5. McAdam, *Freedom Summer*, 81.

6. Carson, *In Struggle*, 82.

7. Moore, *Social Origins;* and Winders, "Maintaining."

8. The term "class relations" refers to how a class or class segment relates to other classes, the market economy, the state, or other social institutions. In part, class relations refers to the relations a class has because of its position in a particular class structure. Thinking about these relations in terms of politics and economics, as I have done here, helps to illuminate how class relations change.

9. Key, *Southern Politics;* Werum, "Sectionalism"; and Winders, "Roller Coaster." Merle Prunty defines plantations as "landholdings of more than 260 acres." Prunty, "The Renaissance," 461. About 5–6 percent of southern farms were plantations from 1930 to 1940. Winders, "Welcome," 256. Oscar Johnston headed one of the largest plantations in the world, which was in Mississippi and covered thirty-eight thousand acres. Nelson, *King Cotton's.*

10. Bloom, *Class, Race;* Royce, *Origins of Southern;* and Schwartz, *Radical Protest.*

11. Prunty, "The Renaissance," 474.

12. Ibid., 468.

13. For a detailed discussion of tenancy, see Prunty, "The Renaissance"; Schwartz, *Radical Protest;* and Woofter et al., *Landlord and Tenant.*

14. Johnson, Embree, and Alexander, *Collapse of Cotton,* 6.

15. Schwartz, *Radical Protest,* 20.

16. Wright, *Old South,* 93. With such greater mobility of labor and termination of contracts, southern tenancy in the twentieth century was distinct from the social property relations of noncapitalist landlord-tenant relations found in feudal Europe or even in the U.S. South in the late 1800s. After the defeat of populism in the 1890s, southern planters reshaped property relations to gain more control over the labor process. Bloom, *Class, Race;* and Wright, *Old South.* Still, the mobility of tenants and croppers was sometimes restricted, and their debt often followed them even when they moved.

17. Woofter et al., *Landlord and Tenant,* 11. Donald Grubbs retells a story that some tenant farmers used to find some wry humor in the crop-lien system: a teacher asked her brightest pupil, "If the landlord lends you twenty dollars, and you pay him back five dollars a month, how much will you still owe him after three months?" "Twenty dollars," the student replied. "You don't understand arithmetic," said the teacher. "You don't understand our landlord!" retorted the student. Grubbs, *Cry from the Cotton,* 9–10.

18. Grubbs, *Cry from the Cotton,* 11.

19. Educational expenditures for blacks students were significantly below that spent on white students. See Bloom, *Class, Race,* 53–56; Grubbs, *Cry from the Cotton,* 11; and Werum, "Sectionalism."

20. Alston and Ferrie, *Southern Paternalism.*

21. Pfeffer, "Social Origins." Importantly, Edward Royce demonstrates that neither planters nor freed blacks favored sharecropping as a replacement for slavery: "As a result of the capacity of each to obstruct the most preferred alternatives of the other, planters and freedpeople found themselves bound together in the unhappy compromise of southern sharecropping." Royce, *Origins of Southern,* 220.

22. USDA, *Statistics on Cotton,* 218.

23. Bloom, *Class, Race;* and Winders, "Roller Coaster," 847–849.

24. Winders, "Roller Coaster," 858 n.10.

25. Key, *Southern Politics;* and Werum, "Sectionalism."

26. Nationally, the number of farms fell from 6.5 million in 1930 to 4 million in 1960 and to 2.8 million in 1975. As the number of farms declined, the average size of farms increased.

27. Daniel, *Breaking the Land;* Kirby, "Transformation."

28. USDA, *Agricultural Statistics, 1938,* 432, Table 555.

29. Woofter et al., *Landlord and Tenant,* 66, Table 24.

30. Fite, *Cotton Fields.* However, the availability of relief was curtailed when farm labor was needed. For example, in Mississippi many "planters opposed [federal relief] to agricultural laborers during the cotton season because such payments undermined their ability to pay low wages." Southworth, "Aid to Sharecroppers," 62.

31. Gilbert and Howe, "Beyond," 212; and Grubbs, *Cry from the Cotton,* 22–26.

32. Winders, "Welcome," 281, Figure 2.14.

33. Calculated from U.S. Census Bureau, *Census of Agriculture, 1959.* After 1959, the *Census of Agriculture* stops counting sharecroppers and instead collapses sharecroppers into the larger category of share-tenants. I estimated the number of sharecroppers for 1964 by assuming that the proportion of sharecroppers to share-tenants remained the same as in 1959, which is a conservative assumption.

34. Kirby, "Transformation," 268–272.

35. Ibid., 272.

36. Among many others, see Fite, *Cotton Fields;* Mann, "Rise of Wage Labor"; and Prunty, "The Renaissance."

37. Aiken, *Cotton Plantation,* 102.

38. Musoke, "Mechanizing Cotton," 348.

39. USDA, *Statistics on Cotton,* 218.

40. Fornari, "Big Change."

41. Winders, "Welcome," 255, Table 2.3.

42. The first wave of blacks and whites leaving the South came during World War I and continued through the 1920s. Nonetheless, there is little question that the effects of the AAA and the depression facilitated the continuation of this exodus from the South. A second wave peaked during World War II, but significant numbers of blacks continued leaving the South through 1960. Flamming, *Bound.*

43. Calculated from U.S. Census Bureau, *Statistical Abstract* (1940), 14–15, Table 17; and U.S. Census Bureau, *Statistical Abstract* (1965), 26, Table 23. Again, by contrast, 50 percent of all blacks lived in the eleven southern states in 1960. So the gap closed considerably during this period.

44. Price, *Changing Characteristics,* 11, Table I-3.

45. U.S. Census Bureau, *Statistical Abstract* (1940), 22–26, Table 24; and U.S. Census Bureau, *Statistical Abstract* (1965), 19–20, Table 14.

46. While I focus on "push" factors in explaining migration out of the rural South, a number of factors also "pulled" blacks out of the rural South between the mid-1920s and 1960. In particular, new opportunities "pulled" blacks as the South industrialized

and northern industries needed workers during World War II. See Piven and Cloward, *Poor People's;* and Wright, *Old South.*

47. U.S. Census Bureau, *Statistical Abstract* (1940), 22–26, Table 24; and U.S. Census Bureau, *Statistical Abstract* (1965), 19–20, Table 14.

48. Before the New Deal, black voters tended to support the Republican Party. Douglas Flamming analyzes this electoral shift in Los Angeles, where blacks rose from 5 percent to 17 percent of the city's population between 1920 and 1960. See Flamming, *Bound,* Chapter 9.

49. Piven and Cloward, *Poor People's,* 214–215.

50. Wexler, "Sorry History," B4.

51. McAdam, *Political Process,* 89, Table 5.5.

52. See, for example, Flamming, *Bound.*

53. McAdam, *Political Process,* 94–106.

54. Morris, *The Origins,* 79.

55. McAdam, *Political Process,* 90–91.

56. Bloom, *Class, Race,* Chapter 5; and Morris, *The Origins.*

57. Calculated from Winders, "Roller Coaster," 836, Table 1.

58. In 1944, the Supreme Court ruled the white primary system in Texas to be unconstitutional in *Smith v. Allwright.*

59. Andrews, "The Impacts," 809.

60. See Bartley, *Rise of Massive;* and Bloom, *Class, Race.*

61. Piven and Cloward, *Poor People's,* 231.

62. Morris, *The Origins.*

63. Winders, "Roller Coaster," 852.

64. Cobb, *Selling of the South.*

65. If southern agriculture no longer rested on labor-intensive cotton cultivation, why then did the planters oppose changing race relations? The answer lies partly in the timing of changes in southern agriculture. Mechanizing and diversifying southern agriculture did lead to the rise of large commercial farmers in place of the planters; however, these changes occurred gradually, not overnight. In fact, these changes were relatively incomplete until the mid-1960s. During the 1950s and even the early 1960s, much of the cotton segment still rested on the old agricultural foundations—without mechanization or diversification. For instance, when Freedom Summer hit Mississippi in 1964, roughly one-third of the state's cotton crop was still harvested by hand. Winders, "Welcome," 283, Figure 5.3. When blacks and industry challenged the power of the planters from 1948 through 1964, the latter's economic interests were in flux and still contained elements of the old plantation system. The change in the political power and economic interests of the cotton segment occurred nearly simultaneously. Regardless of the precision of the timing, however, the resistance of the planters also reflects a cohort effect; that is, the adult generation of planters and other southern whites in the 1950s and 1960s found it difficult to let go of the racist culture in which they had spent their entire lives and that had defined their worldviews.

66. Bloom, *Class, Race,* 91–96; and Bartley, *Rise of Massive,* 251.

67. Jack Bloom outlines how the rural elite organized and led the massive resistance to school integration, in part by forming White Citizens' Councils in 1954. Bloom, *Class, Race,* Chapter 4; see also Bartley, *Rise of Massive,* 84–85. More generally, V. O. Key argues that whites in the Cotton Belt (that is, the planters) set the tone for all of southern politics. Key, *Southern Politics.*

68. Cobb, "Lesson," B2.

69. Bloom, *Class, Race;* and Cobb, *Selling of the South.*

70. Bloom, *Class, Race,* 116.

71. Schulman, *From Cotton Belt,* 131.

72. Of course, not all, or even most, of southern industry played this moderating role. Key southern industries, such as textiles, remained in favor of segregation. This may be partly due to the historical ties between textiles and planters. Additionally, the workforce in these industries was historically all white. Therefore, it may have been too explosive for management to be moderate on the issue of segregation.

73. Bass and De Vries, *The Transformation,* 36–37, Tables 2.3 and 2.4.

74. Key, *Southern Politics;* and Piven and Cloward, *Poor People's.*

75. In 1948, the northern Democrats and President Truman (also a Democrat) supported civil rights measures and included civil rights in the party platform, leading southerners to support Strom Thurmond, the Dixiecrat candidate for president. Frederickson, *Dixiecrat Revolt.* However, the South backed Adlai Stevenson, the Democratic nominee in 1952 and 1956, who gave less support to civil rights. Piven and Cloward, *Poor People's,* 200.

76. In addition, the Senate majority leader from 1937 to 1947 was Alben Barkley of Kentucky, one of the leading tobacco-producing states.

77. Piven and Cloward, *Poor People's.*

78. Lamis, *Two-Party,* 10, Figure 2-1.

79. Bloom, *Class, Race,* 103.

80. As I discuss further in Chapter 7, the poultry industry was especially prevalent and influential in southern agriculture during this period. Between 1950 and 1970, the number of chickens killed annually just in the South increased from 267 million to more than 2.2 billion, and the value of this industry rose from about $200 million to more than $1 billion. Furthermore, the per capita consumption of chickens nearly doubled between 1950 and 1970. Thus, the increased consumption of animals encouraged southern farmers to switch from cotton to soybeans.

81. Congressional Quarterly, *Congressional Quarterly* (1973), 2314.

## Chapter 6. Agriculture and the Changing World Economy

Epigraph. Merlin Plagge quotation from U.S. House, "Formulation, Part III," 162.

1. Cleaver, "Food, Famine," 32.

2. Rensberger, "32 Nations."

3. Rensberger, "Experts Ask," 35.

4. Robbins, "Hunger in U.S."

5. On consumer protests, see Barmash, "Butz Assails." Boyce Rensberger states,

"some casual observers have been led to conclude that this is the beginning of what will eventually envelop the planet in a continuous famine." Rensberger, "Food," 18.

6. Therefore, the carry-over stocks alone would have provided enough wheat for annual consumption. Wheat farmers could have taken a "wheat holiday," as the South had suggested for cotton in the early 1930s. This vast wheat surplus also existed in 1959 and 1961–1963.

7. Annual wheat production in the United States rose from 37 MMT in 1970 to 57 MMT in 1975.

8. World wheat production increased from 306 MMT in 1970 to 352 MMT in 1975.

9. For example, see Sharma, "Indian Agriculture," 3.

10. Rensberger, "Experts Ask," 35.

11. Toma, *Politics of Food*, 28; see also Rensberger, "Experts Ask," 35. The U.S. population, for example, increased from about 140 million to 180 million people between 1945 and 1960 — an increase of almost 25 percent in just fifteen years. This was in large part due to the "baby-boom" generation. Similarly, Australia's population increased by 84 percent between 1948 and 1978. Hefford, *Farm Policy*, 364.

12. Barmash, "Butz Assails," 49.

13. One notable example is Susan George, who makes the point that the mere commodification of food is part of the problem. When food is a commodity, its production and distribution are guided by the market and profit. There is little profit to be made in selling food to people with little money. See George, *How the Other Half*.

14. Brass, "Political Uses," 253; see also Sharma, "Indian Agriculture." Richard Gilmore adds, "The quid pro quo was to be American food in exchange for more emphasis in India on agricultural development, as well as greater hospitality for U.S. investments there, particularly in the fertilizer industry." Gilmore, *Poor Harvest*, 154. In the end, India was the largest recipient of food aid that year, receiving almost 1.2 MMT of grains. Hopkins, "Reform," 245, Table 4.

15. Gilmore, *Poor Harvest*, 155–157.

16. Maidenberg, "U.S. Ending," 1.

17. Hoffmann, "President Urges,"

18. Friedmann, "Political Economy (1982)," 248.

19. Polanyi, *Great Transformation*.

20. Friedmann, "Food Politics," 15.

21. Mintz, *Sweetness*.

22. McMichael, "Introduction," x.

23. Beverly Silver and Giovanni Arrighi make this point clearly: "although Polanyi acknowledged the existence (and sometimes even the importance) of differential power among classes and among states, he nevertheless underemphasized the role that these unequal power relations played in determining the historical trajectory he analyzed." Silver and Arrighi, "Polanyi's 'Double Movement,'" 326.

24. In the late 1800s, a "return to imperialism" occurred as trade barriers reemerged throughout the world economy, partly as a response to worldwide depressions in the 1870s and 1890s. This process involved the major European powers — Great Britain,

Germany, France, and Belgium—scrambling to colonize most of Africa as well as parts of Asia. At this time, the United States took possession of Hawaii, Puerto Rico, and the Philippines, and it briefly put Cuba in a trusteeship. Free trade continued within the colonial systems but diminished between core nations. After the First World War, however, Britain and other countries tried to reestablish free trade in the world economy. This short resurgence of the free market ended with the Great Depression, and tariff barriers increased again throughout the world economy at the end of British hegemony in the late 1920s.

25. The British food regime, with its reliance on settler colonies (and, later, settler states), also "enhanced the competitive principle in the emerging nation-state system," thereby undermining the free-trade dimension of the food regime. Friedmann and Mc-Michael, "Agriculture and the State," 98.

26. At the root of the different contours of these food regimes were varying dominant political coalitions in Britain and the United States. In part, British grain producers were excluded from the dominant coalition. The result was the passage of the Anti-Corn Law Bill in 1846, which established free trade for agriculture in Britain. By contrast, segments of agriculture, in particular cotton and wheat producers, seeking state protection from the market were at the core of the New Deal coalition in the United States. See Winders, "Vanishing."

27. In 1957, the Treaty of Rome created the European Economic Community (EEC; later European Community [EC]) with six original member nations: Belgium, France, Italy, Luxembourg, the Netherlands, and West Germany. Among other things, this treaty outlined principles for a common agricultural policy for the EC. The CAP was formally created at the Stresa Conference in July 1958. Then the six members of the EC adopted the CAP in 1960, and the policy finally went into effect in 1962. Alvarez and Navarrette, "Agrarian Policies."

28. This is not to suggest that no agricultural commodities flowed from the periphery to the core. Indeed, nations in the periphery sent agricultural cash crops—such as cocoa, coffee, and bananas—to the United States and other core nations. Nevertheless, the United States maintained import barriers even on peanuts, sugar, and other agricultural commodities often associated with the periphery. In this way, then, the U.S. food regime was certainly distinct from the British regime, which fostered free trade in such commodities.

29. McMichael, *Development*, 63.

30. Friedmann, "Family Farm," 252.

31. Dudley and Sandilands, "Side Effects."

32. McMichael, *Development*.

33. The U.S. push for free trade and economic liberalism in the world economy was tempered by the communist threat embodied in the Soviet Union. In part because the United States worried about the spread of communism to Europe and the periphery, nations could develop policies to regulate labor markets and other aspects of the economy.

34. There were some limitations on the volume of production. Marketing quotas limited the amount of program commodities that farmers could sell on the market, but

these quotas had to be approved by two-thirds of the producers of each commodity. Nonetheless, "Both the allotment and the [marketing] quota are based on a reduction of the number of acres that a farmer can use for a given crop. Within the specified acreage, he can produce as much as he desires or is able." Toma, *Politics of Food,* 8–13.

35. Other nations recognized that price supports, in particular, had the effect of increasing production, and several nations—Australia, the European Community, Japan, and many others—adopted them for this reason (that is, to increase production).

36. Although wheat production increased much more slowly than corn production, this period (1945–1970) understates the change because 1970 was the only year after 1967 that wheat production did not approach or surpass 40 MMT. Between 1967 and 1973, annual wheat production averaged 41 MMT, and annual wheat production never fell below 48 MMT after 1974.

37. Concentrated animal feeding operations keep animals confined to limit their mobility, control their environment (for example, air temperature and exposure to light), and maximize efficiency and profits. On the effects of the expanding livestock industry on animals and workers, see Nibert, *Animal Rights;* and Winders and Nibert, "Consuming."

38. Brown, *United States,* 42.

39. Matusow, *Farm Policies,* 80. Interestingly, "Britain, its dominions of Canada, Australia, New Zealand, and South Africa, and a number of colonies had turned to protectionism to retaliate against [the] Smoot-Hawley [Tariff of 1930], which denied them access to the large American market, and to combat the Great Depression." Zeiler, *Free Trade,* 8.

40. Gardner, *Sterling-Dollar,* 150–161.

41. Zeiler, *Free Trade,* 66.

42. Brown, *United States;* Gardner, *Sterling-Dollar.*

43. Britain's imperial preference system ended in 1973 when Britain joined the European Community. Britain's opposition to relinquishing its system of imperial preferences was a bargaining chip to prompt the United States to further reduce its tariff levels because "without greater access to the U.S. market, British nations could not phase out preferences." Zeiler, *Free Trade,* 35.

44. Winters, "Road to Uruguay," 1289.

45. Dam, *The GATT;* Winters, "Road to Uruguay."

46. Grant, "Against the Grain," 249.

47. Dam, *The GATT,* 21.

48. Ibid., 258.

49. U.S. House, "Trade Agreements," 253.

50. See ibid.

51. Brown, *United States;* Matusow, *Farm Policies;* and Zeiler, *Free Trade.*

52. U.S. Senate, "International Trade," 382.

53. Ibid., 474–477.

54. Ibid., 418.

55. Opposition to the ITO also came from various business organizations and industries. For example, see Zeiler, *Free Trade,* 150–157. The goal of a governing trade

organization remained unfulfilled until the World Trade Organization was created in 1994.

56. Friedmann, "Political Economy (1993)," 33.

57. Dam, *The GATT;* Dunkley, *Free Trade;* and Winters, "Road to Uruguay."

58. Richard Rubinson offers an impressive analysis of shifting political coalitions in the late nineteenth century, demonstrating how dynamics in the world economy shaped the political preferences of segments of U.S. agriculture. Rubinson, "Political Transformation."

59. See Matusow, *Farm Policies,* 3; and Wilcox, *The Farmer,* 278–280.

60. Quoted in *Fortune,* "Free Trade," 2.

61. When the Republican Party controlled the House and Senate from 1947 to 1949, Joseph Martin (R-MA) served as speaker of the House, and Arthur Vandenberg (R-MI) chaired the Senate Foreign Relations Committee.

62. Dam, *The GATT,* 271.

63. Beane, *United States,* Appendix B.

64. Grant, *Common Agricultural,* 64–65.

65. Friedmann, "Political Economy (1993)," 35; and Morgan, *Merchants of Grain,* 185.

66. Hefford, *Farm Policy,* 64.

67. Sheingate, *Agricultural Welfare State,* 156. During the war, the Japanese government passed the Food Control Law of 1942, which "regulated the prices, production, and distribution of all staple foods." Ibid., 90. The 1955 amendment to this law both solidified supply management policy in Japan and brought the Japanese policy even closer to that of the United States.

68. Ibid., 158.

69. This point may be more evident if we think about the counterfactual: how much more difficult would it have been for Japan, France, Australia, and other nations to keep up protectionist and market-intervening policies had the United States not fought for agriculture's exemption from GATT?

70. Matusow, *Farm Policies,* 84.

71. McMichael, *Development,* 64.

72. Insel, "World Awash," 895; see also, Farnsworth, "International."

73. The United States generally defined "need" against the backdrop of the Cold War.

74. Friedmann, "Political Economy (1982)," 261–263.

75. Friedmann, "The Origins," 17.

76. McMichael, *Development,* 45.

77. Friedmann, "Political Economy (1982)," 261–262; and Matusow, *Farm Policies.*

78. Benedict and Stine, *Agricultural Commodity,* 125. Given the Marshall Plan's focus on reconstructing European agriculture, the true release for U.S. agricultural surpluses during the early 1950s was the Korean War. Gilmore, *Poor Harvest,* 73; and Matusow, *Farm Policies.*

79. Of the thirty-six nations in Africa, twenty-eight became independent between

1955 and 1965. Two African nations gained independence before this period: Egypt (1922) and Libya (1951). Four nations gained independence in the late 1960s: Botswana (1966), Lesotho (1966), Mauritius (1968), and Swaziland (1968). Lastly, Angola gained independence in 1975, and Zimbabwe in 1980. Thus, the 1950s and 1960s were a revolutionary period in Africa. The collapse of colonial structures there opened many potential markets for U.S. exports.

80. Friedmann, "The Origins," 18.

81. McMichael, *Development*, 62.

82. Toma, *Politics of Food*, 52.

83. Peterson, *Agricultural Exports;* U.S. House, "Extend," 88.

84. Peterson, *Agricultural Exports*, 62.

85. Ibid., 74.

86. Schapsmeier and Schapsmeier, *Ezra Taft Benson*, 111–113.

87. Trudy Peterson states that at "the end of 1955, . . . the surplus situation was grim. CCC storage costs were running over a million dollars a day." Peterson, *Agricultural Exports*, 74. PL 480 offered an opportunity to alleviate such costs.

88. Friedmann, "Family Farm," 253, emphasis in original.

89. Hopkins, "Reform," 234.

90. Friedmann, "Political Economy (1982)," 277.

91. McMichael, *Development*, 63.

92. Morgan, *Merchants of Grain*, 180.

93. U.S. House, "Extend," 86.

94. Friedmann, "The Origins," 20.

95. U.S. House, "Extend," 58.

96. Eleven of the nineteen Democrats on the committee represented southern states. Harold Cooley (D-NC) chaired the committee, and W. R. Poage (D-TX) was the vice chair. In addition, the committee included four Republicans from the Wheat Belt. Therefore, fifteen of the committee's thirty-four members represented the cotton-wheat coalition.

97. U.S. House, "Extend," 76–78.

98. Ibid., 85.

99. Ibid., 90.

100. Morgan, *Merchants of Grain*, 185.

101. Friedmann, "Distance."

102. Farnsworth, "International," 217. The primary problem with the International Wheat Agreements was that the exporting nations—the United States, Canada, Australia, and France—"found it difficult to agree on their respective shares of the limited total market." Ibid., 230.

103. In a similar way, the British food regime based on free trade unleashed production levels that the market could not sustain, contributing to the crisis of overproduction discussed in Chapter 3. For detailed discussions on the collapse of the U.S. food regime, see Friedmann, "Political Economy (1982)" and "Political Economy (1993)"; as well as McMichael, "GATT," and "Global Food."

104. These figures come from the "Production, Supply, and Distribution Database"

online by the Foreign Agricultural Service of the USDA. This database provides information for the European Union rather than individual European nations. Here, I have used the figures for the EU-15, which includes Austria, Belgium, Britain, Denmark, Finland, France, Germany, Greece, Ireland, Italy, Luxembourg, the Netherlands, Portugal, Spain, and Sweden.

105. Friedmann, "Political Economy (1982)," 278, Table 8; and Hopkins, "Reform," 234, Table 1.

106. See Runge, "The Assault."

107. Hathaway, *Agriculture*, 10.

108. Grain, millet, and cassava farmers in northern Africa, for instance, could not compete effectively with heavily subsidized imports, which had the deleterious effect of depressing grain prices in the region.

109. The Cairns Group included Argentina, Australia, Brazil, Canada, Chile, Colombia, Fiji, Hungary, Indonesia, Malaysia, the Philippines, New Zealand, Thailand, and Uruguay.

110. McMichael, "Global Food," 100.

111. Peterson, *Agricultural Exports*, 141.

112. McMichael, "GATT," 184, n.4.

113. Friedmann, "Distance."

114. Morgan, *Merchants of Grain*, 182.

115. McMichael, "GATT."

116. Ibid.; and Friedmann, "Food Politics."

117. Lieber, *Rats in the Grain*, 83.

118. Broehl, *Cargill*, 16; and Morgan, *Merchants of Grain*, 148–149.

119. Dudley and Sandilands, "Side Effects," 331.

120. Friedmann, "Political Economy (1982)," 250.

## Chapter 7. The 1996 FAIR Act

Epigraph. Bill Northey quotation from U.S. House, "Formulation (Part III)," 148.

1. The primary exception, of course, was defense spending, which continued to rise substantially.

2. Orden, Paarlberg, and Roe, *Policy Reform*, 72.

3. Controlling for inflation, direct payments to farmers in 1987 totaled $28.5 billion (in constant 2005 dollars).

4. Ibid., 74.

5. For a detailed discussion of this crisis and how farmers responded, see Barlett, *American Dreams*.

6. The Senate and House passed the FAIR Act on March 28 and 29, respectively. President Clinton signed the bill into law a few days later, on April 4, 1996.

7. Hosansky, "House and Senate," 296.

8. Carr et al., "North American," 113.

9. Programs to protect the environment, such as the Conservation Reserve Program, remained. Such programs idle the most environmentally fragile farmland (for ex-

ample, land susceptible to soil erosion) but without the explicit goal of managing supply as found in the ARP.

10. Thus, if the FAIR Act had not been renewed or replaced with new legislation, then agricultural policy would have reverted automatically to the Agricultural Act of 1949.

11. Among others, see Moyer and Josling, *Agricultural Policy;* Orden, Paarlberg, and Roe, *Policy Reform;* Paarlberg and Orden, "Explaining"; and Schertz and Doering, *The Making.*

12. Paarlberg and Orden, "Explaining," 1306.

13. Sheingate, *Agricultural Welfare State,* 201.

14. For example, see ibid., 193–203.

15. Moyer and Josling, *Agricultural Policy,* 159.

16. Since less than 40 percent of those eligible voted in the 1994 election, the "Republican mandate" was actively granted by less than 25 percent of the overall electorate.

17. Schertz and Doering, *The Making,* 81–83.

18. For instance, President Clinton had already vetoed the "Freedom to Farm" bill when it was attached to the larger omnibus budget bill in 1995. Sheingate, *Agricultural Welfare State,* 200–203. And Clinton signed the FAIR Act in March 1996, "despite continuing administration misgivings" about the bill. Congressional Quarterly, "Clinton Signs," 938.

19. From the National Agricultural Statistics Service (USDA), Quick Stats (Agricultural Statistics Data Base), http://www.nass.usda.gov/.

20. Paarlberg and Orden, "Explaining," 1306.

21. Importantly, although Republicans controlled the presidency and both houses of Congress, they could not end supply management policy, as was their goal. Recall from Chapter 4 that Secretary of Agriculture Benson vocally and consistently opposed supply management policy. The fact that the Republican Party failed to make more significant changes—and, especially, left production controls untouched—should raise questions as to the strength of partisan politics as a prime determinant of national policy.

22. Sheingate, *Agricultural Welfare State,* 201.

23. Orden, Paarlberg, and Roe, *Policy Reform,* 59, Table 8.

24. USDA, *Agricultural Statistics, 1957,* Tables 3, 35, 76.

25. Ibid., Table 651.

26. USDA, *Agricultural Statistics, 1966,* Tables 3, 40, 87, 684.

27. USDA, *Agricultural Statistics, 1975,* Tables 1, 35, 74, 632. The support price for wheat in 1973 was $3.39 per bushel. When the Agriculture and Consumer Protection Act was passed in July, the market price for wheat was $2.47 per bushel but rising. By August, the price was $4.45 per bushel. Price supports for cotton were set at $0.415 per pound in 1973. When the farm bill passed that year in July, the market price for cotton was $0.304, and it rose to $0.375 in August.

28. For example, Orden, Paarlberg, and Roe, *Policy Reform.*

29. In fact, the Democratic liberal ideology often pits the party against supply management policy. For instance, northeastern liberals have frequently opposed supply man-

agement programs, especially price supports, that put burdens on urban consumers or taxpayers. Consequently, Democrats' support for welfare-state policies, such as social security, does not automatically translate into support for farmers. From the 1930s to the 1960s, Democrats' support for both welfare-state programs and supply management policy resulted from the makeup of the New Deal political coalition: northern liberals, labor unions, southern Democrats, and midwestern progressives. Without the southern and midwestern Democrats pushing for federal support for agriculture, the Democratic Party would not necessarily have favored supply management policy. Later, the food stamps program helped to gain support for supply management policy from urban liberals. Thus, Democratic liberal ideology in and of itself does not create support for farm subsidies; rather, the underlying class coalitions generate such support.

30. I do not analyze the FAIR Act by examining each step in the bill's passage: the writing and introduction of various bills in committees, debates on the floor of the House or Senate, failed attempts on floor votes, negotiations and compromises, etc. For this kind of detail of the legislative process, see Ferranti, "The FAIR Act"; Orden, Paarlberg, and Roe, *Policy Reform;* Schertz and Doering, *The Making;* and Sheingate, *Agricultural Welfare State.* As with earlier policy formation and shifts, my focus is on the underlying coalitions and how they are evident in hearings and roll-call votes.

31. U.S. Senate, "Farm Programs," 35–37; and U.S. Senate, "Commodity Policy (Subcommittee)," 16–17.

32. U.S. House, "Formulation (Part III)," 376–377, 693; U.S. Senate, "Farm Programs," 35–37. By contrast, the American Corn Growers Association (ACGA) tended to side with the NFU and NAWG regarding supply management. Keith Dittrich, the second vice president of the ACGA stated, "Now at a time when we are all faced with the job of defending farm programs we have the National Corn Growers Association publicly stating that we no longer need Acreage Reduction Programs!" U.S. House, "Formulation (Part III)," 93.

33. U.S. House, "Formulation (Part III)," 152–153.

34. U.S. Senate, "Commodity Policy (Subcommittee)," 39.

35. The livestock segment had one qualification for its support of flexible production: income support payments should not be attached to acres taken out of commodity programs that are then used for haying or grazing livestock. Such a scenario would create competition for current livestock producers, who would not receive support payments. Ibid., 40.

36. For instance, DuWayne Skaar, the president of the Idaho Cattle Association, stated, "Our industry works the best when we have cheap grain prices and high cattle prices." U.S. House, "Formulation (Part I)," 838.

37. Ibid., 649.

38. For Iowa, see U.S. House, "Formulation (Part III)," 173–175; for Idaho, see ibid., 945–954; and for retailers, see ibid., 175–176.

39. U.S. Senate, "Market Effects," 44–45.

40. Orden, Paarlberg, and Roe, *Policy Reform,* 134.

41. U.S. Senate, "Commodity Policy (Committee)," 158. The National Grain and Feed Association is a "trade association representing . . . grain, feed, and processing

firms . . . that store, handle, merchandise, mill, process, and export U.S. grains and oil-seeds." Ibid., 158, n.11. This witness also spoke on behalf of the National Grain Trade Council.

42. Schertz and Doering, *The Making,* 77.

43. The primary exceptions were organizations representing wheat growers in Kansas. Representatives of the Kansas Farm Bureau and the Kansas Association of Wheat Growers (KAWG) each emphasized flexibility in production and endorsed a shift to a whole farm program. U.S. House, "Formulation (Part III)," 502–505. Representatives of neither organization explicitly called for the end of the ARP or other production controls, though the representative for KAWG did call for an end to "set-asides." Ibid., 505. This contrasts with the general tenor of testimony from other Wheat Belt organizations and especially from southern organizations, which were far less welcoming of more flexibility and the whole farm program and tended to explicitly oppose ending the ARP.

44. U.S. Senate, "Farm Programs," 45.

45. U.S. House, "Formulation (Part III)," 906.

46. Ibid., 888.

47. Ibid., 327.

48. See, for example, Orden, Paarlberg, and Roe, *Policy Formation.*

49. U.S. Senate, "Farm Programs," 53–55.

50. Young and Westcott, "The 1996," 7.

51. The primary limitations were on growing fruits and vegetables on base acreage. Fruit and vegetable growers had traditionally not participated in supply management programs, and so they did not receive subsidies. If growers of program commodities, such as cotton or corn, had been allowed to switch to fruits or vegetables and still receive income subsidies, then they would have had an advantage over the traditional fruit growers because the former would continue to receive government supports while the latter would not.

52. In discussing price supports here, my focus is on the primary form of income support for farmers: target prices and deficiency payments. The nonrecourse CCC loans are also price supports, but they rarely come up as a policy issue. Nonrecourse loan rates are set low relative to market prices, and they perform a generally accepted function in agriculture. These loans are in fact price supports because they set a floor beneath which market prices cannot fall. But again, this floor is relatively low. Since 1973, target prices and deficiency payments have been the primary form of income support.

53. The American Corn Growers Association was one of the few nonwheat organizations strongly advocating for retaining the target price system.

54. U.S. Senate, "Commodity Policy (Committee)," 70–72. The NFU proposed a targeted program that aimed to help smaller farmers by offering a high loan rate for a certain number of bushels, after which support gradually declined. For much of the twentieth century, the majority of farm subsidies went to a minority of farmers. In 1992, for instance, the richest 10 percent of farmers received more than 40 percent of government payments. U.S. Census Bureau, *Census of Agriculture, 1992,* 14, Table 5. However, these farmers also contribute the most to overall production, and their absence from

commodity programs would render futile any attempts at production control. Most other farm organizations—including NAWG, the USA Rice Federation, and the Delta Council (cotton)—opposed targeting or means-testing the benefits, in part because of fears that dominant producers would leave programs after their payments were cut or capped. Consequently, the NFU's proposal received little serious discussion, except in opposition to it.

55. Orden, Paarlberg, and Roe, *Policy Reform*, 181.

56. Schertz and Doering, *The Making*, 95.

57. Orden, Paarlberg, and Roe, *Policy Reform*, 136.

58. Ibid., 138–139.

59. See, for example, U.S. House, "Formulation (Part III)," 296–299.

60. Young and Westcott, "The 1996," 22.

61. U.S. House, "Formulation (Part III)," 296–298, 646–648.

62. U.S. Senate, "Farm Programs," 1.

63. Orden, Paarlberg, and Roe, *Policy Reform*, 154.

64. Orden and his colleagues note this important connection between the elimination of price supports and production controls. Ibid., 134–135. Sheingate, however, seems to have missed this subtle link despite his focus on budget pressures and processes. Sheingate, *Agricultural Welfare State*.

65. U.S. Senate, "Farm Programs," 42–43.

66. The Center for Global Food Issues (CGFI), a research center supported by the Hudson Institute that promotes free markets, proposed eliminating price supports altogether. U.S. Senate, "Farm Programs," 15–16. Yet even Dennis Avery of the CGFI stated that he did not oppose a "safety net" for farmers but felt this support should be "as direct payments rather than as a price support." Ibid., 23.

67. U.S. Senate, "Commodity Programs (Committee)," 160.

68. U.S. House, "Farm Programs," 649.

69. Ibid., 945–954.

70. However, Less Guthrie of the National Cattlemen's Association expressed concern that decoupling might allow haying or grazing on base acres, thereby increasing competition for livestock producers. U.S. Senate, "Commodity Policy (Subcommittee)," 48.

71. Orden, Paarlberg, and Roe, *Policy Reform*.

72. U.S. House, "Formulation (Part III)," 719.

73. Ibid., 776. Earlier in his testimony, Sleight indicated that the Feed Grains Council supported the EEP, as long as it did not displace non-EEP commodities (that is, coarse grains). Ibid., 763–765.

74. U.S. Senate, "Market Effects," 2.

75. U.S. House, "Formulation (Part III)," 779.

76. See, for example, U.S. House, "Formulation (Part I)," 735–736; U.S. House, "Formulation (Part III)," 186–188; and U.S. Senate, "Federal Farm," 90–91.

77. U.S. Senate, "Commodity Policy (Subcommittee)," 14.

78. U.S. House, "Formulation (Part III)," 761–762; and U.S. Senate, "Federal Farm," 12–14, 43–46.

79. Libby, *Protecting Markets,* 59. See also, testimony of Robert Paarlberg, U.S. Senate, "Federal Farm," 76.

80. Libby, *Protecting Markets,* Appendix.

81. Morgan, *Merchants of Grain.*

82. See, for example, ibid., 128–129, 139–141.

83. U.S. Senate, "Market Effects," 44.

84. U.S. Senate, "Federal Farm," 20.

85. U.S. House, "Formulation (Part III)," 779.

86. U.S. Senate, "Federal Farm," 71.

87. Some may argue that continuing the Conservation Reserve Program (CRP) was a compromise between retaining and eliminating production controls. Certainly, while programs that regulated production for economic reasons were eliminated, the CRP continued to idle millions of acres of farmland. Nonetheless, the CRP was not a compromise measure used to induce corn producers or other farmers into supporting the FAIR Act. In part, continuing the CRP represented a compromise with environmentalists. In this sense, then, environmentalists were a primary factor for retaining a program that performed a function similar to that of supply management policy—removing significant acreage from production. This is the exact opposite of the common argument that, over the past thirty years, environmental organizations have helped to roll back supply management policy over the objections of farmers. In this scenario, farmers wanted to end production controls but had to compromise with environmental organizations by retaining some elements of regulations.

88. Orden, Paarlberg, and Roe, *Policy Reform,* 148, 183–185.

89. Hosansky, "House and Senate," 296.

90. Zahniser and Coyle note, "Prior to NAFTA, U.S. corn exports to Mexico were controlled by import licenses, with no guarantee as to the amount of U.S. access to the Mexican market." "U.S.-Mexico Corn," 4.

91. Gallagher, "Corn," 51–52.

92. Orden, "Agricultural Interest," 347, Table 7.5.

93. Ibid., 350.

94. U.S. House, "Formulation (Part I)," 700.

95. Zahniser and Coyle, "U.S.-Mexico Corn," 1.

96. See U.S. Senate, "China Accession."

97. U.S. Senate, "Federal Farm," 20.

98. Anania, Bohman, and Carter, "United States," 536, Table 1.

99. Josling, "Agricultural Trade."

100. World Food Institute, *World Food,* 47, Figure 38.

101. U.S. House, "Formulation (Part III)," 776.

102. U.S. Senate, "Market Effects," 2.

103. Among others, see Winders and Nibert, "Consuming."

104. In 1996, southern cotton, soybean, and tobacco production created $4.9 billion, $2.5 billion, and $2 billion, respectively. Winders, "Welcome," 255, Table 2.3. This totals to about $9.4 billion, less than 10 percent more than the value produced by the southern poultry industry.

105. Perhaps the best examples are processed foods and the fast food industry. Among others, see Pollan, *Omnivore's Dilemma*.

106. Only Phil Gramm (R-TX) did not vote on the FAIR Act.

107. Three southern Democratic senators voted against the FAIR Act: Dale Bumpers and Mark Pryor of Arkansas, and Fritz Hollings of South Carolina.

108. Concessions on sugar policy likewise had this purpose.

## Epilogue

Epigraph. Saxby Chambliss quotation from Pear, "Bush Aims," B7.

1. For a clear demonstration of this, see Winders, "Maintaining." This article compares the short-term trajectories of three New Deal policies: agricultural policy, social security, and labor policy.

2. Some scholars, such as Sheingate, assert that commodity prices reached "record high levels." Sheingate, *Agricultural Welfare State*, 205. We need to recognize, however, that while nominal prices reached historic heights, real prices (in constant dollars, controlling for inflation) in 1996 were actually lower than real prices in the 1940s, the 1970s, and even at various points in the 1980s.

3. This estimate is derived from the Foreign Agriculture Service database "Production, Supply and Distribution," including only China, Japan, and South Korea. Using data from *Agricultural Statistics,* which includes more countries to define "Asia," leads to an even larger drop in U.S. corn exports to the region: about 32 percent. See the appendix for more information on these sources.

4. Westcott, Young, and Price, "The 2002 Farm Act," 3.

5. USDA, *Agricultural Statistics, 2003,* IX-39, Table 9-39.

6. Sheingate, *Agricultural Welfare State,* 210–211.

7. Concern over declining budget surpluses and the possibility of deficits was expressed many times throughout the congressional hearings in 2001. For example, Senator Harkin (D-IA) stated, "Thank you very much, Senator Conrad, . . . for ringing the alarms and letting us know . . . [that] we have got to move on this Farm bill rapidly and expeditiously to make sure that we are able to enact the policies that will increase farm income within the confines of that budget." U.S. Senate, "New Federal Farm Bill (June 28)," 6.

8. Paarlberg and Orden, "Explaining U.S.," 1306.

9. Calculated from Congressional Quarterly, *CQ Weekly,* 1180.

10. U.S. Senate, "New Federal Farm Bill (June 28)," 25.

11. U.S. Senate, "New Federal Farm Bill (July 17)," 3–4.

12. U.S. Senate, "New Federal Farm Bill (June 28)," 2.

13. *Des Moines Register,* "Farm Bill," 10.

14. On 1996 opinion, see Fogarty, "Freedom." On 2001 opinion, see Perkins, "Farms Face," 1D.

15. U.S. Senate, "New Federal Farm Bill (June 28)," 21–22.

16. U.S. Senate, "New Federal Farm Bill (July 17)," 10.

17. Ibid., 13.

18. U.S. Senate, "New Federal Farm Bill (June 28)," 26.

19. U.S. Senate, "New Federal Farm Bill: Feed Grains," 11.

20. Ibid., 13.

21. Ibid., 8; and U.S. Senate, "New Federal Farm Bill (June 28)," 87.

22. Although a few scholars, most notably Harriet Friedmann and Philip Mc-Michael, focus heavily on agriculture in the world economy, most studies of agricultural policy either ignore this issue altogether or leave it in the background.

23. Polanyi, *Great Transformation*.

## Appendix

1. Marx focused on several coalitions: petite bourgeoisie and proletariat, large landowners and finance capital, and big industry and finance capital. Marx, *18th Brumaire*.

2. This data base can be found on the NASS website, http://www.nass.usda.gov/.

3. For prices for these years, I used USDA, National Agricultural Statistics Service, "Prices Rec'd by Farmers," accessed June 20, 2008.

4. Bensel, *Sectionalism*.

5. McKeown, "Politics of Corn." McKeown finds that one important segment defected to support ending the Corn Laws: livestock producers.

6. Among many others, see Hansen, *Gaining Access;* Prechel, "Steel and the State"; Quadagno, "Welfare Capitalism"; and Swenson, *Capitalists*.

# Bibliography

**Government Publications**

United States Census Bureau. 1933. *Statistical Abstract of the United States, 1933.* Washington, D.C.: GPO.

———. 1940. *Statistical Abstract of the United States, 1940.* Washington, D.C.: GPO.

———. 1951. *Statistical Abstract of the United States, 1951.* Washington, D.C.: GPO.

———. 1959. *Census of Agriculture, 1959.* Washington, D.C.: GPO.

———. 1965. *Statistical Abstract of the United States, 1965.* Washington, D.C.: GPO.

———. 1975. *Historical Statistics of the United States, Colonial Times to 1970.* Washington, D.C.: GPO.

———. 1994. *Census of Agriculture, 1992.* Washington, D.C.: GPO.

United States Congress. 1924. *Congressional Record.* 68th Congress, 1st Session. Washington, D.C.: GPO.

———. 1926. *Congressional Record.* 69th Congress, 1st Session. Washington, D.C.: GPO.

———. 1927. *Congressional Record.* 69th Congress, 2nd Session. Washington, D.C.: GPO.

———. 1928. *Congressional Record.* 70th Congress, 1st Session. Washington, D.C.: GPO.

———. 1933. *Congressional Record.* 73rd Congress, 1st Session. Washington, D.C.: GPO.

———. 1938. *Congressional Record.* 75th Congress, 3rd Session. Washington, D.C.: GPO.

United States Department of Agriculture (USDA). 1938. *Agricultural Statistics, 1938.* Washington, D.C.: GPO.

———. 1941. *Agricultural Statistics, 1941.* Washington, D.C.: GPO.

———. 1942. *Agricultural Statistics, 1942.* Washington, D.C.: GPO.

———. 1946. *Agricultural Statistics, 1946.* Washington, D.C.: GPO.

———. 1952. *Agricultural Statistics, 1952.* Washington, D.C.: GPO.

———. 1957. *Agricultural Statistics, 1957.* Washington, D.C.: GPO.

———. 1962. *Agricultural Statistics, 1962.* Washington, D.C.: GPO.

———. 1966. *Agricultural Statistics, 1966.* Washington, D.C.: GPO.

———. 1974. *Statistics on Cotton and Related Data, 1920–1973.* Statistical Bulletin No. 535. Washington, D.C.: GPO.

———. 1975. *Agricultural Statistics, 1975.* Washington, D.C.: GPO.

———. 2003. *Agricultural Statistics, 2003.* Washington, D.C.: GPO.

———. Economic Research Service. "Food Availability (Per Capita) Data System." Available at http://www.ers.usda.gov/data/foodconsumption/.

———. National Agricultural Statistics Service. "Prices Rec'd by Farmers: Historic Prices & Indexes, 1908–1992." Data set No. 92152. Available at http://usda.mannlib.cornell.edu/MannUsda/viewDocumentInfo.do?document ID=1243.

———. National Agricultural Statistics Service. "Quick Stats: Agricultural Statistics Data Base." Available at http://www.nass.usda.gov/QuickStats/.

United States House of Representatives. 1932. "Agricultural Adjustment Program." Hearings before the Committee on Agriculture. 72nd Congress, 2nd Session. Washington, D.C.: GPO.

———. 1948. "Trade Agreements Program." Hearings before the Subcommittee on Tariffs and Foreign Trade of the Committee on Ways and Means. 80th Congress, 2nd Session. Washington, D.C.: GPO.

———. 1949. "General Farm Program (Testimony of Farm Organizations)." Hearings before the Special Subcommittee of the Committee on Agriculture. 81st Congress, 1st Session. Washington, D.C.: GPO.

———. 1954. "Long Range Farm Program." Hearings before the House Committee on Agriculture. 83rd Congress, 2nd Session. Washington, D.C.: GPO.

———. 1958. "Extend Public Law 480: Agricultural Trade Development and Assistance Act of 1954." Hearings before the Committee on Agriculture. 85th Congress, 2nd Session. Washington, D.C.: GPO.

———. 1958. "Program Proposals for Feed Grain Producers." Hearings before the Subcommittee on Livestock and Feed Grains of the Committee on Agriculture. 85th Congress, 2nd Session. Washington, D.C.: GPO.

———. 1964. "Extension of Public Law 480 — Titles I and II." Hearings before the Subcommittee on Foreign Agricultural Operations of the House Committee on Agriculture. 88th Congress, 2nd Session. Washington, D.C.: GPO.

———. 1964. "Wheat Legislation." Hearings before the Subcommittee on

Wheat of the House Committee on Agriculture. 88th Congress, 2nd Session. Washington, D.C.: GPO.

———. 1973. "General Farm Program." Hearings before the Committee on Agriculture. 93rd Congress, 1st Session. Washington, D.C.: GPO.

———. 1995. "Formulation of the 1995 Farm Bill, Part I." Hearings before the Committee on Agriculture. 104th Congress, 1st Session. Washington, D.C.: GPO.

———. 1995. "Formulation of the 1995 Farm Bill, Part III (Cotton, Feed Grains, Wheat, Rice and Oilseeds)." Hearings before the Subcommittee on General Farm Commodities of the Committee on Agriculture. 104th Congress, 1st Session. Washington, D.C.: GPO.

United States Senate. 1933. "Agricultural Adjustment Relief Plan." Hearings before the Committee on Agriculture and Forestry. 72nd Congress, 2nd Session. Washington, D.C.: GPO.

———. 1947. "International Trade Organization." Hearings before the Committee on Finance. 80th Congress, 1st Session. Washington, D.C.: GPO.

———. 1952. "Farm Price Supports and Production Goals." Hearings before the Subcommittee of the Committee on Agriculture and Forestry. 82nd Congress, 2nd Session. Washington, D.C.: GPO.

———. 1964. "Wheat Programs." Hearings before the Senate Committee on Agriculture and Forestry. 88th Congress, 2nd Session. Washington, D.C.: GPO.

———. 1995. "Farm Programs: Are Americans Getting What They Pay For?" Hearing before the Committee on Agriculture, Nutrition, and Forestry. 104th Congress, 1st Session. Washington, D.C.: GPO.

———. 1995. "Commodity Policy (Committee)." Hearing before the Committee on Agriculture, Nutrition, and Forestry. 104th Congress, 1st Session. Washington, D.C.: GPO.

———. 1995. "Commodity Policy (Subcommittee)." Hearing before the Subcommittee on Production and Price Competitiveness. 104th Congress, 1st Session. Washington, D.C.: GPO.

———. 1995. "Market Effects of Federal Farm Policy." Hearing before the Committee on Agriculture, Nutrition, and Forestry. 104th Congress, 1st Session. Washington, D.C.: GPO.

———. 2000. "China Accession to the World Trade Organization." Hearing before the Committee on Agriculture, Nutrition, and Forestry. 106th Congress, 2nd Session. Washington, D.C.: GPO.

———. 2001. "The New Federal Farm Bill (June 28)." Hearing before the Committee on Agriculture, Nutrition, and Forestry. 107th Congress, 1st Session. Washington, D.C.: GPO.

———. 2001. "The New Federal Farm Bill (July 17)." Hearing before the Committee on Agriculture, Nutrition, and Forestry. 107th Congress, 1st Session. Washington, D.C.: GPO.

———. 2001. "The New Federal Farm Bill: Feed Grains and Oilseeds." Hearing before the Committee on Agriculture, Nutrition, and Forestry. 107th Congress, 1st Session. Washington, D.C.: GPO.

## Books, Articles, and Periodicals

Aiken, Charles S. 1998. *The Cotton Plantation South Since the Civil War*. Baltimore: Johns Hopkins University Press.

Alston, Lee J., and Joseph P. Ferrie. 1999. *Southern Paternalism and the Rise of the American Welfare State: Economics, Politics, and Institutions in the South: 1865–1965*. Cambridge: Cambridge University Press.

Alvarez, Antonio Fernandez, and Donato Fernandez Navarrette. 1990. "Agrarian Policies and the Agricultural Systems of the European Community: A Historical Overview." In *Agrarian Policies and Agricultural Systems*, edited by Alessandro Bonanno. Boulder: Westview Press.

Anania, Giovanni, Mary Bohman, and Colin A. Carter. 1992. "United States Export Subsidies in Wheat: Strategic Trade Policy or Expensive Beggar-Thy-Neighbor Tactic?" *American Journal of Agricultural Economics* 74(3):535–545.

Andrews, Kenneth T. 1997. "The Impacts of Social Movements on the Political Process: The Civil Rights Movement and Black Electoral Politics in Mississippi." *American Sociological Review* 62(5):800–819.

Baker, Benjamin. 1951. *Wartime Food Procurement and Production*. New York: King's Crown Press.

Baldwin, Sidney. 1968. *Poverty and Politics: The Rise and Decline of the Farm Security Administration*. Chapel Hill: University of North Carolina Press.

Barlett, Peggy F. 1993. *American Dreams, Rural Realities: Family Farms in Crisis*. Chapel Hill: University of North Carolina Press.

Barmash, Isadore. 1974. "Butz Assails Restrictive Food Actions." *New York Times*. October 29:49.

Bartley, Numan V. 1969. *The Rise of Massive Resistance: Race and Politics in the South during the 1950's*. Baton Rouge: Louisiana State University Press.

Barton, Weldon V. 1976. "Coalition-Building in the United States House of Representatives: Agricultural Legislation in 1973." In *Cases in Public Policy-Making*, edited by James E. Anderson. New York: Praeger.

Bass, Jack, and Walter De Vries. 1995. *The Transformation of Southern Politics*. Athens: University of Georgia Press.

Beane, Donald G. 2000. *The United States and GATT: A Relational Study*. New York: Pergamon.

Becker, Geoffrey S. 2002. "Farm Commodity Legislation: Chronology, 1933–2002." Congressional Research Service (CRS) Report for Congress. Washington, D.C.: Library of Congress.

Benedict, Murray R. 1953. *Farm Policies of the United States, 1790–1950: A Study of Their Origins and Development*. New York: Twentieth Century Fund.

Benedict, Murray R., and Oscar C. Stine. 1956. *The Agricultural Commodity Programs: Two Decades of Experience*. New York: Twentieth Century Fund.

Bensel, Richard Franklin. 1984. *Sectionalism and American Political Development: 1880–1980.* Madison: University of Wisconsin Press.

Benson, Ezra Taft. 1960. *Freedom to Farm.* New York: Doubleday.

Black, Conrad. 2003. *Franklin Delano Roosevelt: Champion of Freedom.* New York: Public Affairs.

Bloom, Jack M. 1987. *Class, Race, and the Civil Rights Movement.* Bloomington: Indiana University Press.

Boli, John, and George M. Thomas. 1997. "World Culture in the World Polity: A Century of International Non-Governmental Organization." *American Sociological Review* 62(2):171–190.

Bonnen, James T., William P. Browne, and David B. Schweikhardt. 1996. "Further Observations on the Changing Nature of National Agricultural Policy Decision Processes, 1946–1995." *Agricultural History* 70:130–152.

Brass, Paul R. 1986. "The Political Uses of Crisis: The Bihar Famine of 1966–1967." *Journal of Asian Studies* 45(2):245–267.

Broehl, Wayne G., Jr. 1998. *Cargill: Going Global.* Hanover: University Press of New England.

Brown, William Adams, Jr. 1950. *The United States and the Restoration of World Trade.* Washington, D.C.: Brookings Institution.

Browne, William P. 1995. *Cultivating Congress: Constituents, Issues, and Agricultural Policymaking.* Lawrence: University of Kansas Press.

Cagin, Seth, and Philip Dray. 1988. *We Are Not Afraid: The Story of Goodman, Schwerner, and Chaney and the Civil Rights Campaign for Mississippi.* New York: Macmillan.

Campbell, Christiana McFayden. 1962. *The Farm Bureau and the New Deal: A Study of the Making of National Farm Policy, 1933–1940.* Urbana: University of Illinois Press.

Carr, Barry, Klaus Frohberg, Hartley Furtan, S. R. Johnson, William Meyers, Tim Phipps, and G. E. Rossmiller. 1988. "A North American Perspective on Decoupling." In *World Agricultural Trade: Building a Consensus,* edited by William M. Miner and Dale E. Hathaway. Halifax: Institute for Research on Public Policy.

Carson, Clayborne. 1981. *In Struggle: SNCC and the Black Awakening of the 1960s.* Cambridge: Harvard University Press.

Cheever, Lawrence Oakley. 1948. *The House of Morrell.* Cedar Rapids: Torch Press.

*Chicago Daily Tribune.* 1933. "Process Taxes Likely to Face Court Attacks." July 17:2.

———. 1933. "Little Pigs Go to Market, but Many Stay Home." August 24:24.

———. 1933. "Packers Pile Up Fertilizer from U.S. Bonus Pigs." September 8:32.

———. 1933. "U.S. to Kill More Bonus Pigs; Aid Areas Hurt by Drought." September 15:35.

———. 1933. "Butter—Millions of Pounds of It—May Go to the Needy." October 3:11.

———. 1933. "Butter and Beef to be Purchased by Government." October 17:26.

———. 1933. "U.S. Will Spend Millions More in Buying Pork." November 5:4.

———. 1933. "Farmers Say They Pay Hog Processing Tax." November 26:A10.

Choate, Jean. 2002. *Disputed Ground: Farm Groups That Opposed the New Deal Agricultural Program.* Jefferson: McFarland.

Clarke, Sally H. 1994. *Regulation and the Revolution in United States Farm Productivity.* New York: Cambridge University Press.

Cleaver, Harry. 1977. "Food, Famine and the International Crisis." *Zerowork.* http://libcom.org/library/food-famine-international-crisis-harry-cleaver-zerowork. Last accessed on June 19, 2008.

Cobb, James C. 1993. *The Selling of the South: The Southern Crusade for Industrial Development, 1936–1990.* 2nd ed. Urbana: University of Illinois Press.

———. 1997. "The Lesson of Little Rock." *Atlanta Journal-Constitution.* September 21:B-2.

Cochrane, Willard W., and Mary E. Ryan. 1976. *American Farm Policy, 1948–1973.* Minneapolis: University of Minnesota Press.

Congressional Quarterly. 1962. *Congressional Quarterly Weekly Report.* Washington, D.C.: Congressional Quarterly.

———. 1973. *Congressional Quarterly Weekly Report.* Washington, D.C.: Congressional Quarterly.

———. 1996. "Clinton Signs Farm Bill Despite Misgivings." *Congressional Quarterly Weekly Report* 54(14):938.

———. 2002. *CQ Weekly.* Washington, D.C.: Congressional Quarterly.

Conrad, David Eugene. 1965. *The Forgotten Farmers: The Story of Sharecroppers during the New Deal.* Urbana: University of Illinois Press.

Constance, Douglas H., Jere L. Gilles, and William D. Heffernan. 1990. "Agrarian Policies and Agricultural Systems in the United States." In *Agrarian Policies and Agricultural Systems,* edited by Alessandro Bonanno, pp. 9–75. Boulder: Westview.

Conze, Werner. 1969. "The Effects of Nineteenth-Century Liberal Agrarian Reforms on Social Structure in Central Europe." In *Essays in European Economic History, 1789–1914,* edited by F. Crouzet, W. H. Chaloner, and W. H. Stern. London: Edward Arnold.

Coppa, Frank. 1970. "The Italian Tariff and the Conflict between Agriculture and Industry: The Commercial Policy of Liberal Italy, 1860–1922." *Journal of Economic History* 30(4):742–769.

Dam, Kenneth W. 1970. *The GATT: Law and International Economic Organization.* Chicago: University of Chicago Press.

Daniel, Pete. 1985. *Breaking the Land: The Transformation of Cotton, Tobacco, and Rice Cultures since 1800.* Chicago: University of Illinois Press.

Dean, Virgil W. 2006. *An Opportunity Lost: The Truman Administration and the Farm Policy Debate.* Columbia: University of Missouri Press.

*Des Moines Register.* 2002. "Farm Bill: A Blessing and a Curse." May 5:10.

Domhoff, G. William. 1996. *State Autonomy or Class Dominance? Case Studies on Policy Making in America.* New York: Aldine de Gruyter.

Dudley, Leonard, and Roger Sandilands. 1975. "The Side Effects of Foreign Aid: The Case of Public Law 480 Wheat in Colombia." *Economic Development and Cultural Change* 23(2):325–336.

Dunkley, Graham. 1997. *The Free Trade Adventure: The Uruguay Round and Globalism—A Critique.* Victoria: Melbourne University Press.

Farnsworth, Helen C. 1956. "International Wheat Agreements and Problems, 1948–1956." *Quarterly Journal of Economics* 70:217–248.

Ferranti, Michael Robert. 2007. "The FAIR Act of 1996: Party, Production and Practicality in the Passage of a Farm Bill." M.A. Thesis, Virginia Polytechnic Institute and State University, Blacksburg.

Finegold, Kenneth. 1981. "From Agrarianism to Adjustment: The Political Origins of New Deal Agricultural Policy." *Politics & Society* 11(1):1–27.

Finegold, Kenneth, and Theda Skocpol. 1995. *State and Party in America's New Deal.* Madison: University of Wisconsin Press.

Fite, Gilbert C. 1954. *George N. Peek and the Fight for Farm Parity.* Norman: University of Oklahoma Press.

———. 1981. *American Farmers: The Minority.* Bloomington: Indiana University Press.

———. 1984. *Cotton Fields No More: Southern Agriculture, 1865–1980.* Lexington: University of Kentucky Press.

Flamming, Douglas. 2005. *Bound for Freedom: Black Los Angeles in Jim Crow America.* Los Angeles: University of California Press.

Fogarty, Thomas A. 2002. "Freedom to Farm? Not Likely." *USA Today.* January 2. http://www.usatoday.com, accessed on September 16, 2007.

Fornari, Henry D. 1979. "The Big Change: Cotton to Soybeans." *Agricultural History* 53(1):245–253.

*Fortune.* 1947. "Free Trade vs. Control." 35(Feb.):2–4.

Frederickson, Kari. 2001. *The Dixiecrat Revolt and the End of the Solid South, 1932–1968.* Chapel Hill: University of North Carolina Press.

Friedmann, Harriet. 1982. "The Political Economy of Food: The Rise and Fall of the Postwar International Food Order." *American Journal of Sociology* 88(Supplement):248–286.

———. 1987. "The Family Farm and the International Food Regime." In *Peasants and Peasant Societies: Selected Readings,* edited by Teodor Shanin. 2nd ed. New York: Blackwell.

———. 1990. "The Origins of Third World Food Dependence." In *The Food Question: Profits Versus People,* edited by Henry Bernstein, Ben Crow, Maureen MacKintosh, and Charlotte Martin. New York: Monthly Review Press.

———. 1992. "Distance and Durability: Shaky Foundations of the World Food Economy." *Third World Quarterly* 13(2):371–383.

———. 1993. "The Political Economy of Food: A Global Crisis." *New Left Review* 197:29–57.

———. 1995. "Food Politics: New Dangers, New Possibilities." In *Food and Agrarian Orders in the World-Economy,* edited by Philip McMichael. Westport: Praeger.

Friedmann, Harriet, and Philip McMichael. 1989. "Agriculture and the State System: The Rise and Decline of National Agricultures, 1870 to the Present." *Sociologia Ruralis* 29(2):93–117.

Gallagher, Paul W. 2000. "Corn." In *Competition in Agriculture: The United States in the World Market,* edited by Dale Colyer, P. Lynn Kennedy, William A. Amponsah, Stanley M. Fletcher, and Curtis M. Jolly. New York: Food Products Press.

Gardner, Richard N. 1956. *Sterling-Dollar Diplomacy.* Oxford: Clarendon.

George, Susan. 1977. *How the Other Half Dies: The Real Reasons for World Hunger.* Montclair: Allanheld and Osmun.

Gilbert, Jess. 2000. "Eastern Urban Liberals and Midwestern Agrarian Intellectuals: Two Group Portraits of Progressives in the New Deal Department of Agriculture." *Agricultural History* 74(2):162–180.

Gilbert, Jess, and Carolyn Howe. 1991. "Beyond 'State vs. Society': Theories of the State and New Deal Agricultural Policies." *American Sociological Review* 56(2):204–220.

Gilmore, Richard. 1982. *A Poor Harvest: The Clash of Policies and Interests in the Grain Trade.* New York: Longman.

Gourevitch, Peter. 1986. *Politics in Hard Times: Comparative Responses to International Economic Crises.* Ithaca: Cornell University Press.

Grant, Richard. 1990. "Against the Grain: Agricultural Trade Policies of the U.S., the European Community and Japan at the GATT." *Political Geography* 12(3):247–262.

Grant, Wyn. 1997. *The Common Agricultural Policy.* New York: St. Martin's.

Grubbs, Donald H. 1971. *Cry from the Cotton: The Southern Tenant Farmers' Union and the New Deal.* Chapel Hill: University of North Carolina Press.

Hacker, Jacob S. 2002. *The Divided Welfare State: The Battle over Public and Private Social Benefits in the United States.* New York: Cambridge University Press.

Hadwiger, D. F., and R. B. Talbot. 1965. *Pressures and Protests: The Kennedy Farm Program and the Wheat Referendum of 1963.* San Francisco: Chandler.

Hallberg, M. C. 1992. *Policy for American Agriculture: Choices and Consequences.* Ames: Iowa State University Press.

Hamilton, David E. 1991. *From New Day to New Deal: American Farm Policy from Hoover to Roosevelt, 1928–1933.* Chapel Hill: University of North Carolina Press.

Hansen, John Mark. 1991. *Gaining Access: Congress and the Farm Lobby, 1919–1981.* Chicago: University of Chicago Press.

Hardin, Charles. 1954. "The Republican Department of Agriculture: A Political Interpretation." *Journal of Farm Economics* 36:210–227.

Hathaway, Dale E. 1987. *Agriculture and the GATT: Rewriting the Rules.* Washington, D.C.: Institute for International Economics.

Heffernan, William D. 1998. "Agriculture and Monopoly Capital." *Monthly Review* 50:46–59.

Hefford, R. K. 1985. *Farm Policy in Australia.* St. Lucia: University of Queensland Press.

Hoffmann, Paul. 1974. "President Urges Global Strategy for Food and Oil." *New York Times.* September 19:1, 18.

Hooks, Gregory. 1990. "From an Autonomous to a Captured State Agency: The Decline of the New Deal in Agriculture." *American Sociological Review* 55(1):29–43.

Hopkins, Raymond F. 1992. "Reform in the International Food Aid Regime: The Role of Consensual Knowledge." *International Organization* 46(1):225–264.

Hosansky, David. 1996. "House and Senate Assemble Conflicting Farm Bills." *Congressional Quarterly.* February 3:295–296, 298.

Hosen, Frederick E. 1992. *The Great Depression and the New Deal: Legislative Acts in Their Entirety (1932–1933) and Statistical Economic Data (1926–1946).* Jefferson: McFarland.

Hurt, R. Douglas. 2002. *Problems of Plenty: The American Farmer in the Twentieth Century.* Chicago: Ivan R. Dee.

Insel, Barbara. 1985. "A World Awash in Grain." *Foreign Affairs* 64:892–911.

Jenkins, J. Craig, and Barbara G. Brents. 1989. "Social Protest, Hegemonic Competition, and Social Reform: A Political Struggle Interpretation of the Origins of the American Welfare State." *American Sociological Review* 54(6):891–909.

Johnson, Charles S., Edwin R. Embree, and W. W. Alexander. 1935. *The Collapse of Cotton Tenancy: Summary of Field Studies and Statistical Surveys, 1933–35.* Chapel Hill: University of North Carolina Press.

Josling, Tim. 1993. "Agricultural Trade Issues in Transatlantic Trade Relations." *World Economy* 16(5):553–573.

Katznelson, Ira. 2005. *When Affirmative Action Was White: An Untold History of Racial Inequality in Twentieth-Century America.* New York: W. W. Norton.

Katznelson, Ira, Kim Geiger, and Daniel Kryder. 1993. "Limiting Liberalism: The Southern Veto in Congress, 1933–1950." *Political Science Quarterly* 108(2):283–306.

Kester, Howard. 1936. *Revolt among the Sharecroppers.* New York: J. J. Little and Ives.

Key, V. O., Jr. 1949. *Southern Politics.* New York: Vintage.

Kindleberger, Charles P. 1973. *The World in Depression, 1929–1939.* Berkeley: University of California Press.

Kirby, Jack Temple. 1983. "The Transformation of Southern Plantations, c.1920–1960." *Agricultural History* 57(3):257–276.

Lamis, Alexander P. 1988. *The Two-Party South*. Expanded ed. New York: Oxford University Press.

Lawson, Steven F. 1985. *In Pursuit of Power: Southern Blacks and Electoral Politics, 1965–1982*. New York: Columbia University Press.

Leuchtenburg, William E. 1963. *Franklin D. Roosevelt and the New Deal*. New York: Harper & Row.

Libby, Ronald T. 1992. *Protecting Markets: U.S. Policy and the World Grain Trade*. Ithaca: Cornell University Press.

Lieber, James B. 2000. *Rats in the Grain: The Dirty Tricks and Trials of Archer Daniels Midland*. New York: Four Walls Eight Windows.

Lipson, Charles. 1982. "The Transformation of Trade: The Sources and Effects of Regime Change." *International Organization* 36(2):417–455.

*Los Angeles Times*. 1930. "California Vegetables Go into River." July 20:30.

Lowi, Theodore J. 1969. *End of Liberalism: Ideology, Policy, and the Crisis of Public Authority*. New York: Norton.

Lyons, Michael S., and Marcia Whicker Taylor. 1981. "Farm Politics in Transition: The House Agriculture Committee." *Agricultural History* 55:128–146.

Maidenberg, H. J. 1974. "U.S. Ending 'Food for Peace' despite Rising Hunger Abroad." *New York Times*. October 29:1, 51.

Mann, Susan A. 1987. "The Rise of Wage Labor in the Cotton South: A Global Analysis." *Journal of Peasant Studies* 14(2):226–242.

Marx, Karl. 1904 [1859]. *A Contribution to the Critique of Political Economy*. Chicago: Charles H. Kerr.

———. 1994 [1852]. *The 18th Brumaire of Louis Bonaparte*. New York: International Publishers.

Marx, Karl, and Frederick Engels. 1987 [1848]. *The Communist Manifesto*. New York: Pathfinder.

Matthews, Donald R., and James W. Prothro. 1966. *Negroes and the New Southern Politics*. New York: Harcourt, Brace & World.

Matusow, Allen J. 1967. *Farm Policies and Politics in the Truman Years*. New York: Atheneum.

McAdam, Doug. 1982. *Political Process and the Development of Black Insurgency, 1930–1970*. Chicago: University of Chicago Press.

———. 1988. *Freedom Summer*. New York: Oxford University Press.

McConnell, Grant. 1969. *The Decline of Agrarian Democracy*. New York: Atheneum.

McKeown, T. J. 1989. "The Politics of Corn Law Repeal and Theories of Commercial Policy." *British Journal of Political Science* 19:353–380.

McMichael, Philip. 1994. "GATT, Global Regulation and the Construction of a New Hegemonic Order." In *Regulating Agriculture*, edited by Philip Lowe, Terry Marsden, and Sarah Whatmore. London: David Fulton.

———. 1995. "Introduction: Agrarian and Food Relations in the World-Economy." In *Food and Agrarian Orders in the World-Economy*, edited by Philip McMichael. Westport: Praeger.

————. 1998. "Global Food Politics." *Monthly Review* 50(3):97–111.

————. 2000. *Development and Social Change: A Global Perspective.* 2nd ed. Thousand Oaks: Pine Forge.

Mintz, Sidney W. 1986. *Sweetness and Power: The Place of Sugar in Modern History.* New York: Penguin.

Mooney, Patrick H. 1983. "Toward a Class Analysis of Midwestern Agriculture." *Rural Sociology* 48:563–584.

Moore, Barrington, Jr. 1966/1993. *Social Origins of Dictatorship and Democracy: Lord and Peasant in the Making of the Modern World.* Boston: Beacon.

Morgan, Dan. 1980. *Merchants of Grain.* New York: Penguin.

Morris, Aldon D. 1984. *The Origins of the Civil Rights Movement: Black Communities Organizing for Change.* New York: The Free Press.

Moyer, Wayne, and Tim Josling. 2002. *Agricultural Policy Reform: Politics and Process in the EU and US in the 1990s.* Burlington: Ashgate.

Murphy, Paul L. 1955. "The New Deal Agricultural Program and the Constitution." *Agricultural History* 29:160–169.

Musoke, Moses E. 1981. "Mechanizing Cotton Production in the American South: The Tractor, 1915–1960." *Explorations in Economic History* 18(4):347–375.

Nelson, Lawrence J. 1999. *King Cotton's Advocate: Oscar G. Johnston and the New Deal.* Knoxville: University of Tennessee Press.

*New York Times.* 1933. "Hog Plan Dooms 5,000,000 Animals." August 19:17, 22.

————. 1933. "$246,000,000 Rise Given to Cotton." September 3:12.

————. 1933. "6,000,000 Total Ends Pig Buying." September 30:25.

Nibert, David. 2002. *Animal Rights, Human Rights: Entanglements of Oppression.* New York: Rowman & Littlefield.

Orden, David. 1996. "Agricultural Interest Groups and the North American Free Trade Agreement." In *The Political Economy of American Trade Policy,* edited by Anne O. Krueger, pp. 335–384. Chicago: University of Chicago Press.

Orden, David, Robert Paarlberg, and Terry Roe. 1999. *Policy Reform in American Agriculture: Analysis and Prognosis.* Chicago: University of Chicago Press.

Paarlberg, Don. 1989. "Tarnished Gold: Fifty Years of New Deal Farm Programs." In *The New Deal and Its Legacy: Critique and Reappraisal,* edited by Robert Eden. New York: Greenwood.

Paarlberg, Robert, and David Orden. 1996. "Explaining U.S. Farm Policy in 1996 and Beyond: Changes in Party Control and Changing Market Conditions." *American Journal of Agricultural Economics* 78(December):1305–1313.

Pear, Robert. 2005. "Bush Aims to Cut Farm Subsidies." *Atlanta Journal-Constitution.* February 6:B7.

Perkins, Jerry. 2001. "Farms Face Uncertainty: Poll Gauges Support for 1996 Farm Law." *Des Moines Register.* November 14:1D.

Peterson, Trudy Huskamp. 1979. *Agricultural Exports, Farm Income, and the Eisenhower Administration.* Lincoln: University of Nebraska Press.

Pfeffer, Max J. 1983. "Social Origins of Three Systems of Farm Production in the United States." *Rural Sociology* 48(4):540–562.

Piven, Frances Fox, and Richard A. Cloward. 1977. *Poor People's Movements: Why They Succeed, How They Fail.* New York: Random House.

Polanyi, Karl. 1957. *The Great Transformation.* Boston: Beacon.

Pollan, Michael. 2007. *The Omnivore's Dilemma: A Natural History of Four Meals.* New York: Penguin Books.

Porter, Kimberly K. 2000. "Embracing the Pluralist Perspective: The Iowa Farm Bureau Federation and the McNary-Haugen Movement." *Agricultural History* 74(2):381–392.

Prechel, Harland. 1990. "Steel and the State: Industry, Politics, and Business Policy Formation, 1940–1989." *American Sociological Review* 55:648–668.

Price, Daniel O. 1969. *Changing Characteristics of the Negro Population.* Washington, D.C.: GPO.

Prunty, Merle, Jr. 1955. "The Renaissance of the Southern Plantation." *Geographical Review* 45(4):459–491.

Quadagno, Jill. 1984. "Welfare Capitalism and the Social Security Act of 1935." *American Sociological Review* 49(5):632–647.

Rasmussen, Wayne D., and Gladys L. Baker. 1979. "Price-Support and Adjustment Programs from 1933 through 1978: A Short History." United States Department of Agriculture, Agricultural Information Bulletin No. 424.

Rensberger, Boyce. 1974. "Experts Ask Action to Avoid Millions of Deaths in Food Crisis." *New York Times.* July 26:35, 66.

———. 1974. "Food: A Crisis for All." *New York Times.* September 19:1, 18.

———. 1974. "32 Nations Close to Starvation." *New York Times.* October 20: section 4, page 4.

Robbins, William. 1974. "Hunger in U.S., a Problem of Want Amid Plenty." *New York Times.* October 28:39, 60.

Roberts, Owen Josephus. 1936. "Opinion of the Court." Supreme Court of the United States, *United States v. Butler,* 297 U.S. 1, pp. 53–78.

Royce, Edward. 1993. *The Origins of Southern Sharecropping.* Philadelphia: Temple University Press.

Rubinson, Richard. 1978. "Political Transformation in Germany and the United States." In *Social Change in the Capitalist World Economy,* edited by Barbara Hockey Kaplan. Beverly Hills: Sage.

———. 1986. "Class Formation, Politics, and Institutions: Schooling in the United States." *American Journal of Sociology* 92(3):519–548.

Rubinson, Richard, and Joan Sokolovsky. 1988. "Patterns of Industrial Regulation: Railroads in the World Economy." In *Rethinking the Nineteenth-Century World-Economy,* edited by Francisco Ramirez. New York: Greenwood.

Runge, Carlisle Ford. 1988. "The Assault on Agricultural Protectionism." *Foreign Affairs* 67(1):133–150.

Schapsmeier, Edward L., and Frederick H. Schapsmeier. 1975. *Ezra Taft Benson and the Politics of Agriculture: The Eisenhower Years, 1953–1961*. Danville: Interstate Printers and Publishers.

———. 1979. "Farm Policy from FDR to Eisenhower: Southern Democrats and the Politics of Agriculture." *Agricultural History* 53(January):352–371.

Schertz, Lyle P., and Otto C. Doering, III. 1999. *The Making of the 1996 Farm Act*. Ames: Iowa State University Press.

Schlesinger, Arthur, Jr. 1959. *The Age of Roosevelt: The Coming of the New Deal.* Boston: Houghton Mifflin.

———. 1960. *The Age of Roosevelt: The Politics of Upheaval*. Boston: Houghton Mifflin.

Schulman, Bruce J. 1991. *From Cotton Belt to Sunbelt: Federal Policy, Economic Development, and the Transformation of the South, 1938–1980*. Durham: Duke University Press.

Schwartz, Michael. 1976. *Radical Protest and Social Structure: The Southern Farmers' Alliance and Cotton Tenancy, 1880–1890*. Chicago: University of Chicago Press.

Sharma, Devinder. 2004. "Indian Agriculture: Back to Square One." *Global Ecology*. May:3–6.

Sheingate, Adam D. 2001. *The Rise of the Agricultural Welfare State: Institutions and Interest Group Power in the United States, France, and Japan*. Princeton: Princeton University Press.

Shover, John L. 1965. *Cornbelt Rebellion: The Farmers' Holiday Association*. Urbana: University of Illinois Press.

Silver, Beverly J., and Giovanni Arrighi. 2003. "Polanyi's 'Double Movement': The *Belle Epoques* of British and U.S. Hegemony Compared." *Politics & Society* 31(2):325–355.

Snyder, Robert E. 1984. *Cotton Crisis*. Chapel Hill: University of North Carolina Press.

Southworth, Caleb. 2002. "Aid to Sharecroppers: How Agrarian Class Structure and Tenant-Farmer Politics Influenced Federal Relief in the South, 1933–1935." *Social Science History* 26(3):33–70.

Steinbeck, John. 1985 [1939]. *The Grapes of Wrath*. New York: Penguin.

Steinmo, Sven. 1989. "Political Institutions and Tax Policy in the United States, Sweden, and Britain." *World Politics* 41(4):500–535.

Stone, Harlan Fiske. 1936. "Dissenting Opinion." Supreme Court of the United States, *United States v. Butler*, 297 U.S. 1, pp. 78–88.

Swenson, Peter. 2002. *Capitalists against Markets: The Making of Labor Markets and Welfare States in the United States and Sweden*. New York: Oxford University Press.

———. 2004. "Varieties of Capitalist Interests: Power, Institutions, and the Regulatory Welfare State in the United States and Sweden." *Studies in American Political Development* 18(1):1–29.

Tesche, W. C. 1933. "Stabilize or Agonize!" *Los Angeles Times*. July 9:H3, H6.

Toma, Peter A. 1967. *The Politics of Food for Peace: Executive-Legislative Interaction.* Tucson: University of Arizona Press.

Tweeten, Luther. 1970. *Foundations of Farm Policy.* Lincoln: University of Nebraska Press.

Wallerstein, Immanuel. 1974. *The Modern World-System: Capitalist Agriculture and the Origins of the European World-Economy in the Sixteenth Century.* New York: Academic Press.

*Wall Street Journal.* 1958. "House Committee Hears Charge Communists Back One Cotton Plan." January 30:8.

Warden, Philip. 1958. "House Group Farm Session Ends in Uproar." *Chicago Daily Tribune.* January 30:B5.

*Washington Post and Times Herald.* 1958. "Bid to End Issue in Alley Disrupts Farm Hearing." January 30:B4.

Weller, Cecil Edward, Jr. 1998. *Joe T. Robinson: Always a Loyal Democrat.* Fayetteville: University of Arkansas Press.

Wells, Mariam J. 1996. *Strawberry Fields: Politics, Class, and Work in California Agriculture.* Ithaca: Cornell University Press.

Werum, Regina. 1997. "Sectionalism and Racial Politics: Federal Vocational Policies and Programs in the Predesegregation South." *Social Science History* 21(3):399–453.

Werum, Regina, and Bill Winders. 2001. "Who's 'In' and Who's 'Out': State Fragmentation and the Struggle over Gay Rights, 1974–1999." *Social Problems* 48(3):386–410.

Westcott, Paul C., C. Edwin Young, and J. Michael Price. 2002. "The 2002 Farm Act: Provisions and Implications for Commodity Markets." United States Department of Agriculture, Agriculture Information Bulletin No. 778. Washington, D.C.: GPO.

Wexler, Laura. 2005. "A Sorry History: Why an Apology from the Senate Can't Make Amends." *Washington Post.* June 19:B1, B4.

Wilcox, Walter W. 1947. *The Farmer in the Second World War.* Ames: Iowa State College Press.

Winders, Bill. 1999. "The Roller Coaster of Class Conflict: Class Segments, Mass Mobilization, and Voter Turnout in the U.S., 1840–1996." *Social Forces* 77(3):833–862.

———. 2000. "The Vanishing Free Market: Comparing International Food Orders under British and U.S. Hegemony." Paper presented at the Annual Meeting of the American Sociological Association, Washington, D.C.

———. 2005. "Maintaining the Coalition: Class Coalitions and Policy Trajectories." *Politics & Society* 33(3):387–423.

Winders, Bill, and David Nibert. 2004. "Consuming the Surplus: Expanding 'Meat' Consumption and Animal Oppression." *International Journal of Sociology & Social Policy* 24(9):76–96.

Winders, William P. 2001. "Welcome to the Free Market: Class Bases of U.S.

Agricultural Policy, 1938–1996." Ph.D. Dissertation, Emory University, Atlanta.

Winters, L. Alan. 1990. "The Road to Uruguay." *Economic Journal* 100(December):1288–1303.

Woofter, T. J., with Gordon Blackwell, Harold Hoffsommer, James G. Maddox, Jean M. Massell, B. O. Williams, and Waller Wynne, Jr. 1936. *Landlord and Tenant on the Cotton Plantation.* Washington, D.C.: Works Progress Administration, Research Monograph V.

World Food Institute. 1988. *World Food Trade and U.S. Agriculture, 1960–1987.* Ames: World Food Institute.

Wright, Gavin. 1986. *Old South, New South: Revolutions in the Southern Economy since the Civil War.* New York: Basic Books.

Young, Edwin C., and Paul C. Westcott. 1996. "The 1996 U.S. Farm Act Increases Market Orientation." United States Department of Agriculture, Information Bulletin No. 726. Washington, D.C.: GPO.

Zahniser, Steven, and William Coyle. 2004. "U.S.-Mexico Corn Trade during the NAFTA Era: New Twists to an Old Story." United States Department of Agriculture, Economic Outlook Report from the Economic Research Service. Washington, D.C.: GPO.

Zeiler, Thomas W. 1999. *Free Trade, Free World: The Advent of GATT.* Chapel Hill: University Press of North Carolina.

# Index

Page numbers marked *f* refer to figures, *t* to tables.

agricultural segments, competing interests
    among, 15–17, 81, 169, 178–180, 179t,
    184–185, 202. *See also specific commodity
    segments*
Agricultural Trade Development and Assis-
    tance Act. *See* Public Law *480*
agricultural transnational corporations, 153,
    155–157
agriculture, U.S., international markets for,
    49, 82, 136, 138, 140, 146–149, 151,
    181–185, 203
Agriculture and Consumer Protection Act
    (1973), 7t, 8–9, 82–83, 97, 99t, 102, 125,
    207, 241n27
Aiken bill, 88
Algeria, 135
AMA. *See* Agricultural Marketing Act (1929)
American Corn Growers Association, 202
American Council of Agriculture, 42, 44t
American Farm Bureau Federation. *See* Farm
    Bureau
American Soybean Association, 170, 177, 180,
    202
Amstutz, Dan, 157, 183
Anderson, Tony, 202
Anderson Clayton and Company, 155
Andre & Co., 155
Andreas, Dwayne, 156, 177
Andrews, Kenneth, 119
Anti-Corn Law Bill (1846), 236n26
Archer Daniels Midland, 156–157, 177, 180,
    229n68
Argentina, 130, 135, 149, 156
Armour & Co., 65
ARP. *See* Acreage Reduction Program
Arringhi, Giovanni, 235n23
ASA. *See* American Soybean Association
Australia, 130, 135, 141, 145–146, 149, 154–
    156, 177, 184
Avery, Dennis, 244n66
Avery, Sewell, 223n43

BAE. *See* Bureau of Agricultural Economics
Baker, Howard, Jr., 160
Ball, Don, 178
Bangladesh, 129, 132
Bankhead, John, 58
Barrett, Bill, 176
Barton, Weldon, 97–98
Benson, Ezra, 78–79, 82–83, 85–86, 88
Bilbo, Theodore, 49
Black, Hugo, 68

blacks
    churches, 118, 120
    industrial sector, 121
    political voice, 117–120, 123–124
    segregation, 25, 107, 109–111, 116, 118,
        120–122, 124, 234n72
    and urbanization, 118
    violence against, 117
    voter registration, 106–107, 119, 120f
Bloom, Jack, 124, 234n67
Brandeis, Louis, 67, 224n64
Brannan, Charles, 79, 83–84
Brannan Plan, 83–84, 207
Brazil, 48
*Brown v. Board of Education,* 121–122
Bumpers, Dale, 246n107
Bunge, 155
Bureau of Agricultural Economics, 70, 72
Bush, George W., 199
Butler, Pierce, 224n64
Butler, William M., 66–67
Butz, Earl, 79, 101, 131
Byrns, Joseph, 57

Cairns Group, 15
Cambodia, 132
Canada, 130, 135, 141, 146, 149, 154–155, 177,
    184
CAP. *See* Common Agricultural Policy
Cardozo, Benjamin, 67
Cargill, 155–157, 177, 229n68
Carter, Jimmy, 159
Casement, Dan, 61
CBLL. *See* Corn Belt Liberty League
CCC. *See* Commodity Credit Corporation
CCFAS. *See* Coalition for a Competitive Food
    and Agricultural System
Center for Global Food Issues, 244n66
Chad, 129
Chaney, James, 106
Cheever, Lawrence, 52
chemical fertilizers, 17
Chile, 132
China, 99, 182–183, 184, 191, 197
Civilian Conservation Corps, 222n20
Civil Rights Act (1964), 107
civil rights movement, x, xv, xvi, 22, 105–107,
    115–123, 128
class, in agriculture, defined, 19
class segments. *See also specific commodity
    segments*
    coalition building, 2, 16, 21, 22–24, 180